MW01252840

Criminal Behaviour in Context

INTERNATIONAL SERIES ON DESISTANCE AND
REHABILITATION

Series editor: Stephen Farrall

Published titles

The Dynamics of Desistance: Charting pathways through change,
by Deirdre Healy

Criminal Behaviour in Context: Space, place and desistance from crime,
by Nick Flynn

Criminal Behaviour in Context

Space, place and desistance from crime

Nick Flynn

WILLAN
PUBLISHING

Published by

Willan Publishing
2 Park Square
Milton Park
Abingdon
Oxon
OX14 4RN

Published simultaneously in the USA and Canada by

Willan Publishing
270 Madison Avenue
New York
NY 10016

First published 2010

ISBN   978-1-84392-811-9 hardback

British Library Cataloguing-in-Publication Data

A catalogue record for this book is available from the British Library

FSC
Mixed Sources
Product group from well-managed
forests and other controlled sources
Cert no. SGS-COC-2482
www.fsc.org
© 1996 Forest Stewardship Council

Project managed by Deer Park Productions, Tavistock, Devon
Typeset by GCS, Leighton Buzzard, Bedfordshire
Printed and bound by T.J. International, Padstow, Cornwall

For Shirley and Bob (Mum and Dad)

Contents

Acknowledgements

I would like to thank the following. Roger Matthews for getting me started, money, and enthused; Karen Duke for sage, practical advice and the bottle of champagne; and Anthony Goodman for pastoral care and the seafood risotto. Others at Middlesex University who chipped in along the way include Ken Lupton (RIP), Theresa Wilson, David Jarrett, David Porteous, Rhona Stephen and Margaret Davis; and at De Montfort University, Rob Canton and Roger Smith. Pat Dowdeswell, Veronica Hollis, Richard Lane and Sarah Gough at the Home Office provided access to statistical information. Nicky Young in HMP Wandsworth, Claire Smith in HMP Pentonville, and (an especial big 'hello' to) Cheryl Brown and Jasmine Scott in HMP Brixton, arranged the interviews. Obviously I am grateful for the quality time provided by each of the prisoners. I'd like to think they got something out of it too. Stephen Farrall has been an encouraging and helpful editor. It goes without saying that all errors and omissions are my own. And finally, on the home front, to Jo and Jack for everything really. 'Space *is* the place' and living with you *in it* is just ... *x*.

Nick Flynn
De Montfort University

Participant list

Adusa, a 43-year-old black African man, first convicted at the age of 14, imprisoned 14 times.

Barry, a 33-year-old white British man, first convicted at the age of 9, imprisoned 10 times.

Billy, a 27-year-old black British man, first convicted at the age of 14, imprisoned five times.

Dalmar, a 23-year-old African man, first convicted at the age of 18, imprisoned three times.

Declan, a 37-year-old Irish man, first convicted at the age of 35, imprisoned twice.

Eric, a 29-year-old black British man, first convicted at the age of 14, imprisoned eight times.

Freddie, a 42-year-old Afro-Caribbean man, first convicted at the age of 17, imprisoned five times.

Hari, a 26-year-old Asian British man, first convicted at the age of 14, imprisoned 20 times.

Harvey, a 21-year-old white British man, first convicted at the age of 14, imprisoned three times.

Ian, a 33-year-old black British man, first convicted at the age of 21, imprisoned five times.

Jimmy, a 33-year-old white British man, first convicted at the age of 21, imprisoned five times.

John, a 22-year-old white British man, first convicted at the age of 17, imprisoned 12 times.

Joshua, a 31-year-old black British man, first convicted at the age of 16, imprisoned five times.

Keifer, a 40-year-old black British man, first convicted at the age of 22, imprisoned three times.

Kev, a 49-year-old black British man, first convicted at the age of 16, imprisoned 15 times.

Liam, a 21-year-old black British man, first convicted at the age of 14, imprisoned five times.

Maurice, a 30-year-old black British man, first convicted at the age of 17, imprisoned six times.

Mika, a 28-year-old black British man, first convicted at the age of 15, imprisoned 25 times.

Nige, a 22-year-old white British man, first convicted at the age of 16, imprisoned three times.

Paul, a 29-year-old black British man, first convicted at the age of 15, imprisoned three times.

Peter, a 23-year-old white British man, first convicted at the age of 20, imprisoned four times.

Raja, a 23-year-old Asian British man, first convicted at the age of 17, imprisoned nine times.

Rick, a 31-year-old black British man, first convicted at the age of 17, imprisoned three times.

Robert, a 39-year-old black British man, first convicted at the age of 21, imprisoned three times.

Sammy, a 37-year-old white British man, first convicted at the age of 14, imprisoned over 50 times.

Sean, a 22-year-old white British man, first convicted at the age of 13, imprisoned nine times.

Stuart, a 40-year-old black British man, first convicted at the age of 18, imprisoned six times.

Tanveer, a 27-year-old Asian British man, first convicted at the age of 19, imprisoned three times.

Theo, a 21-year-old black British man, first convicted at the age of 15, imprisoned eight times.

Tim, a 31-year-old black British man, first convicted at the age of 11, imprisoned six times.

Glossary of terms and phrases

baby mother	woman who has one's child but with whom one may not actually live
bullshitted	lied
burn	a smoke, a cigarette
buzz	a sensation, thrill
cane the shops	wreck
chase the dragon	to smoke heroin by burning it on kitchen foil and inhaling the smoke through a tube
crack	a mixture of cocaine, baking powder and water which is smoked rather than snorted
fanny me off	deceive
'Groundhog Day'	from the film *Groundhog Day*, the idea that every day is exactly the same as the one before
living it large	in an unrestrained way, excessively enjoyable
Mr T	American actor, known for wearing large amounts of gold jewellery and for his tough-guy image
piss test	drug testing by urinalysis
puff	cannabis
road	the street settings in which many criminals survive and earn a living

Rizla	a brand of cigarette papers
ruck up	to get angry with, fight
screw	prison officer
sofa surfing	staying with friends or acquaintances in accommodation that is not secure
'Space is the Place'	film and song by Sun Ra
speedballs	a mixture of cocaine and heroin, either injected or sniffed
spunking the money	spending it on instantly gratifying, enjoyable pursuits
tear granny out of it	significantly reduce in importance, humiliate

Introduction

A common frame of spatial reference

Raja walks into the cell, sits down and stares at a spot on the wall behind me. There is a ruckus going on outside: prisoners and prison officers shouting on the landing, what sounds like a tin cup being banged repeatedly against a wall. I am in Brixton prison in London to interview prisoners for research I am conducting on prisoner rehabilitation and criminal desistance. I want Raja to tell me his life story. This is not a promising start. I go through the motions of telling him a little about myself, the purpose of the research, and that a pseudonym will be used in any published material to ensure his non-identification. I also inform him he is not obliged to answer any questions he does not like and that he can stop the interview at any point. As the noise outside gets louder, he continues to stare vacantly at the wall. The situation is unnerving me. I ask him if he wants to postpone or cancel the interview. There is a long silence, which I finally break by getting out of my chair and suggesting that the shouting and banging is too loud and it is perhaps not a good time to talk. He suddenly comes to life, looks at me for the first time, and splutters, 'It's like this in here all the time.' No, he wants me to start the interview. 'Go on, ask me your questions,' he says. I sit back down but explain I have no set questions. I want him to tell me where he used to live and how he passed the time; about school, work, his crimes; how many times he has been to prison, what it is like for him inside; and where he normally lives after he is released. I explain that he can choose what to tell me and what he thinks is important. I want to know his opinions and ideas, how he thinks about things; not about his crimes so much as about him as an individual.

As with all the interviews included in this book, encouraging Raja to feel relaxed enough to confide in me and express his innermost feelings and attitudes took time. As the participants were initially reluctant to express themselves in any other way than monosyllabically, it was usual to instigate discussion through prompts: 'Tell me where you lived; how many brothers and sisters you have; as a child, who your were friends'. The noise outside subsides, and eventually, slowly, painfully, Raja becomes more animated. He tells me he is 23 and that he grew up in Whitechapel in the East End of London with his mum, who is a pensioner, and his two brothers. He last saw his dad, who is now in Bangladesh, eight years ago. Raja stopped going to school at the age of 13 and has no friends, but I'll let him speak for himself:

> I was lonely a lot in the house and outside. I'd drink and smoke cannabis. Did that from the age of 11. I don't watch much television. Listened to music, pop music. Outside I'd just walk to the shop and come back, 'cause I never got close to anyone. No one talked to me 'cause I was drinking and smoking. I just had my mother to look after. Brothers moved out when I was 15. Sometimes I see them. They come and see my mum when they feel like it. They work in restaurants but I have nothing to do with them. I was lonely and I just thought that was the end of my life and I still feel the same today. I was 16 when I started shoplifting. I did it to buy my alcohol and cannabis. I was shoplifting from 10 or 12 shops a day, from shops in the local area. I was getting the drugs from elder people, the drug dealers. I was spending about £1,000 a week on drugs. I was also working in Sainsbury's and McDonald's and a clothing factory. When I was working, I was not committing crime. I was gambling with the elder Asians, playing cards in snooker clubs, coffee shops. Some days I could win £10,000. I was playing big games. I spent the lot on crack. I didn't commit much crime. They sent me to prison for being drunk and abusive. Four of my offences are for being drunk and abusive. One was a commercial robbery and one ABH [actual bodily harm] and two offensive weapons. When I was really drunk or paranoid from the crack, that's the time I'd carry a knife or something.

Raja goes on to tell me about prison. It is 'the same old shit every day'. He has been attacked 'about 14, 15 times in prison, by Irish and white and black people'. Fighting back is futile; it 'would just make things worse'. After each prison sentence, he goes back to Whitechapel. He would prefer to live 'anywhere else, 'cause there's many Asians there, and where there's Asians there's problems, drugs and crime, but I can't leave my mum.' For the last four years he has been living in his car. I ask him why.

> Because of prison and the community. I've been to prison so many times the community of the people around, the residents, give a hard time to my mum, asking her, 'Why's your son in prison?' It was just too distressing for her, so I just left. My car is parked about 10 minutes from my mum's, but just my mum knows where I am. The police try to move me on but I just drive off, then come back later. I've got used to it, but it's hard, very hard. Cold, freezing, uncomfortable, can't move your legs, can't spread your legs, no duvet, no pillow, just lie down on the seat.

I continue by enquiring why he has not found somewhere better to live:

> Everyone's let me down. The council promises me this and that but nothing. I've had nothing but trouble, grief, sweared at, racially attacked, bullying. In a couple of weeks I'm probably going to shoot myself. That's it, that's the end, I've had enough. What can I make happen? I've been to prison, destroyed my body, destroyed my health, bullshitted my mum, I can't go back to school, can't go to college. If no one helps me I can't do it, but no one comes to see me.

Raja is becoming quite upset and agitated now so I attempt to bring the discussion to a close. But he wants to carry on. 'Please keep asking me stuff, I'll tell you more for your research,' he insists. We continue for a few more minutes but when a prison officer knocks and says Raja must return to his cell, the interview comes to an end.

All prisoners are different of course; their autobiographies and outlook on life are unique. Nevertheless, Raja's interview illustrates some common characteristics and themes: a disrupted and chaotic family background; low educational attainment; drug and alcohol abuse; a propensity for violence; early and progressively serious criminal activity; unemployment interspersed with sporadic, low-wage work; numerous prison sentences; social marginalisation and deprivation after release; and on a more personal basis, perhaps also a need to talk. Living in a car is probably not a course of action most ex-prisoners would resort to, but homelessness in one form or another – on the streets, bed-and-breakfast accommodation, night shelters, or 'sofa surfing' at friends and acquaintances – is common enough. Pick up any book on offender resettlement and you will find a detailed commentary on why reoffending is associated with various forms of economic and social deprivation. But, there is something else in Raja's testimony which is essential to the life histories of many persistent offenders. His narrative plays out according to a common frame of spatial reference. Evidence suggests that large numbers of persistent offenders grow up in poor, marginalised urban neighbourhoods, experience imprisonment for a significant number of times, and return repeatedly to the same or similar places after release. Raja's story reveals what this means as an everyday life experience. The way he thinks – his attitudes, beliefs, feelings and expectations; in totality, his sense of self – is geographically bounded by two precise and parallel locations. At 23, all he knows and has ever known is loneliness, drug taking, crime and social isolation in Whitechapel; and boredom, bullying, insularity and despair in prison.

This illustrates another facet of Raja; an obvious one perhaps, but important nonetheless. It is simply that he has a story to tell. The social context of offender resettlement does not simply constitute a list of objective problems to overcome. It is how Raja feels about living in his car, his poor education, unemployment, drug taking, lack of friends and social networks, the need to take care of his mother, the hostile attitudes of local people, his prison experiences, bullying, racism and limited opportunities after release. These subjective experiences and responses reveal Raja to be utterly weighed down by his problems. Wholly reliant on the support of others, he appears to be incapable of summoning the motivation to address his needs through his own efforts. And yet, as his interview progressed, and once Raja had overcome his initial reluctance to talk, he was willing at least to articulate his predicament and explain why he felt so overwhelmed by life – a start perhaps.

The way in which persistent offenders perceive themselves to be in relation to the places they inhabit over the life course is the subject matter of this book. By tracing the 'pathways' taken by them between the community and prison, its overall purpose is to examine the extent to which criminal desistance – a theoretical perspective on the change process involved in the ending of criminal behaviour – is affected by life circumstances, experiences and events which are space and place specific. To do this, as well as assessing criminal desistance developmentally, the content of the book is grounded spatially. Informed by an ontological perspective 'that just as people construct places, places construct people' (Holloway and Hubbard 2001: 7), it considers how behavioural change is constituted in the places routinely inhabited by convicted criminals: the places they grow up, prison and the places they return to after they are released from prison. The purpose of this introduction is to explain broad themes and define key terms. The context is set first of all by explicating space and place; then by articulating the relationship between space, place and the offender; and finally by delineating the spatial dimensions of criminal desistance and the meanings and justifications of prisoner resettlement. The chapter ends with a brief summary of the structure of the book.

Local life in the global economy

Integral to the project overall is a human geographical understanding of space and place. It is commonly assumed that space is a more abstract term than place in that it denotes expanse, a distance between two points (Augé, 1995). Place, on the other hand, is bounded; a specific locale geographically situated and given meaning and substance by the people who live there. In short, place is 'a locus for identity' (Hubbard *et al.* 2004). However, the terms are also often used synonymously. Because space, like place, is socially produced and therefore can only be understood in relation to human experience and activity, '"space" and "place" require each other for definition' (Tuan 1977: 6). According to Harvey (1990: 302), 'everyone occupies a space of individuation (a body, a room, a home, a shaping community, a nation), and how we individuate ourselves shapes identity.' To the extent that individuals assign meaning to particular 'place communities' (Davies and Herbert 1993) there is supposed to be an 'intertwining of personal identity and of place attachment' (Kintrea *et al.* 2008: 12). The social life of an area affects how people think and the forms of behaviour they engage in. Moreover, they develop collective attachments to places which engender shared meanings and responses (Thrift 1985). How individuals conceive themselves and others around them to be, and how they reason and act upon the decisions they make, betray their social location. Therefore, 'place identity' – 'the extent to which a person can recognize or recall a place as being distinct from other places' (Oktay 2002: 264) is an elemental constituent of 'self identity' (Proshansky *et al.* 1983). So, relationships between people and place matter. As Giddens (1984: 367) has commented generally:

A sense of place seems of major importance in the sustaining of ontological security precisely because it provides a psychological tie between the biography of the individual and the locales that are the settings of the time–space paths through which that individual moves.

Yet, over the past few decades, there has been an important and sustained challenge to the view that there is a co-variation between place and identity. It is a significant feature of the contemporary world that 'we are all complexly constructed through different categories, of different antagonisms, and these have the effect of locating us socially in multiple positions' (Hall 1991: 57). It follows that, place identity can no longer be thought of simply as a product of specific neighbourhoods, communities, towns or cities. New reflexive relationships between global and local processes have caused the 'dissolution of traditional spatial identities and their reconstitution along new lines' (Zukin 1992: 221). Personal and social life has been 'detraditionalised' by economic and social forces of globalisation and consumer capitalism. Economic restructuring – occasioned by advances in communications technology, the deregulation of national economies, the demise of Fordist processes of mass production, the emergence of 'flexible specialisation' in the workplace, and new spatial divisions of labour – has transformed the urban landscape of Western capitalist countries. The result is that ever changing life situations have engendered new reciprocal relationships between the mind of the individual and society (Beck 1992).

It is far from certain how these relationships play out. Increasingly rapid flows of labour, capital and information have 'distanciated' social relations across time and space (Giddens 1990). As people around the world have been brought into contact with one another instantaneously, communal bonds have been de-localised, engendering a sense of 'placelessness' (Relph 1976). To some, this social transformation has brought about an overall demise in traditional place-based communities (Wellman 1979). Face-to-face communal interaction no longer matters (Meyrowitz 1985). Places have lost their significance. The borders and features that once made them distinct have been flattened by the impress of globalism (Friedman 2005). An important consequence of this is that decision making about the right course of action to take under such circumstances has become more uncertain. 'Risk' has supplanted traditional features of class, gender, community and family as the primary constituent of social relations and social identity (Beck 1992). As social life has become more precarious, individuals have been forced to become more responsible for controlling their destinies. Without traditional markers and supports to fall back on, they have had to 'produce, stage and cobble together their biographies for themselves' (*ibid*.: 13). Through having increasingly 'to negotiate lifestyle choices among a diversity of options' (Giddens 1991: 5), it follows that 'where a person lives, after young adulthood at least, is a matter of choice organised primarily in terms of the person's life planning' (*ibid*.: 147).

A benefit of this is that large numbers of people are no longer tied to places of work – 'for richer and poorer, in health and in sickness, and until death them do part' (Bauman 2001: 22). And yet, notwithstanding the freer flow of resources brought about by market capitalism, cities remain beset by complex social problems. The displacement effect of late modernity is not all-encompassing. Separation and segregation, as much as mixing and flow, remain fundamental characteristics of the global economic system. While deindustrialisation and a shift to a world economic system of 'disorganised capitalism' (Lash and Urry 1987) have resulted in greater opportunity and increasingly self-determined ways of life for some, others have found themselves 'on the receiving end of space-time compression' (Massey 1993: 62). Some have the capacity to 'initiate flows and movement, others don't … some are effectively imprisoned by it' (Massey 1997: 317). Under these circumstances, 'life planning becomes impossible, except for the elite inhabiting the timeless space of flows of global networks and their ancillary locales' (Castells 2004: 11). Social, environmental and cultural situations remain firmly segmented by structural division and spatial inequality (Furlong and Cartmel 1997). As cities have grown in size, public services have failed to provide for even the most basic needs of large sections of the population. Unemployment and reductions in public spending have been felt most keenly in areas where, relying on family and friends, the poor have become dependent 'on the smallest spatial scales of the home and neighbourhood' (Fuller and Gough 2001: 269). The meaning of place is far from homogeneous; it would appear that 'its degree of importance depends on who you are and where you are' (Forrest 2000: 30).

Space, place and criminality

In the light of all this, an apposite question to ask is whether a shared experience of spatial disadvantage in the city shapes offending behaviour. Indeed, relationships between criminality and certain urban locations have been drawn ever since the emergence of industrial cities in the nineteenth century (Taylor 1999). But while this is an obvious question, it is by no means a straightforward one. Bound up with intractable disagreements over the aetiology of crime generally, the relationship between crime and place has been conceptualised in wholly divergent ways. Baldly stated, on the one hand, criminal behaviour is explained in relation to economic, social, cultural and political factors; and, on the other hand, as a product of biological and/or psychological deficiencies, which, because they form early in life, are thought to influence criminal behaviour long before place or community processes can take effect. Neither position rests on a certainty. More than most factors, place structures the life paths and destinies of persistent offenders. But although the attachment to place is more likely to be local and less susceptible to change for offenders than other people, there is not a straightforward causal relationship between place and criminal activity. Individuals are affected by place, and places are produced by the people living there. Poverty, disadvantage and crime are mediated by place, and places are affected by the poverty, disadvantage and crime of their inhabitants. The reasons people occupy the places they do may not be their own (Canter 1977), but they are never conditioned to behave in set ways as a result of this. Prolonged geographical and social segregation can be stifling and inhibiting, but, as human agents, offenders, like everybody else, retain the capacity to respond purposefully to the situations they find themselves in.

The role of place in the (re)production of human action is an abstract concept. Different understandings of people and place and the individual's relationship to society are embedded in symbolic interactionist, existential and phenomenological traditions of social enquiry, which, rather than consider individual agency and social structure separately, attempt to draw these dualisms together (e.g. Mead 1934; Berger and Luckman 1966; Douglas 1977; Layder 1981; Lefebvre 1984 [1968]; Sampson 1989; Bourdieu 1990a; Giddens 1990). That is, the ability of individuals and groups to act and make purposive choices and decisions which shape their lives, on the one hand; and the environments and social interrelationships structured around social class, the global economy, and political institutions which govern and shape values and beliefs, on the other hand. The challenge therefore is to disentangle social/environmental characteristics from individual/subjective ones. Because individuals exposed to the same environment experience, interpret and react to it differently (Caspi and Moffitt 1995), the ways they relate to place is never uniformly apparent. For instance, group or collective identity may be as substantial and real as personal identity (Jenkins 2004), and unconscious, imagined representations of reality as crucial to the development of purposeful human agency as objective and material conditions of existence (Castoriadis 1975). As such, the impact of place can only be understood in relation to the way people make sense of the world in which they live (see Giddens 1976, 1984, 1987, 1990, 1991).

The intention is to break down the dichotomy; to affirm that 'despite the objectivity that marks the social world in human experience, it does not thereby acquire an ontological status apart from the human activity that produced it' (Berger and Luckmann 1966: 78). In order to expose this 'absurd opposition between individual and society' (Bourdieu 1990b: 31) as an intellectual artefact, it is necessary to arrive at a conception of space and place which, while it impacts on the subjective experience of people, may be altered through human action. To do this, the various dialectics that characterise the relationships between choice and constraint must be investigated and made clear: the inner and outer, internal and external, individual and social, subjective and objective, personal and general, private and public, behavioural and phenomenal, psychological and sociological, and mental and natural (Pile 1996).

The stakes are high. Within criminology, the need to bridge agentic and structural explanations of behaviour and conduct has been identified 'as the most urgent task confronting a social science that wishes to be politically relevant in the new millennium' (Pitts 2003: 118). To an extent, there is theoretical knowledge and understanding to draw upon. Although there is a tendency for theoretical positions to develop either side of the dichotomy, the separation of psychological and sociological explanations of criminal behaviour has never been absolute. Based on the premise that 'man is neither driven by inner forces nor buffeted helplessly by environmental influences' (Bandura 1973: 43), an important tradition of criminological enquiry has recognised 'the reality' of criminal behaviour to lie somewhere at a level which is neither completely free nor completely determined (e.g. Burt 1925; Friedlander 1947; Matza 1964; Mays 1964; Evans 1980; Rutter and Giller 1983; Wikström and Sampson 2006; Gadd and Jefferson 2007). However, as we shall see, despite calls for the convergence of scientific disciplines to assess criminality in relation to both individual development (the psychological approach) and social context (the sociological approach), finding a non-ideological methodology capable of integrating what are often incompatible perspectives remains an ambitious undertaking (Wikström and Sampson 2006).

The spatial dimensions of criminal desistance

This is not a philosophy book. It is not the aim to bridge this divide. Attempts to resolve the binary opposition between individual agency and social structure are highly contested and subject to ongoing theoretical elaboration. Moreover, and more to the point, in terms of the methodologies employed, despite the attention given to uniting criminological and geographical disciplines in 'multi-level analysis', the uncertainty of applying wide-ranging theoretical concerns to the narrower issue of crime has often led to intellectual disarray and a blurring of disciplinary boundaries (Herbert 1982). Nevertheless, by referring to some of the arguments presented in these debates, it is intended to draw out some of the meanings and interpretations that place and changing social contexts have for persistent offenders which exemplify how criminal desistance occurs, or does not occur, over the life course. In tracing the 'pathways' taken by persistent offenders between the community and prison, the aim is to tease out experiences and social circumstances central to the lives of persistent offenders while exploring how more generally criminality and place are mutually constituted.

This analysis is intended to support a practical aim of the book. A primary purpose is to discuss the implications of the evidence presented and the arguments discussed for prisoner-reintegration policy and practice – or 're-entry', as it is called in the United States – the process by which offenders are released from prison and supervised after release in the community. No doubt owing to the abstractness of the concepts involved, to date understandings of the relationship between subjective experience and place have not been applied in a considered manner to programmes or services concerned with reducing rates of reoffending by ex-prisoners. Throughout, it is argued that, given reintegration is commonly assumed to be a process which aims to restore offenders to the social environment which preceded their imprisonment, this is an oversight. As pointed out by Raynor (2007: 27), 'the problem with this view is that it may have been an actively criminogenic environment, and even the main reason why they found themselves in prison in the first place.' Although it may not be a precondition of successful criminal desistance to administer a 'geographic cure' (Maruna 2001: 153–4) and help ex-prisoners move out of home areas, for persistent offenders who profess a willingness to give up crime and plan their lives accordingly, continued attachment to the places in which they began their criminal careers may hinder the behavioural transformations they need to make in order to follow through.

Another reason for the oversight perhaps is that because the causes of crime are traditionally thought to lie within the individual at a level beyond conscious awareness or control, or else outside in the structural details of the world, much criminology has remained relatively unconcerned with the lived reality of crime, how it is influenced by foreground factors, including 'what goes on in people's heads' (Burnett 2004a: 153). Moreover, in terms of penal policy specifically, as a result of an overall tendency to treat offenders as criminals first and authentic human beings second (Duguid 2000), prison rehabilitation programme staff have not attempted to ascertain how offenders themselves account for the propensity to reoffend. Guided by this fundamental omission and methodologically, through building up a composite picture of the meanings, interpretations and values persistent offenders attach to the places they inhabit over the life course, it is a primary intention of the book to assess the extent to which prisoner reintegration and resettlement policy may be usefully operationalised around the spatial dimensions of criminal desistance.

The structure of the book

Undoubtedly this is an ambitious enterprise. It involves the integration of criminological, sociological, psychological, geographical and broader social scientific disciplines, and it introduces both quantitative and qualitative analysis to illustrate and justify the overall conclusions it presents. As such, it affords only a cursory examination of some highly complex and contested theoretical positions and ideas. Its overall intention, however, is to argue that the context of criminal behaviour and how it helps or hinders criminal desistance can only be understood in relation to wider social and cultural perspectives than criminological spatial analysis has traditionally accommodated to date. This broad perspective is necessary to consider the geographical distribution of offenders, inform approaches to offender rehabilitation and reintegration, and, on a broader policy scale, cast critical light on present-day spatial management and control of crime.

The book is organised into the following chapters. Chapter 1 summarises theoretical work on criminal desistance. It provides a brief historical account of the emergence of desistance research from the margins of life-course criminological analysis to the mainstream. In particular, it charts the development of three primary perspectives: ageing, social context and identity change. A discussion of the extent to which space and place are pivotal to these, in that they engender meanings and a sense of self which obstructs or supports criminal desistance, structures the evidence and analysis presented.

Chapter 2 introduces new quantitative data on the spatial distri-bution of former prisoners throughout the metropolitan area of Greater London. This supplements evidence previously published on other parts of the UK and also the United States, showing that a majority of prisoners return to a small number of urban neighbourhoods. It reveals that in comparison to cities which display clearly defined geographical concentrations of ex-prisoners, the distribution of prisoner addresses in Greater London is relatively diffuse. These findings are assessed in relation to the context of changing urban geographies – neo-liberal globalisation, the capital investment in land, and the role of the housing market. The conclusion drawn is that the context of offender rehabilitation differs spatially according to the uneven historical trajectory of urban economic development and the disparate economic and political circumstances that stem from this.

These themes are expanded in Chapter 3. In presenting broad theoretical positions on geographical differentiation, social deprivation and the spatial concentration of crime and criminals, the chapter discusses divergent discourses on the role of the community to tackle crime. Linking these to equally broad accounts of the development of criminal motivation, the chapter argues that many of the criminological explanations of crime and place have little purchase on the observation that prison populations are drawn from certain neighbourhoods. As a consequence, crime control policies which redefine issues of social order in spatial terms continue to prioritise prevention, protection and exclusion over rehabilitation, resettlement and reintegration.

The failure of criminological spatial analysis to satisfactorily explain geographical concentrations of offenders leads in Chapter 4 to consideration of spatial analysis in other areas of social scientific investigation. With reference to both sociological and geographical materials on everyday life experiences in the contemporary city, the pathways and choices open to different people in different spaces and places – in both the community and prison – are discussed. It is argued that although these, too, have a tendency to drift either side of the structure agency dichotomy, they provide a much closer reading of the relationship.

Having established the necessity of incorporating the specificity of place, its structural characteristics and function, as well as the self-conscious sense of place and shared meanings derived from everyday lived experience – what Williams (1973) referred to as 'local structures of feeling' – Chapters 5, 6 and 7 assess how structural and personal differences interrelate to affect offending and criminal desistance over the life course. Introducing findings from new qualitative research, they explore the meanings and interpretations prisoners attach to the places they inhabit. By adopting a longitudinal framework which encompasses pre-prison (Chapter 5), in-prison (Chapter 6) and after-prison (Chapter 7) circumstances and experiences, these chapters explore changing dimensions of age, family life, social background, peer groups, social networks and so on, while also assessing the ways in which, more generally, crime, criminality and place are mutually constituted. Together, in seeking personal accounts of offending, reoffending and re-imprisonment over the life course, they organise subjective meanings and perceptions of reoffending and criminal desistance into a form which has a beginning, a middle and an end: a narrative structure.

Finally, Chapter 8 assesses the significance of the research findings for prisoner reintegration policy and practice with particular reference to the UK. Three key areas are highlighted: relationship work, partnership working and area-based initiatives. The book concludes with some general observations on the deficits in capabilities experienced by people living in areas of economic and social deprivation and the need for rehabilitation and reintegration approaches to address these as a specific criminal justice policy intervention which dovetails with wider policy strategies implemented to address structural impoverishment and social exclusion.

Chapter I

Criminal desistance in context

Introduction

This chapter presents the main theoretical positions advanced to explain why nearly all criminals stop offending by the time they reach their late twenties (Blumstein and Cohen 1987). It is usual in studies of reoffending to examine separate processes – the deterrent effect of different sentencing options, for example, or the role of supervision after release from prison in the community. In search of 'a new paradigm in reintegration practice' (Maruna *et al.* 2004), criminological research in recent years has broadened the understanding of reoffending and reconviction to encompass interrelated processes of behavioural change. The overall aim of this work is to understand how, why, when and under what circumstances criminals naturally change their behaviour and desist from offending without the assistance of discrete correctional interventions. In contrast to recidivism, which traditionally is measured in relation to specific outcomes such as rearrest, re-conviction and re-imprisonment – each of which fails to reveal anything about the complex of factors and processes involved (Maltz 1984) – criminal desistance is conceptualised as a gradual, long-term process. Labelling perspectives suggest that while some offenders experiment with crime only for a short while (primary deviance), others adopt it as a character role which persists over time (secondary deviance) (Lemert 1951). Reversing this process, desistance writers are interested in why most offenders vacillate and lapse in and out of criminality (primary desistance) but eventually abandon crime for good (secondary desistance) (Maruna and Farrall

2004). In attempting to reveal the dynamics of how offenders reform on their own, it is intended that practical interventions will emerge which facilitate offender rehabilitation and reintegration during this developmental process.

After charting the emergence of criminal desistance research, the chapter turns to perhaps the most pressing issue facing the implementation of desistance-focused rehabilitation and reintegration: the untangling of personal and social factors. In presenting the developmental stages of reintegration and the various personal and situational characteristics offenders must confront as they make the life course transition from prison to the community, it concludes with a lengthy discussion of local habitats, and the extent to which these influence the criminal behaviour of released prisoners. The three main themes which emerge from this – social deprivation, social interaction patterns, and social capital – are returned to throughout the remainder of the book as key characteristics which shape how prisoners reconnect with physical environments and local communities.

From margins to mainstream

Until relatively recently, to the extent criminal desistance was considered at all in criminology, it was generally accepted as a predictable outcome of the ageing process. Preferring to look within the individual for indications of behavioural change, most criminologists identified 'ontogenetic processes of maturational reform' (Gove 1985) as the primary reason offenders eventually 'burnt out' both biologically and psychologically (Glueck and Glueck 1940). Generally considered to be the strongest predictor of criminal desistance, age today remains such a primary factor that it is thought to operate 'regardless of what else happens' (Gottfredson and Hirschi 1990: 136). It is 'invariant across social and cultural conditions' (*ibid.*: 128) and its effects work independently of any other possible correlates (Wilson and Herrnstein 1985). Commonly linked to rational choice theory, it is argued, that as offenders get caught more often (Clarke and Cornish 1985) and become disillusioned at spending increasing amounts of time in prison (Cusson and Pinsonneault 1986), they begin to reflect on the opportunities they have wasted and eventually reach the rational decision that it is in their best interests to give up a life ill spent.

The problem with this overall perspective is that it commits a basic 'ontogenetic fallacy' (Dannefer 1984). In assuming criminal desistance is natural and invariant over the life course, it fails to explain why criminal behaviour has a tendency to ebb and flow, and why offenders 'drift' in and out of crime (Matza 1964). It also fails to acknowledge the differential effects of ageing on the development of criminal careers; for example on individuals who commit particular offence types, subgroups of offenders, or who begin to commit crime earlier rather than later in life. Seeking to address these problems, a seminal taxonomy of criminal desistance devised by Moffitt (1993) makes a distinction between a small group of 'life-course-persistent' offenders, who begin committing crime during childhood, crime which becomes progressively serious as they grow into adulthood; and 'adolescence-limited offenders', who begin committing crime in their teenage years and are involved in less serious forms of offending. In the sense that criminal activity subsides as they mature into adulthood, the criminal behaviour of 'adolescence-limited' offenders is thought to be situationally specific. 'Life-course-persistent' offenders on the other hand are shaped early on by dispositional personality traits such as various neuropsychological disorders, which, in conjunction with bad parenting or school failure, continue to affect them throughout the life course. Farrington (1994: 511–12) charts the predictable course of events: 'hyperactivity at age two may lead to cruelty to animals at six, shoplifting at 10, burglary at 15, robbery at 20, and eventually spouse assault, child abuse and neglect, alcohol abuse, and employment and accommodation problems later in life.'

But there are problems with this account too. Although it assesses ageing in relation to different categories of offender and offending histories, subsequent research has found that early childhood propensities do not consistently predict persistent criminality in later life (Ezell and Cohen 2005). As Shover (1996) has observed, persistent offenders undergo phases of criminal career characterised by temporal shifts in identity, subjective changes in goals and aspirations, and qualitative differences in opportunities and constraints, all of which may affect the propensity to offend. Moreover, Pitts (2003) has questioned whether the developmental trajectory suggested by Moffitt should be reversed, in that individual risk factors such as hyperactivity and impulsivity are as likely to be symptoms of persistent offending as causes.

A broader criticism is that in isolating the early development of dispositional traits linked to offending within the individual, family and school, persistent offenders are assessed as if they are somehow unaffected by wider social structures and institutions. Undoubtedly, stability of family background is important for instilling a degree of informal social control early in life. However, the propensity to act criminally is not simply a product of chaotic or lax parenting. Poverty, stress and social dislocation can impede the ability of parents to exercise appropriate standards of supervision, making it more likely children will develop delinquent behaviours as they grow older (Sampson and Laub 1994). The need to consider the extent to which criminal behaviour is mediated by factors other than ageing or the family is addressed in Sampson and Laub's (1993) 'theory of age-graded social control'. This explains life-course changes in criminal behaviour in relation to various social ties and relationships which in bonding individuals to society, are thought to exert control over them (Hirschi 1969). In rejection of the notion that behavioural change is not possible for life-course-persistent offenders, education and completing schooling (Farrington *et al.* 1986), gaining employment (Graham and Bowling 1995), getting married (Warr 1998) and becoming a parent (Leibrich 1993) are all thought to 'create interdependent systems of obligation and restraint that impose costs for translating criminal propensities into action' (Sampson and Laub 1993: 141).

Sampson and Laub's work has been heralded for marking 'a watershed in research into criminal careers' (Farrall and Sparks 2006: 9). Yet as with the desistance theories outlined above, it has not always received unequivocal support. Most notably, and as acknowledged by Laub and Sampson themselves, it has been criticised for privileging social over person-based factors, rather than suggest how and under what circumstances they may be intertwined. For example, reviewing the research, Modell (1994) found that 'the authors cannot divorce themselves from a variable focus.... Nor are they adept at discerning (or portraying) the inner logic of lives revealed in data such as these' (in Laub and Sampson 2003: 8). In sum, Sampson and Laub fail to account for the dialectical interplay between human agency and social context, which together are thought to shape the trajectories of life-course criminality. As it has developed in recent years, criminal desistance research has arrived at this fundamental problem: how to untangle subjective and social characteristics of criminal behaviour. Alongside other attempts to broaden understandings of criminal desistance (see Farrall and Bowling 1999; Giordano *et al.* 2002; Maruna and Farrall 2004), Laub and Sampson (2003: 9) have responded to these 'challenges and unresolved questions' by bringing into account 'the interplay of human agency and choice, situational influences, routine activities, local culture, and historical context'. In so doing, they have advanced the proposition that 'desistance stems from a variety of complex processes – developmental, psychological and sociological – that bear on termination and the processes of desistance from crime' (Laub and Sampson 2001: 3). The various factors associated with it interact to produce different outcomes (see also Farrall 2002; Maruna *et al.* 2004; Burnett 2004a). Desistance may be prompted by a singular event such as imprisonment, marriage or gaining employment; but it is shaped and reshaped gradually by the way individuals respond to the constraints and opportunity structure of the social world in which they live (Maruna 1999). Offenders retain the capacity to make internal changes necessary to initiate a crime-free life through their own efforts (Maruna 2001), but they do so in a variety of social contexts which structure their decisions and actions (Laub and Sampson 2001). As such, developmental and psychological factors are as important to understanding why offenders desist from crime as is social and environmental context.

Untangling personal and social factors

To what extent is it possible to untangle personal and social factors in the analysis of life-course behavioural change? While they acknowledge the interplay, according to Laub and Sampson (2001: 41) the dilemma facing criminal desistance research is irresolvable. There is simply 'no way to disentangle the role of subjective vs. objective change as the cause of desistance'. For others, however, it is a matter of finding the right methodologies to establish the sequential order in which subjective and social factors interrelate. On the foundational proposition that cognitive transformations come first (Giordano *et al.* 2002), it has been proposed, for example, that 'subjective changes may precede life-changing structural events and, to that extent, individuals can act as agents of their own change' (LeBel *et al.* 2008: 155). The following section discusses the most recent developments in criminal desistance research.

Responding to the criticisms made of their previous work, Laub and Sampson (2001) have since proposed that criminal desistance is related to significant events and/or turning points which 'serve as the catalyst for sustaining long-term behavioural change' (*ibid.*: 149). Offenders who have successfully given up crime, they contend, 'often selected these structural and situational circumstances (for example, they decided to get married, get that job, hang out with those friends), but these institutions and relationships in turn influenced the men as well' (Laub and Sampson 2003: 279). This general observation departs from their previous position, in that criminal persistence and criminal desistance are now considered to be intrinsically personal processes. A failure to develop pro-social relationships frees offenders to pursue full-blown criminal careers. During childhood and adolescence, the absence of social controls such as those exerted within the family, school, and work, or with peer groups and marriage partners, results in crime being purposefully embraced by offenders for the rewards, as well as the excitement and pleasure it brings. Alternatively, crime is rejected when, as they get older, involvement in family life, education, work, and marriage engenders a purposeful commitment to quit. Succinctly put:

> Persistence in crime is explained by a lack of social controls, few structured routine activities, and purposeful human activity. Simultaneously, desistance from crime is explained by a confluence of social controls, structured routine activities, and purposeful human agency (Sampson and Laub 2005: 166).

There is an important proviso to this chain of events: social relationships have to be of sufficient quality to be valued by the offender. There is nothing inherently meaningful in social relationships *per se*. It is what they mean to the offender that really matters. Employment has to be stable and marriages have to be good, or at least of a quality supportive of the efforts of the offender to desist. If not, they are likely to have the reverse effect and reinforce the propensity to engage in criminal activity. Moreover, the impact of employment or marriage is mediated by other issues such as housing or drug dependency, and so alone is not sufficient to turn offenders' lives around. This reveals an important subjective characteristic of the relationships involved. Many offenders get jobs, get married and have children, but these are not fixed or bounded entities which offenders experience uniformly. Family life, employment, marriage and children can spur offenders on to contemplate giving up crime, and also provide the stability of lifestyle necessary for the maintenance of law-abiding behaviour; but the quality of such relationships to fundamentally change psychological and emotional outlooks on life is affected by the amount of personal investment they are prepared to put into them. As Farrall and Calverley (2006: 104) have observed, forging a new non-criminal identity 'is as much about changes in feelings as it is about changes in behaviour, family formation, employment and so on'. Therefore, it is necessary to assess how offenders think, reason and act upon the decisions they make, and how this increases or decreases the likelihood they will avoid crime in the future. For

Farrall (2005: 368), this necessitates an existentialist approach, one which attempts to capture 'internal changes in self identity and the processes which foster such changes, but does not lose sight of the wider social world and the problems which it can create for those wishing to desist'.

In contrast to the view that events and turning points in life precede behavioural change, another recent taxonomy of criminal desistance contends that offenders who successfully give up crime are agents of their own change. According to Maruna (2001), given the 'dire' circumstances of their lives – their criminogenic traits, backgrounds and environments – many persistent offenders feel 'doomed to deviance'. Therefore, criminal desistance research should concentrate on understanding how it is that offenders who do turn their lives around and successfully give up crime are able to overcome such daunting obstacles. Because 'families, jobs, age, or time cannot change a person who does not make a personal effort to change on the inside' (ibid.: 32), 'making good' is dependent on the formation of a new non-offending identity (Gove 1985; Leibrich 1993; Graham and Bowling 1995; Shover 1996; Baskin and Sommers 1998; Burnett 2000; Uggen et al. 2004). Irrespective of the risk factors that consign persistent offenders to a recurring life cycle of crime, imprisonment and re-imprisonment, offenders who desist demonstrate a capacity to construct a 'coherent, prosocial identity for themselves' (Maruna 2001: 7). In the process 'not only is the desisting ex-offender "changed"... he or she is also reconstituted' (ibid: 10). By forming within themselves a fundamental commitment to attain a desired goal, offenders who give up crime are able to 'recast their criminal pasts not as the shameful failings that they are but instead as the necessary prelude to some newfound calling' (ibid.: 9).

There is no problem with this idea other than the old sociological one of where to draw the line between 'personal troubles' and 'public issues' (Mills 1959). That is: the extent to which unemployment, divorce, illness, addiction, poverty, chaotic family life and so on may be controlled and overcome through individual agency and responsibility, or are beyond voluntary action because they have historical and structural antecedents which require larger-scale economic or social reform. Criminal desistance is dependent on the response offenders make to the difficulties they face, as well as the nature of the difficulties themselves. As much as offenders might want to purposefully turn their lives around, 'the circumstances in which they do so may not enable them to live up to these decisions. Moreover, their decisions may be constrained in ways of which the subjects themselves are unaware' (Farrall and Bowling 1999: 260). For instance, the confidence they express may be misguided and unrealistic, or they may spurn the offer of support because they think they can 'go it alone'. Furthermore, offenders often give up crime without recourse to what Maruna (2001) has termed a 'redemption script'. They 'can and do desist without a conscious decision to "make good"… and offenders can and do desist without a"cognitive transformation"' (Laub and Sampson 2003: 279). They do so haltingly and at different rates because choice is always 'linked to situations and larger structures (cultural, social and psychological), past, present and future' (*ibid.*: 54). It is of note that Maruna (2001: 39–40) draws on the sociology of Giddens (1991) to formulate the theoretical position that identity change is brought about through a process of 'narrative development' and 'reflexive awareness'. In response to this insistently rational view of human behaviour, Layder (2004: 130) has written:

> The actual extent to which the self-narrative is revisable is always limited, conditioned and constrained by external circumstances. It is never simply a reflexive project at the behest of the desires and transformative powers of the individual.

These critiques are not dismissed by Maruna. It is acknowledged that offenders who express confidence in the future do not simply solve their own problems by dint of the motivation to do so, and that for some 'the impact of hope shrinks as the number of problems encountered rises. If faced with dire circumstances upon release, such as homelessness, bereavement, extreme poverty, then feelings of self-efficacy are likely to be vanquished or have little impact' (Burnett and Maruna 2004: 399). Overall, this suggests a twin-track approach which focuses 'on motivation as well as on risk' (Ward and Maruna 2007: 165); the aim being to instil in offenders the personal competencies to solve their own problems, and also focus on 'the external conditions necessary for a person to function effectively within his social, cultural and physical environment' (*ibid.*). The social and situational contexts in which processes of criminal desistance and offender reintegration are played out are discussed below. For the most part this section focuses on local structural influences – in particular the physical and social characteristics of the places inhabited by persistent offenders – and is intended to serve as a preamble to the evidence for geographical concentrations of ex-prisoners outlined in the next chapter and explained in Chapter 3. The equally important consideration of how persistent offenders make sense of, and respond to the situational and social context of the places they inhabit, is introduced theoretically in Chapter 4, and presented from the life-course perspective of persistent offenders themselves in Chapters 5–7.

The role of place and community

It has been proposed that there are four key stages to prisoner reintegration, each of which contains a range of personal, social and situational characteristics which affect criminal desistance. These include the following:

- *pre-prison circumstances* (e.g. demographic profile, work history and job skills, criminal history, substance abuse involvement, family characteristics),

- *in-prison experiences* (e.g. length of stay, participation in treatment programmes, contact with family and friends, pre-release preparation),

- *immediate post-prison experiences* (e.g. moment of release, initial housing needs, transition assistance, family support), and

- *post-release integration experiences* (e.g. employment experiences, influence of peers, family connections, social service support, criminal justice supervision). (Visher and Travis 2003: 94)

This longitudinal, life-course framework indicates that the personal histories of ex-prisoners are contextually distinctive in that they are structured along a pathway which leads back and forth, sometimes repeatedly, between prison and the outside community. Criminal desistance is conceived as a process influenced by past experiences, interpretations and actions; present attitudes, self-concepts and responses to problematic situations; and future plans of action to confront perceived and real constraints. In focusing on individual characteristics, the home and the family, community contexts, and the state institutions of work and imprisonment, it also highlights the importance of changing environmental and social contexts in the reproduction of key dispositions, experiences and events (Loeber and Wikström 1993). Criminal desistance may be based on an individual decision to change, but personal identities are constituted in and through different family and neighbourhood contexts, as well as the relationships and interconnections between them. These in the round shape offending and substance-abuse histories, work skills and job histories, mental and physical health, prison experiences, attitudes, beliefs, and personality traits (Visher and Travis 2003: 91).

In particular, therefore, this framework highlights the significance of place; in the obvious sense of neighbourhood or place of residence, but also the situational contexts of the family home, school and work and, of course, prison. We will return to the role of place generally in criminal desistance towards the end of the chapter, but for now the crucial impact of the incarceration experience is considered. It is important to differentiate prisoners from offenders, re-imprisonment from reoffending, and reconviction from recidivism (Maltz 1984) for the simple reason that prison affects people. In and of itself, prison is an extraordinarily 'powerful social context that can have destructive, even criminogenic consequences on the persons confined there' (Haney 2005: 84). On top of the problems offenders have accrued already in their lives – a lack of education and skills, and a history of serious drug abuse, for example – the experience of imprisonment arrests maturation and depletes human resources. It also imparts stigma, which in later life causes many ex-prisoners to conceal their pasts from the people they come into contact with in everyday social situations or at work (Goffman 1968). Notwithstanding evidence of marginal reductions in reoffending (Posner 1985), such views are generally supportive of the argument that prisons are counterproductive. Rather than deter offenders, or encourage them to lead 'good and useful lives' through reformist measures, imprisonment 'causes recidivism [and it] cannot fail to produce delinquents. It does so by the very type of existence that it imposes on its inmates' (Foucault 1977: 265–66).

The failure of imprisonment to reform offenders has been recognised throughout its history (Rothman 1980). It is generally believed that prisoners reoffend because 'shortly after release the ex-inmate forgets a great deal of what life was like on the inside and once again begins to take for granted the privileges around which life in the institution was organized' (Goffman 1961: 70). Moreover, lengthy spells of inactivity and the routine nature of everyday life inculcate a sense of irresponsibility such that many young offenders fail to mature into adulthood and continue to treat 'life as a party' (Shover 1996). It follows that they are often unable or unwilling to form lasting attachments and commitments to friends or marriage partners (Laub and Sampson 2003). Therefore, in order to overcome the effects of imprisonment on them, they must fashion a new life for themselves by controlling the often chaotic personal and social circumstances they return to outside. Some of the barriers they face are generic, such as the requirement to disclose criminal convictions to potential employers, or restrictions on housing and higher education. Others are situational, such as disrupted family relationships, a wariness and mistrust of people towards them, and ongoing exposure to criminal opportunities and criminal networks. And others still are personal, such as a lack of appropriate habits, values and skills. All told, if they are to successfully give up crime, ex-prisoners must make good 'in the face of widespread social stigma, limited career opportunities, and social exclusion' (Maruna 2001: 27).

It is common for prisoners to receive little help to overcome these problems. For the most part, individual programmes of rehabilitation have had preference over broader social issues associated with resettlement (Maruna *et al.* 2004). In general, there has been a 'lack of attention [on] the impact of social constraints ... and [the] incentive to desist from crime' (Gray 2005: 952). An important consequence of this is that without 'transitional experiences and other resources with which to buffer them' (Haney 2005: 83), prisoners returning home are left to their own devices to renegotiate the criminogenic contexts and situations from which they came, and which probably impacted on their propensity to commit crime in the first place. Petersilia (2003: 7-8) has described the process by which prisoners are released in the United States:

> Most of them will be given a bus ticket and told to report to the parole office in their home community on the next business day. Their 'home' is usually defined as their last legal residence or, in some states, the county in which their current conviction occurred. If they live in a state that provides funds upon release (about one-third of states do not), they will be given $25 to $200 in gate money.... Sometimes, a list of rental apartments or shelters is provided, but the arrangements are generally left up to the offender to determine where to reside and how to pay for basic essentials such as food, housing, and clothing during the first months. Employment is also mostly left up to the offender.... The notion is that convicts can 'make it', if they so desire.

Release procedures in the UK are similarly haphazard. Prisoners are released back into the community with little money (Hagell *et al.* 1995), limited career opportunities (Farrall 2002), and few prospects of finding somewhere stable to live (Lewis *et al.* 2003). Research has shown that 70 per cent of ex-prisoners have no employment, training or education arranged for them on release (Niven and Stewart 2005). Even so, once they return to their home communities, the supervision procedures to which they are required to conform are directed mainly towards ensuring individual compliance and control rather than addressing specific barriers to resettlement. For the most part, 'offending related' rather than 'desistance focused' (Farrall 2004) probation practice has developed in recent years to emphasise risk management and public protection over 'broader social contexts and conditions required to support change' (McNeill 2002: 5). Although historically, the role of the probation service has been to *advise, assist and befriend* offenders through the delivery of interventions customised to address such issues as accommodation and employment, today probation practice has been completely realigned to focus 'on the management of supervision rather than its content' (Worrall and Hoy 2005: 84).

According to Farrall (2002: 26), 'this general neglect of social and personal factors is extraordinary in view of the well established fact that there is a strong link between some forms of offending and some social and personal circumstances.' In a study of 199 probationers, it was found that although over half had made progress towards giving up crime, successful desistance could be attributed to specific interventions in only a few cases, although help with securing permanent employment and forming stable family relationships was shown to be of particular relevance. The overall conclusion drawn is that rehabilitation and reintegration are processes which unfold not in treatment rooms or probation centres but in the places routinely inhabited by offenders during the course of everyday life. Offenders respond best to programmes when they provide advice and guidance based on a close understanding of the local environmental and community contexts in which they make decisions and act upon them. As such, probation interventions need to assess the 'social circumstances and relationships with others [which] are both the object of the intervention and the medium through which ... change can be achieved' (Farrall 2002: 214). This view accords with other recent research on prisoner programmes and offender reintegration which has found that behavioural change effected in prison is best maintained after release by addressing accommodation and employment issues (Elliott-Marshall *et al.* 2004). Advice is most readily received by prisoners 'provided it [is] based on a demonstrated understanding of themselves and their situation' (Rex 1999: 376). While it is recognised that 'offender management models that adopt a generic or integrated, rather than specialist or fragmented, approach are likely to be more effective in reducing re-offending' (Chitty 2004: 74), as 'gains made in prison can be quickly lost if there is insufficient aftercare for prisoners once they are released' (Harper and Chitty 2005: xx), 'it is important (and necessary) for such approaches to reflect local circumstances' (Chitty 2004: 74).

Assessing local circumstances

What are the local circumstances to which prisoners return, and to what extent can they be categorised and delineated? In the next chapter, research evidence is presented that reveals that large numbers of prisoners return to the same socially deprived and high-crime communities from which they originated. As noted by Visher and Travis (2003: 104), the continual movement of offenders between prison and certain urban neighbourhoods has the potential to further embed criminal behaviour 'because the social network of the community and its ability to maintain order is already weakened'. Criminological analysis has affirmed the importance of place in the (re)production of criminal events generally (Bottoms and Wiles 1992). However, as pointed out by Farrall and Sparks (2006: 8), its role 'in fostering (or indeed, inhibiting) rehabilitation is something that for many years eluded many studying criminal careers'.

A proper investigation of people–place relationships in these terms inevitably involves 'the study of social relations and the spatial structures that underpin those relations' (Johnston *et al.* 2000: 753). And perhaps the most obvious change in social relations to consider is the relative impact of structural inequality; in particular, the differential effect of poverty and whether individuals are more likely to desist from crime if they move from a poor to a prosperous neighbourhood. This spatial problem was addressed in some relatively early desistance research which found that, allowing for differences in police procedures and risk of detection – although in other respects social behaviour and lifestyle remained unchanged – offenders who moved out of an inner-city neighbourhood in London to counties in south-east England were hindered from committing crime at the same rate (Osborn 1980). This was taken to affirm the prior assumption that 'moving out was significantly associated with a smaller incidence of subsequent convictions … [and] circumstances associated with living out of London provided less opportunity and temptation' (*ibid.*: 61). However, although this is an interesting finding, as no analysis was subsequently carried out to ascertain why this might be the case, it raises more questions than it answers (Farrall and Sparks 2006).

More recently, the 'Moving to Opportunity' (MTO) housing experiment, conducted by the Department of Housing and Urban Development in the United States, and piloted in the cities of Baltimore, Boston, Chicago, Los Angeles and New York, has assessed neighbourhood effects on life-course criminality in relation to individual outcomes. By allocating housing vouchers to families in poor neighbourhoods, it has attempted to isolate various neighbourhood factors thought to account for adolescent delinquency from individual or family differences. Families participating in the programme have been allocated to one of three groups: a group required to move to low-poverty neighbourhoods, a group whose option to move was not restricted to certain neighbourhoods, and a control group that received no benefits at all. Analysis to date has found that moving from a highly deprived to a more affluent area has a positive effect on reducing crime rates for violent male and female offenders. In the short term, it also has a positive effect on property offending, although for males this is not sustained over time. In fact, in the longer term, males register arrest rates for property crime some 30 per cent higher than males in the control group (Kling *et al.* 2005). The findings therefore are mixed, although it has been claimed that the increase in male property crime is generally compensated for by the overall reduction in violent crime, which is both more damaging and costly to society (*ibid.*).

To an extent, these findings have been replicated in research carried out recently to investigate factors leading to involvement in offending and the development of criminal desistance in Scotland. Once again, the results are mixed. For instance, it has been found that, although neighbourhood characteristics 'do play a part in predicting whether a young person gets involved in property offending during early adolescence … these are not as numerous as individual level factors in determining such behaviour' (McVie and Norris 2006a: 26). Nevertheless, in more general terms it has been observed that 'delinquency, cannabis and hard drug use … thrives within areas experiencing structural adversity and economic deprivation' (McVie and Norris 2006b: 24). Moreover, in relation to criminal desistance specifically, the researchers concluded that the findings are

> consistent with other recent evidence… that shows that those living in deprived neighbourhoods were less likely to desist from offending than those living in more affluent

neighbourhoods (Smith 2006). Such evidence highlights the contextual importance of the places that young people grow up and is broadly supportive of Sampson and Laub's (1993) theory that social stress within neighbourhoods acts as an inhibitor to the formation of strong social bonds which are necessary to enable young people to 'grow out' of crime. (*ibid.*)

To some observers, both of these studies are part of a much larger research agenda which has consistently provided evidence that neighbourhood processes are strongly linked to crime (Sampson *et al.* 2002). Unequivocally, it has been suggested that, overall, the findings indicate that, 'a causal effect of community does not necessarily require individuals as units of analysis' (Sampson 2006: 31). Moreover, according to Sampson (2008), disagreements concerning whether the results from the MTO programme are distorted by selection bias, or criticisms that the overall sample is too small to significantly affect the social composition of the areas to which the families moved and therefore reveals nothing about the social dynamics involved (Goering and Richardson 2003), obscure the value of assessing neighbourhood effects in their own right. Because the results of neighbourhood research may be interpreted in relation to any number of social processes, including the experience of moving itself, they are not reducible to changes in the impact of poverty on individuals alone. Spatial variations in crime may be explained by social mechanisms which have nothing to do with who actually commits it. The implications of this argument for public policy on crime and criminal desistance are profound. They suggest that 'neighborhood- or population-level interventions may be more cost-effective than those targeted to individuals' (Sampson 2008: 195), a conclusion which is discussed further in the final chapter.

Another theme to consider in investigations of place-based factors is the extent to which social relations and interaction patterns characteristic of particular places are linked to crime and criminal desistance. For example, Meisenhelder (1977, 1982) has found that social relationships and activities in certain public spaces, such as bars or street corners, are conducive to criminal activity. Whereas time spent in the family home, school, or legitimate places of employment can encourage the formation of new law-abiding identities, unstructured time spent mixing with peer groups likely to condone or engage in antisocial behaviour and crime can reaffirm the ex-prisoner's status as a persistent offender. More recently, and in a similar vein, Farrall and Sparks (2006: 12-13) have revealed how spatial relationships based on 'deviant consumption' may be transformed to ones of 'respectable reproduction' when reordered and reinforced around different routines and activities such as going to work every day in town and city centres rather than to drink, watch fights, pursue women and so on. It follows that 'knifing off' immediate criminogenic environments (Caspi and Moffitt 1995), avoiding contact with 'law-violating or norm-violating peers' (Akers 1990), and developing new social networks and attachments (Baskin and Sommers 1998) are important requisites for successful criminal desistance.

A final theme to consider is the differential distribution of mainstream resources and the effect this has on whether offenders desist from crime and engage fully in civil society. As we have seen, access to education, training, employment and housing is considered a prerequisite of criminal desistance in the long term (Farrall 2002; Elliott-Marshall *et al.* 2004). Unless legitimate opportunities to reintegrate back into society are available to ex-prisoners in the places they return to 'then no assistance – regardless of intensity, design or commitment of staff – will be of any help' (Farrall 2004: 71). As pointed out by Visher and Travis (2003), and assessed in much greater detail in the following chapter, many of the residential locations to which prisoners return lack the organisational infrastructure and capital to provide mainstream education, training and employment opportunities. To the extent that it is possible to influence wider meso- and macro-level circumstances, interventions should therefore attend to the physical settings and wider economic and social contexts in which ex-prisoners attempt to 'make good their lives' (Laub and Sampson 2003; Bottoms 2006; Farrall and Calverley 2006; Farrall and Sparks 2006).

In order to establish social networks and build up resources which support offenders to maintain desistance from crime, Farrall (2002, 2004) has emphasised the importance of interventions which generate 'social capital'. In comparison to 'human capital' which refers to personal resources such as motivations, skills and knowledge, social capital is constitutive of the relationships, networks and opportunities that exist in families, communities and places (Coleman 1988). In order to develop social capital in ways that enable offenders to maintain behavioural change, it is recommended that probation services tackle family relationship problems and build community relations. They should also seek to improve local employment opportunities, as, for example, by liaising with local employers to ensure that ex-offenders are not discriminated against if and when they disclose criminal records during job interviews (Fletcher *et al.* 1998). Social capital is returned to in more detail in Chapter 4. It is also referred to again in the final chapter, which assesses the role of partnership working and area-based interventions to support criminal desistance. For now, however, in order to justify the central argument of this book, that the economic, social, institutional and cultural characteristics of the places and communities prisoners return to after release are important factors in whether they engage in, or refrain from, further offending, the next chapter reviews the evidence that the majority of prisoners are drawn from and return to certain socially deprived urban neighbourhoods.

Chapter 2

From A to B and back again: the revolving door between place of residence and imprisonment

Introduction

In this chapter research is presented to demonstrate that in both the United States and the UK large numbers of ex-prisoners return to specific urban areas characterised by high levels of economic and social disadvantage. Notwithstanding differences in urban structure, the evidence reveals a strong link between certain neighbourhoods, crime and imprisonment. Importantly however, this is not indicative of uniform patterns of spatial concentration between or within these countries. In the second part of the chapter, employing Greater London as a case example, data are introduced to examine the systematic tri-variation between neighbourhoods, crime and imprisonment in the contemporary city. This is then compared to other parts of the UK where the socio-economic consequences of deindustrialisation have impacted on urban development, economic infrastructure, and social mobility in different ways. The conclusion drawn is that policy approaches to urban and social deprivation, as well as crime and offender reintegration, operate in physical and social locations characterised by a high degree of social ambiguity and difference. Taking context seriously in offender reintegration policy and practice requires a close appreciation of this.

'We know who you are and we know where you live'

As prison populations have risen dramatically throughout all

Western countries over the past quarter of a century, researchers and policymakers have analysed ways of reducing the rising levels of crime committed by prisoners who each year are released back into the community in ever increasing numbers. It has been found that of the 1.4 million prisoners in state and federal prisons in the United States, nearly a third are rearrested within the first six months, 44 per cent within the first year, and over two-thirds within three years of their release (Langan and Levin 2002). In total, 52 per cent of prisoners are returned to prison within three years for either a new crime or a technical violation of parole conditions (*ibid.*). Similarly, in the UK, the Social Exclusion Unit (SEU) has acknowledged that 'prison sentences are not succeeding in turning the majority of offenders away from crime' (SEU 2002: 5). A total of 47 per cent of prisoners are reconvicted within one year of being released, and the reconviction rate for prisoners serving less than one year is 60 per cent (Ministry of Justice 2009a). Furthermore, about 40 per cent of prisoners are recommitted to custody within two years of release; and 96 per cent of prisoners under the age of 20 who have 11 or more previous convictions are recommitted to custody within two years of release (Home Office 2004a). Unsurprisingly, in both countries, this has led to heightened public and professional interest in the crime profile and social status of ex-prisoners. While control-orientated activities have been introduced to manage the risk of reoffending alongside new systems of rehabilitation and resettlement, the social and communal contexts to which prisoners return after release have also begun to receive more attention.

As noted in the previous chapter, whereas treatment approaches to prisoner rehabilitation concentrate on changing individual behaviour, social approaches focus on the social context of rehabilitation within the family, housing, schools and the work place. Recently, in the United States, research has begun to look beyond these micro- locations to explore the demographic profile of the prison population and the social characteristics of the residential areas prisoners return to after release (Petersilia 2003). This needs putting into a wider economic, social and penal context. The first issue to note is that increasing economic inequality in market societies has created areas of urban deprivation occupied by marginalised groups of people who have become isolated from mainstream employment opportunities (Harvey 1997). The second is that spatial segregation has cleaved along racial lines (Kodras 1997). The United States remains one of the most racially unequal countries in the world, with large sections of the black and Hispanic population living in 'apartheid' conditions socially isolated from broader society (Massey and Denton 1993). And third is the claim that prison is used increasingly to contain and manage the threat to public order presented by this surplus population, colloquially referred to as the 'underclass' (Feeley and Simon 1992). Together, these factors have created deeply polarised cities. The implications of this for prisoner reintegration are of major significance. According to Petersilia (2003: 30), the fact that socially marginalised groups of Latino and African-American people comprise some 70 per cent of the prison population in the United States (Peck 2003) 'affects every aspect of reentry, including communities, labor markets, family welfare, government entitlements and program innovations'.

Exactly where do these prisoners come from? Research has shown that a disproportionate number of prisoners are drawn from, and after release return to, a small number of socially deprived urban neighbourhoods creating, what has been described as, a 'carceral continuum', 'a self-perpetuating cycle of escalating socio-economic marginality and legal incapacitation' (Wacquant 2001: 114). The recurrent 'churning' of large numbers of male, black offenders out of and back into these rundown urban neighbourhoods has damaged social cohesion and trust, tipping community life into a downward spiral of ever increasing crime, violence and victimisation (Clear *et al.* 2003). Subject to coercive policing tactics (Sun *et al.* 2008), and strict penal sanction (Feeley and Simon 1992), interpersonal violence and aggression have become permanent features of everyday life for the residents who live there. Ethnographic research has revealed the ways people learn to 'handle themselves' under such circumstances. It suggests that once the judicial system is perceived to be 'a hostile imposition rather than a social institution that serves the community' (Anderson 2001: 136), residents consciously reject social and legal conventions enshrined in civil law. Bound together by a shared 'politics of location' (hooks 1990), coded, interpersonal behaviours develop, founded on a currency of reputation, respect, retribution and retaliation, and given a threatening visual presence by particular styles of dress and communicating with physical gestures (Anderson 1999). This new 'oppositional culture' (*ibid.*), 'with its ardent imperative of individual "respect" secured through the militant display and actualization of readiness to mete out physical violence' (Wacquant 2001: 110–11) is then exported to prisons where it supplants long standing 'inmate codes' of camaraderie and mutual trust, only to be exported back to further disrupt the neighbourhoods from which it evolved. The result is a constantly revolving door between prison and certain inner-city locations. Some details:

- In 1998, five states – California, Florida, New York, Ohio and Texas – accounted for just under half of all prisoners released nationally (Lynch and Sabol 2001).

- In the late 1980s, three-quarters of all prisoners in New York State came from just seven neighbourhoods in New York City, of whom 47 per cent were re-imprisoned within a year of their release (Ellis 1993 in Wacquant 2001).

- In Brooklyn, New York 11 per cent of the city blocks are home to 50 per cent of ex-prisoners, yet only 20 per cent of the Brooklyn population as a whole lives in these neighbourhoods (Lynch and Sabol 2001).

- Imprisonment rates in the Brownsville neighbourhood of Brooklyn are 150 times that of another Brooklyn neighbourhood which is only a few blocks away (Clear *et al*. 2003).

- In some parts of Washington, DC, 25 per cent of adult black males are imprisoned per day (Lynch and Sabol 1992 in Clear *et al*. 2003).

- In the state of Ohio, 22 per cent of prisoners return to Cuyahoga County, which is home to just 12 per cent of the state's population. Of these, 79 per cent return to the city of Cleveland, and just under a third return to just five communities within Cleveland (La Vigne and Thomson 2003).

- In 1998, Los Angeles County in California received 30 per cent of all state parolees, even though its residents comprised only 12 per cent of the total state population (Petersilia 2000).

- In the city of Tallahassee, Florida, crime rates have been shown to increase dramatically in a small number of neighbourhoods one year after large numbers of prisoners return to live there (Rose *et al*. 1999). All 125 residents included in a sample of people living in two small neighbourhoods in Tallahassee reported that they had a close relative in prison (*ibid*.).

- In the state of Maryland, 59 per cent of prisoners return to Baltimore, and under a third of these return to just six of Baltimore's 55 communities (La Vigne and Kachnowski 2003).

- In the state of Illinois, 51 per cent of prisoners return to Chicago, and over a third of these return to just six of Chicago's 77 communities (La Vigne *et al*. 2003).

How does this compare with the UK? In the most general terms, prisoner surveys have revealed that the prison population in the UK is overwhelmingly young, male, and socially and economically disadvantaged (Walmsley *et al.* 1992). Relative to the population generally, a disproportionate number of prisoners have no educational qualifications, experience high rates of unemployment, and live in social housing or rented accommodation. Many also come from unstable family backgrounds, suffer from some form of antisocial personality disorder, and have a history of alcohol and/or drug misuse (SEU 2002). These social and economic characteristics reflect the fact that the prison population is mostly comprised of people who live in poor material and financial circumstances. National prisoner surveys reveal that, compared to 18 per cent of the general population, nearly 70 per cent of prisoners have been unemployed prior to imprisonment (*ibid*), and that just under half of male prisoners have been employed in unskilled or partly skilled occupations (Walmsley *et al.* 1992). In terms of education, 65 per cent have a reading ability that is at, or below, the level expected of an average 11-year-old (Home Office 2001a); and just less than a half of all male prisoners have been excluded from school (Singleton *et al.* 1998). Prisoners also suffer from a range of family problems. For example, 43 per cent come from a family background in which a family member has been convicted of a criminal offence (Dodd and Hunter 1992), and just under a third have been taken into care as a child (SEU 2002). Nearly half have run away from home (Singleton *et al.* 1998), and over 30 per cent are homeless prior to imprisonment (SEU 2002). Furthermore, nearly a half have a history of serious drug addiction involving heroin or crack cocaine (Ramsay 2003). They also suffer much poorer mental health than the general population, with over 70 per cent suffering from two or more mental disorders (Singleton *et al.* 1998). Finally, in terms of race, although the prison population remains predominately English and white, numbers of black and minority ethnic prisoners, as well as foreign-national prisoners, have risen disproportionately in recent years. Between 1999 and 2002, as the total prison population increased by 12 per cent, the number of black prisoners increased by 51 per cent (HM Prison Service and Commission for Racial Equality 2003). Overall, black prisoners account for 56 per cent of ethnic minority prisoners (Ministry of Justice 2009b). Today, the prison population is comprised of 27 per cent ethnic minority prisoners compared to one in 11 of the general population (*ibid.*).

Of course, much of this is well known. A long tradition of class analysis has repeatedly drawn a link between imprisonment and inequality, and, more recently, race and gender. Ever since 1878, when prisons in the UK were brought under central government control, only rarely have the wealthy been seen as a problem population requiring prosecution and imprisonment (Reiman 1979). According to Marxist criminological perspectives, the reason for this is that imprisonment is used primarily to regulate surplus populations of labour (Rusche and Kirchheimer 2003 [1939]). In contrast, recent analyses of bureaucratic and individual decision making suggest that it is a consequence of differing perceptions of what constitutes seriousness and harm. Owing to variations in the complexity of criminal investigations, street crime and property crime, for example, commonly receive more police attention than tax evasion and corporate fraud (Clarke 1990). Not only do such processes set a precedent for sentencers to imprison more working-class than middle-class offenders who commit the same offence(s) (Cavadino and Dignan 1997), they serve to 'criminalise' areas of public space, especially disadvantaged neighbourhoods, while downplaying the importance of private locations – the everyday settings of business crime, for example (Coleman 2004).

What is less well known, however, is the extent to which in the UK, as in the United States, prisoners are drawn from specific areas which suffer high levels of urban deprivation. Again, this needs to be put into a wider context. Generally, European cities do not exhibit the same spatial scales of poverty, and income disparities are also much narrower than is the case in the United States (Atkinson *et al.* 2005). Owing to lower migration levels, neither are European cities as segregated by race (Musterd and Ostendorf 1998). Most ethnic minority groups in Britain live in mixed areas rather than polarised 'ghettoes' (Johnston *et al.* 2002). Furthermore, such intense levels of 'concentrated incarceration' (Clear *et al.* 2003) are not so evident. Penal policymakers have been more inclined than their American counterparts to implement measures designed to divert less serious young offenders from custody, obviating the need for incarceration on such a mass scale (Pitts 2003).

Recently, however, research has shown how the economic, social and penal situation may be changing. Over the past ten years, there has been a significant increase in inequality generally throughout the UK (Brewer *et al.* 2007). Evidence suggests there is now an urban mosaic of wealth and deprivation throughout England and Wales (Dorling *et al.* 2007) such that 'most of [the] examples of socio-economic collapse are concentrated in relatively small neighbourhoods (Robson *et al.* 2000: 25). As higher-income groups have exercised a 'right to buy' into private sector property markets (Hamnett 1999), the less well off have been forced to relocate to designated areas of social housing (Murie 1998). Nearly a half of this is located within the most deprived fifth of neighbourhoods, where poverty rates are double that of the population as a whole (Hills 2007). As a consequence, distinct communities of social deprivation have emerged, characterised by depleted public services, large numbers of low-income families, and, in some cases, levels of unemployment topping 60 per cent (Pitts 2003). Moreover, there is evidence that growing numbers of ethnic minorities live in pockets of social deprivation (Ratcliffe 1997). In London, 70 per cent of residents in the most deprived housing estates are from ethnic minorities (Power and Tunstall 1997), and over a dozen cities in England exhibit distinct spatial concentrations of Asian people, especially Bangladeshis and Pakistanis (Darden 2001). Finally, there is also evidence that the connection between socio-economic disadvantage and criminal behaviour has become clearer in recent years. Analyses of probation caseloads have shown that in 1965 just over a fifth of probation clients were unemployed compared to nearly 60 per cent in 1991 (Smith and Stewart 1997). Furthermore, as in the United States specific groups are increasingly found to express a lack of trust and confidence in the criminal justice system and as a consequence are unlikely to report crime to the police, a cultural characteristic which serves to further marginalise them from mainstream society (Pennant 2005).

Comparisons with the United States should not be pushed too far, however. In particular, it needs to be remembered that the increase in incarceration rates in the UK has not been anywhere near as steep. Unsurprisingly, therefore, the social consequences of large numbers of prisoners removed from and returning to disadvantaged areas has not been such a prominent feature of academic and policy-related research in recent years. Nevertheless, the few studies that have been carried out do suggest that spatial concentrations of former prisoners are certainly not exclusive to the context of the United States. In the most general terms, it has been found that prisoners in the UK are drawn primarily from metropolitan areas, a consequence of differential sentencing procedures practised by the courts, as well as contrasting crime patterns between urban and shire areas (Howard 1994), and that disproportionate numbers of ex-prisoners return to 'metropolitan areas such as Greater London, Merseyside and the West Midlands, where there are also the highest rates of deprivation and family poverty' (SEU 2002: 18). Furthermore, high rates of reoffending have been linked to a 'sharp rise in social exclusion, in areas such as child poverty, drug use, social exclusion, inequality' (*ibid*.: 5).

Of course, this meso-level analysis is far too broad to reveal whether prisoners are drawn and return to certain urban neighbourhoods. This has been the focus of more recent research which has found that in south Yorkshire, for example, ex-prisoners live predominately in relatively small areas characterised by high levels of poverty and poor-quality housing (Craglia and Costello 2005). And that within the metropolitan district of Gateshead, in the north-east of the country, half of the offenders known to the Northumbria Probation Service live in just five electoral wards characterised by the highest levels of multiple deprivation (Allen *et al.* 2007). Moreover, in Scotland, it has been found that a quarter of prisoners come from just 53 (4 per cent) of the 1,222 local government election wards, and half from the most deprived 12 per cent of wards (Houchin 2005). This equates to an imprisonment rate of 953 per 100,000 compared to 237 per 100,000 for Scotland as a whole. Of the 53 wards most represented, 35 are in Glasgow, eight in Edinburgh, three in Aberdeen and two in Dundee, compared to 269 wards which appear to produce no prisoners at all. As was made clear in the introductory chapter, it is important to emphasise here that poverty and disadvantage do not cause crime, or result in imprisonment, directly. Poverty and disadvantage are strong correlates of high-crime neighbourhoods, but not all disadvantaged neighbourhoods have high levels of crime (Hirschfield and Bowers 1997). Of course, it is also the case that not all people who live in high-crime neighbourhoods are criminals. However, the conclusion drawn from the research that social deprivation, crime and imprisonment are linked is unequivocal:

> If you are a man and come from some of our communities, not only is it likely that you will remain poor, you will be unemployed and will have poor health; it is also likely that you will spend part of your life in prison. The increased probability of spending time in prison is both a consequence and indicator of the deprivation of the community from which you come. (Houchin 2005: 23)

The next section presents new data on the residential distribution of prisoners who come from within the metropolitan area of Greater London. In doing so, it assesses social relations and practices in contemporary urban society, and the extent to which differences in urban geography throughout the UK influence the spatial organisation of criminal networks and communities.

Offender residence in the contemporary city: the case of Greater London

In important ways, the geography of social deprivation varies both between and within cities. Because the economic histories and trajectories of urban areas are never the same, there are few physical or social characteristics which unite them. According to Amin and Thrift (2002: 7), differential patterns of urban development construct contemporary cities in ways that multiply 'their extraordinary variety and vitality'. The history of economic restructuring, housing, transport and urban governance within the metropolitan area of Greater London is illustrative of this general point. Cities expand and develop in a variety of ways. For instance, they expand outwards in circles (Burgess 1925); in sectors, along lines of communication or adjacent to natural features such as lakes or rivers (Hoyt 1939); and around nuclei of social and economic activity – transport facilities, warehouse space, financial districts, residential areas and so on (Harris and Ullman 1945). As it is a global city, which throughout its history has undergone major economic restructuring, the social geography of London exemplifies all of these models of development (Pacione 2009: 143). As such, the specificity of London, its mixture of old and new economies, and diverse and constantly changing population, makes comparisons with other cities in the UK, and, vice versa, difficult to sustain.

A brief description of its historical development reveals that, as London grew rapidly during the second half of the nineteenth century, rural migrants settled in what became known as the 'rookeries', pre-existing housing blocks hastily subdivided for multiple occupation by acquisitive private landlords in the boroughs north and east of the city centre – Kings Cross, Bethnal Green, Bermondsey, Stepney and Southwark. Disease-ridden, without clean water, and traversed by open sewers, these areas rapidly became synonymous with corruption, violence and political insurrection (Hall 1988). Popularly imagined as places in which licentiousness and crime were contagious, Victorian social reformers mapped the residential location of offenders across the city. It was found that crime and criminality coalesced in neighbourhoods characterised by the highest levels of poverty. For example, between 1841 and 1850, two of the seven Metropolitan Police Divisions, containing the districts of Hoxton and Westminster, produced 65 per cent of the city's alleged criminals (Mayhew 1862 in Morris 1957: 62).

Anxious to protect their commercial and industrial interests, in response the propertied middle classes privately fortified their houses and factories (Taylor 1999). More generally however, the price of peace of mind was 'municipal socialisation'. No longer inclined to treat the poor with casual disregard (Ignatieff 1978), the ruling classes pressed for improvements in sanitation, health, and civil engineering. Moreover, building and planning regulations established single-purpose neighbourhoods to physically separate the 'dangerous classes' from the 'urban bourgeoisie', some of whom had already begun to take flight to the expanding suburbs (Jones 1971). The response to the threat and fear of crime specifically was the introduction of policing and the nationalisation of prisons, an explicit indication that government was prepared through punishment to regulate unequal class relations by incorporating the criminal classes into mainstream working life as disciplined and productive members of society (Melossi and Pavarini 1981). Deliberately situated in areas of dense working-class population, the high brick walls of Victorian prisons served as a stark reminder that a failure to accept the norms of society would result in enforceable quarantine from the rest of society as a 'foreign body' (Combessie 1998).

Throughout the twentieth century, as suburban manufacturing grew, the spatial separation of the social classes throughout Greater London intensified. Skilled workers able to take advantage of new work opportunities left the inner city for towns circling the 'green belt', leaving behind a residue of poorly skilled and unemployed labourers. Later in the century, slum clearance and the replacement of old Victorian housing stock with new council estates and high-rise flats, broke up traditional working-class areas, which, over time, increasingly came to be occupied by immigrant populations, particularly people from the Commonwealth countries of the Caribbean and the Far East (Smith 1987). During the 1960s and 1970s, these populations were the first to suffer the effects of deindustrialisation as the decline of manufacturing spread to the suburbs and beyond. Unemployment, physical dereliction and social deprivation once more became synonymous with the inner city. Then suddenly, from this position of overall economic decline, in the early 1980s London capitalised on global markets and revitalised its industrial base by attracting new financial and service sector employment (Sassen 1991). London 'boomed'. Flagship developments – Canary Wharf, Wembley Stadium, the South Bank, Kings Cross – spatially reorganised the urban landscape as large numbers of people moved into the city, including the inner city where, between 1992 and 2003, the population increased more quickly than in outer areas (Champion 2006).

It might appear from this that the recent history of London has been an unqualified economic and social success. But, as clearly documented by economic and social geographers, hand in hand with the economic and urban restructuring of London as a dominant command centre within the global economy and financial system, there has been a marked increase in poverty and systemic inequality (Massey 2007). For instance, a recent survey of social and spatial inequalities throughout the UK as a whole has shown that, apart from some areas of Glasgow, poverty is now most concentrated in east central London (Dorling and Thomas 2004). Such developments are not unique to London. Extreme spatial concentrations of affluence and deprivation are a feature of all global financial cities (Sassen 1991). While the comprehensive (re)development of office complexes and rehabilitation of housing markets have attracted growing numbers of high-income residents, a major feature of the economic transformation of contemporary cities built on the new financial services sector has been a significant increase in social polarisation. Today, London is the most unequal city in the UK. It remains spatially divided in terms of household income, housing tenure, economic activity, unemployment, health, crime, ethnic origin, and religion (Greater London Authority (GLA) 2002). As rising property prices have reorganised the physical and social geography of the city, resident Londoners and companies not involved in financial services have been priced out of the market. Rather than securing jobs for local people, the demand for high-skill workers to fill professional and managerial occupations has been met by attracting commuters and drawing on foreign workers. As a result, Londoners, without the relevant qualifications, face long-term social exclusion from the labour market (*ibid*). In an effort to regulate the openness of the economy and address widening inequality, interventionist programmes struggle 'to provide affordable housing [and] to support public services periodically in crisis because their workers can no longer afford to live in the area they serve' (Massey 2007: 158). The result is 'homelessness and overcrowding, and the stresses and strains that accompany these things' (*ibid*.: 68).

Using Greater London as a case example, the following section assesses the extent to which the economic restructuring and social demography of contemporary cities impacts on the spatial distribution of crime and criminals, and whether there are significant differences between so-called 'world' and older industrial cities. First, in terms of offences, recent statistics show that domestic burglary, for example, is prevalent across London as a whole, including in outlying areas which are relatively sparsely populated. However, the highest rates are concentrated in inner London, especially the boroughs of Lambeth, Southwark, Hackney and Tower Hamlets (GLA 2002). A similar picture emerges in relation to offenders. As referred to in the introductory chapter, and described in more detail in the Appendix, the statistics and maps presented below are based on an analysis of the address locations of prisoners who live within the Greater London area. They reveal that prisoners are drawn from Greater London at a rate of 204 per 100,000 of the population, compared to 153 per 100,000 of the population for England and Wales as a whole (Walmsley 2009). Prisoner addresses are dispersed throughout Greater London, with the exception of clusters of wards towards the periphery, in particular the far south- west, south-east, and north-west of the city. However, there is clear evidence of geographical differentiation between areas. For example, the addresses of 1,695 prisoners (a third of the sample) are contained in 16 per cent of wards, and 3,328 (just under two-thirds) in 34 per cent of wards, while the remaining third are drawn from 60 per cent of wards. As visually presented in Figure 2.1, a disproportionate number of prisoners are drawn from inner London wards, particularly an area that runs roughly north to south through the central area of the city, bounded by the wards of Northumberland Park in the north, New Cross in the east, Ferndale in the west, and South Norwood in the south.

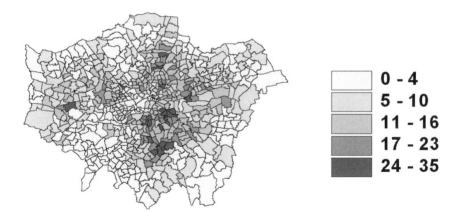

	0 - 4
	5 - 10
	11 - 16
	17 - 23
	24 - 35

Figure 2.1 Number of prisoners per ward in Greater London

Moreover, the data show there is a significant correlation between the inner London wards which contain a disproportionate number of prisoner addresses and indices of multiple deprivation. Wards which run in a roughly north to south direction through the central and north-eastern parts of the inner city, including large parts of Hackney, Tower Hamlets, Newham, Haringey and Enfield to the north of the river, and Lambeth, Southwark, Lewisham and Greenwich to the south, suffer the highest levels of social deprivation. In addition, there are small clusters of wards further out towards the west of the city, within the areas of Ealing, Hounslow and Brent, which also contain disproportionate numbers of prisoner addresses and suffer high levels of deprivation. For example, of the 16 per cent of inner- city wards which contain a third of prisoner addresses, there is a significant correlation with 'unemployment' (0.731 on the Pearson coefficient [in statistics, a ratio scale used to measure the relationship between two variables]), 'long-term unemployment' (0.729), 'population who have never worked' (0.570), 'population with no qualifications' (0.459), 'population in council accommodation' (0.579), and 'population not having good health' (0.615). For reference, a map of multiple deprivation throughout Greater London is presented in Figure 2.2.

However, although this is evidence of broad spatial differences in prisoner addresses throughout Greater London as a whole, it does

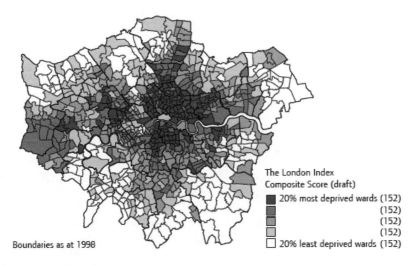

The London Index
Composite Score (draft)
■ 20% most deprived wards (152)
■ (152)
▨ (152)
□ (152)
□ 20% least deprived wards (152)

Boundaries as at 1998

source   Greater London Authority

Figure 2.2 Quintile distribution of London wards on the draft London Index

not reveal whether there are distinct concentrations at neighbourhood levels, which as we have seen, are found in the United States and other parts of the UK. Because wards are administrative units which contain artificial transitions of population densities within their boundaries, they do not provide a breakdown of population distribution according to smaller geographical units such as housing estates. So, in order to assess whether prisoner addresses are contained within micro-geographical areas within wards, the population density of prisoner addresses was calculated. In keeping with the residential distribution of prisoners by ward, Figure 2.3 again reveals that prisoner addresses are distributed diffusely, although a few small areas within the inner city and to the west of the city show disproportionate numbers of prisoner addresses. This finding is consistent with previous research showing that offenders, rather than being distributed over large metropolitan areas, tend to be clustered within smaller urban neighbourhoods (Baldwin and Bottoms 1976).

Cosmopolitan boundaries and neighbourhood relations

In order to explain why specific concentrations of offenders occur in urban space, detailed local knowledge of the physical and social characteristics of specific neighbourhoods is required (Bottoms and Wiles 1997). For instance, it would be necessary to overlay offence and

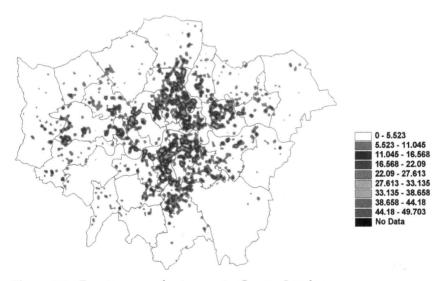

	0 - 5.523
	5.523 - 11.045
	11.045 - 16.568
	16.568 - 22.09
	22.09 - 27.613
	27.613 - 33.135
	33.135 - 38.658
	38.658 - 44.18
	44.18 - 49.703
	No Data

Figure 2.3 Density map of prisoners in Greater London

offender statistics on a range of spatial data sets on housing tenure, employment, education, lifestyle choice and so on. Nevertheless, it is possible to draw some general conclusions. Although prisoners in Greater London appear to originate in greater numbers from some parts of the city than others, patterns of geographical concentration are not as dense or clearly defined as those found in Yorkshire, Gateshead or Scotland, for example. Consistent with this is the observation that urban neighbourhoods within contemporary global cities such as London have become far less segregated than they once were (Amin and Thrift 2002). Some of the communal bonds that exist in cities remain localised and characterised by face-to-face social interaction; but, increasingly, they 'successfully persist at a distance, posing new tests of reciprocal resolution and commitment, constructing new forms of intentionality, building new types of presence' (*ibid.*: 43). Within this social context, in order to understand the reasons for spatial distributions of crime and criminals, it is necessary to assess 'relations *across* neighbourhoods – not merely as a function of geographical distance (e.g. ties to adjacent neighbourhoods) but of the actual networks of connections that cross-cut neighbourhood and even cosmopolitan boundaries' (Sampson 2006: 44; emphasis in the original). This has been clearly articulated by Young (2002: 475), for whom the contemporary city

> is a world where borders blur, where cultures cross over, hybridize and merge, where cultural globalization breaks down, where virtual communities lose their strict moorings to space and locality. The late modern city is one of blurred boundaries ... gentrification occurs in the inner city; deviance occurs in the suburbs. It is a world of globalization, not separation; of blurring, not strict lines of demarcation.

This point should not be overextended and taken to apply to all urban contexts, however. It needs to be considered in relation to London specifically and other parts of the UK by comparison. Deindustrialisation and the switch from Fordist processes of mass production to an economic system based on 'flexible specialisation' (Lash and Urry 1994) have resulted in the increasing casualisation of labour and pervasive job insecurity throughout the UK. Hardest hit have been cities that once provided the workforce for what is now defunct or declining heavy industry. Physically isolated from temporary, agency and subcontract work in the new information and financial service sector occupations characteristic of modern urban agglomerations, populations within older industrial regions have been consigned to eke out a living in conditions of almost permanent recession and marginal economic significance.

This is a fundamentally different social context from the active labour market, and far more ethnically diverse and transient population in London, where, owing to its recent economic transformation, straightforward connections between spatial and social exclusion are more difficult to identify (Folwell 1999). Compared to northern and western cities, for example, where research shows that nearly two out of every three of the poorest 10 per cent of neighbourhoods are located (Turok *et al.* 2006), concentrated poverty in London is much less closely associated with primary deprivation indices such as chronic ill-health and long-term unemployment. Although the highest rates of unemployment are concentrated in central and eastern areas of the inner city (GLA 2002), rather than being fixed in specific neighbourhoods, unemployment remains consistently high throughout the inner city as a whole (*ibid.*). Moreover, even though concentrations of high- and low-income households are evident in relatively small parts of the city (*ibid.*), social deprivation is particularly fine-grained. Even small areas of the city are quite heterogeneous in terms of housing (Buck *et al.* 2002). As such, compared to the large, homogeneous and socially deprived housing areas characteristic of many midland and northern cities (Mooney 1999), the physical geography of London comprises a variety of mixed-income and mixed-tenure neighbourhoods, many of which are subject to continuous urban development and change (Robson *et al.* 2000).

An important consequence of this is that the social classes in London tend not to be as physically separated from each other as in other parts of the country. As much as the rich might want to insulate themselves from the visible signs and effects of unemployment and social deprivation by using, for example, private transport and sending their children to private schools, they often occupy the same boroughs, wards, postcode areas, and even streets and housing blocks as the poor. An important benefit of this is that social networks tend to be wider and more extensive than in areas of the country where social interaction is limited to a close circle of family, neighbours and friends, and where territorial introspection often develops as a distinctive feature of everyday community life (Kearns and Parkinson 2001). Residential mobility is more frequent, and movement in and around the capital is relatively easy (Church *et al.* 2000). According to Ball *et al.* (2000: 149), space remains 'relatively unfettered … opportunity and imagination, rather than fearfulness' characterise the 'socioscapes' of many London residents. In particular, housing, education, work and leisure options, because they are 'marked by movement and boundary crossing' (*ibid*.), are relatively numerous and accessible, especially to young people, who in recent years have been attracted to the capital in ever increasing numbers (Dorling and Thomas 2004). Comparing London to Glasgow, Atkinson *et al*. (2005: 168) have commented that:

> In Scotland some of the evidence points to a poor neighbourhood being a drag upon people's opportunities, but this is much less clearly so in London. In London, neither analyses of data relating to segregation nor the evidence of interviews suggest a notable growth of high concentrations of highly excluded people living in large scale and highly segregated areas. There is, though, a concentration of deprived neighbourhoods, including a small proportion who could be regarded as 'truly excluded', on some social housing estates. The most difficult of these have poor housing, poor environments and high crime and incivility, and consequently heightened feelings of insecurity. However, in London, neither the housing nor the job markers are so divided as to extend this limited form of area-based deprivation and exclusion across large parts of the inner city.

This immediately suggests the need to apply different policy responses to area-based deprivation and exclusion in different social contexts. At the national level, in terms of macro-economic policy, it raises a justifiable objection to the decision of government to 'distribute more funds to London and the South East than would be expected according to definitions of need' (Simmie *et al*. 2006: 12). As Massey (2007: 121) has written, the concentration of power at the heart of London 'reflects and reinforces the thinness of democracy nationally... The "other" regions do not have their own, equal, voices or recognised trajectories.' And at the local level, it provides evidence of the need for specific policy interventions which take into account contextual diversity. Simply put, what might work in one area is not necessarily appropriate for another. Most important is the need to assess how urban physical environments affect social life, the social networks and interaction patterns, within particular areas; and how, in crucial ways, the relationships between people and place, as they play out in everyday life, create or restrict possibilities and opportunities.

The previous chapter presented the argument that criminal desistance is affected by social context. This chapter has attempted, at least in part, to pin down what this might mean in the sense that social context varies between and within different urban environments. In the next chapter, it is argued that 'one size fits all' approaches to crime reduction and community safety, because they fail to appreciate contextual diversity, have a tendency to reinforce certain community typologies – some real, some symbolic – which, rather than improve prospects for offenders attempting to give up crime, tend to militate against them. Not only is this an inappropriate response to the problems of high-crime communities, where poverty, wealth and crime are spatially and contextually relative, but it can also have a negative impact on the social life of areas where poverty and crime are spatially and contextually bound up together. The assumption is often made that deprived urban areas generate distinctive criminal subcultures. As a result, they become socially demarcated as problem areas which require distinct forms of spatial control. A recurring theme which informs urban policy management is that social problems such as crime can be resolved through physical means. As such, they warrant particular strategies of control which emphasise the rehabilitation of urban space rather than people (Coleman 2003). In fact, all communities, irrespective of the degree of social isolation or crime they suffer, demonstrate a diversity of experience that warrants a far more considered and sophisticated response than one which addresses issues of social order simply in spatial terms.

Chapter 3

Place, the community and the offender

Introduction

In this chapter the spatial concentration of offenders is explained with reference to theories of geographic differentiation, social deprivation and community. Throughout the last century, urbanisation, suburban- isation and high levels of mobility have led to a decline in the spatially defined urban community. The understanding that patterns of behaviour, identity and culture are now much less spatially defined is applied to the criminal careers of persistent offenders, who appear to share highly localised experiences before, during and after prison. A number of antithetical discourses are presented situated in various traditions – behavioural, cultural, structural and institutional – which privilege different readings of the relationship between crime, place and the community. There follows a discussion of the general policy responses that derive from each of these divergent theoretical positions with respect to individual and social approaches to crime reduction and community safety. Broadly, they suggest a Russian doll geographical perspective which extends outwards from the individual, home, neighbourhood and community through local and national government to the global economy. In the light of this, the chapter ends with some general observations concerning the extent to which local urban communities are equipped, or engaged to address, the reintegration of ex-prisoners.

Free will versus determinism: explaining divergent theories of crime and place

The evidence for a strong correlation between imprisonment and place of residence suggests that resettlement activities should be targeted within the local communities to which offenders return after release from prison (Travis and Petersilia 2001). It is an aim of this chapter to assess the potential of local communities to support and engage with efforts to reintegrate offenders. First, however, the evidence presented in the previous chapter for a link between area of residence and imprisonment needs accounting for. Throughout the history of criminological spatial analysis, it has been shown that specific places are strongly linked to crime and criminality (Herbert 1993); yet, devising a methodology and framework to explain this is far from straightforward.

As we have seen, the majority of crimes detected, prosecuted and sanctioned reflect the social background of prisoners, which is disproportionately working class (Mathiesen 1974). Throughout the time that imprisonment has been the cornerstone of the penal system, prison populations have comprised aggregate populations of the destitute and marginalised. Ever since the early nineteenth century when traditional place-based communities fragmented across Europe and people flocked to newly expanding urban areas in search of work, crime and the fear of crime have been fused in the public imagination with the threat to public order presented by surplus populations of labour – *la classe dangereuse*. In France, social cartographers compared arrest data obtained from provincial public prosecutor departments with broad 'moral statistics' affecting society such as illegitimacy, poverty and suicide (see Guerry 1833; Quetelet 1842). For the first time, it was shown that the areal distribution of crime and offenders is not random but conforms to distinct socio-demographic features such as population density and social class. As cities expanded and populations increased, it was found that the areas 'where frequent mixture of the people takes place; those in which industry and trade collect many persons and things together, and possess the greatest activity; finally, those where the inequality of fortune is most felt, all things being equal, are those which give rise to the greatest number of crimes' (Quetelet 1842: 27). But while nineteenth-century developments in statistical cartography cemented the connection between crime and place, and new forms of disciplinary punishment established the prison as the most effective means of regulating the urban poor (Rusche and Kirchheimer 2003 [1939]), the debate over whether urban environments somehow cause criminal behaviour was just beginning.

In fact, disagreements over whether there is a connection between social status, poverty and crime go back further than the period of capitalist industrial expansion. Ever since the Enlightenment, when it was first advanced that human nature derives from background and circumstance rather than fate and original sin, the premise that human beings are essentially rational and endowed with free will and self-control has underpinned the notion that crime is a course of action open to all individuals who decide that the benefits of breaking the law outweigh the perceived costs. Enlightenment scholars proposed that, as man is naturally accumulative, criminality stems from a normal and therefore understandable desire for personal gain and self-improvement. Moreover, because criminality is fixed, the product of a rational calculation of the perceived pains and pleasures to be derived from it, its solution should be fixed equally in return. Therefore, in order to effectively deter would-be and persistent criminals, punishment should be immediate, consistent and proportionate to its severity (see Beccaria 1767; Bentham 1789).

But while the Enlightenment introduced the notion of the 'rational individual subject', it also problematised personal choice and voluntary action by opening up the possibility that human beings, at least in part, are determined by the actions they take. In fact, attitudes towards the poor during the Enlightenment were ambiguous. While some held that vice, corruption and crime were self-induced, others blamed social circumstance. Most notably, a new movement of Enlightenment environmentalism argued that the capitalist farming system of 'enclosure', used to forcibly evict labourers from agricultural land, had effectively widened social divisions between the leisured classes and the labouring poor and reduced a new class of 'unfortunates' to pauperdom, vice and crime. Even the arch-rationalist Beccaria (1767: 53) was ambivalent on the subject, regarding the widening of social divisions between rich and poor to have spawned 'the crime of poverty and desperation, the crime of that unhappy section of men to whom the perhaps "terrible" and "unnecessary" right to property has allowed nothing but a bare existence.' Furthermore, Bentham (1791), in designing the 'panopticon' prison as 'a machine to grind rogues honest', acknowledged the necessity of removing criminals from the corrupting influence of their immediate environment.

Some 50 or so years later, by offering divergent explanations for the distinct geographical patterns they charted across urban space, the early 'moral statisticians' served to intensify the debate over where to draw the line between free will and determinism. Whereas Guerry (1833) explained the relationship with reference to the spatial distribution of 'opportunity', to areal differences in the availability of property worth stealing, for example, Quetelet (1842) was more inclined to point to the influence of 'need' and the differential areal effects of education and poverty (Morris 1957: 47). Today these debates persist. Explanations of the evident correlation between crime, criminality and place continue to differ markedly on the role of the physical and social environment to (re)produce criminal motivation. Mirroring aetiological explanations which suppose the causes of crime to lie within the individual at a level beyond conscious awareness, or outside in the structural details of the world, criminological spatial analysis has persisted in reading criminal behaviour as either a rational, voluntary response to spatial opportunity; or a function of geographic differences in economic and social inequality (Bottoms and Wiles 1992).

Just as explanations of criminality continue to be positioned either side of this dichotomy, so, too, do explanations for its spatial distribution. It is traditional within criminology to conceive of space as either a geometric container of physical particularities and behavioural cues, or in terms of geographically bounded socio-economic structures such as poverty and class. The failure to conceptualise the criminal subject as anything but a self-determining rational actor or passive dupe of environmental forces has meant that for the most part criminological analysis has failed to provide a meaningful response to the central question: do places act as 'criminogenic *generators* of crime, or merely more attractive *receptors* of crime.... [Do they] vary in their capacity to help cause crime, or merely in their frequency of hosting crime that was going to occur some place inevitably, regardless of the specific place?' (Sherman *et al.* 1989: 46; emphasis in the original). Bottoms and Wiles (1992: 16) neatly summarise the reasons for the deficiency:

Explanations of where offences occur, or where offenders live, can all too easily assume that place or design acts as a deterministic and monocausal variable. Alternatively, they may assume that place can stand as an operational construct for other aspects of social structure, such as class, or employment status, or family structure; or that it is simply a sorting mechanism which brings together in one place those individuals who possess criminogenic attributes (generally of a genetic or psychological kind).

Nevertheless, over the past few decades, macro-physical and social transformations – 'neo-liberalism', 'globalisation', 'the risk society' – have recast understandings of the criminal subject and, in doing so, changed the parameters of the debate concerning the spatial distribution of crime. Critiques of wider economic and social forces suggest that crime and criminality can no longer be explained by location factors alone. Instead, criminological research must turn to 'processes of convergence and divergence, similarities and differences between different spaces and scales and also the unevenness of seemingly global trends' (Hughes 2007: 2). Yet, although the need to integrate knowledge on individuals and social environments and avoid assigning causal effects to single factors remains a concern of comparative criminology, rather than resolve important differences over the criminal subject, these debates have generally tended to fragment along traditional lines. Exemplified best perhaps by the reception accorded the reintroduction of classical rational man, today reborn as *Homo economicus*, this widely embraced discourse has severed the economic basis of offending from the social reality of crime (Young 1999). So the debate remains fundamentally the same: either criminals continue to act 'purely on the basis of reason or "choice", interested only in the maximization of utility', or they are 'the products of their social circumstances ... pure social constructions' (Gadd and Jefferson 2007: 1).

The concept of community

The historical preface to this chapter is intended to be of more than academic interest. It is necessary to elucidate the assumptions that lie behind divergent theories of crime and place because in fundamental respects they mirror those which inform theoretical approaches to punishment and, associated with it, offender rehabilitation and reintegration. Whichever theory is espoused at the time underpins penal law and practice. For example, depending on whether criminals are viewed as free agents responsible for their own moral decisions or shaped by forces largely beyond their control, the measures taken to reduce reoffending have drawn on either classical or positivist traditions of offending behaviour. Whereas classicism views crime as essentially normal, commonplace and rational, and therefore privileges penal responses 'selected as to make the most efficacious and lasting impression on the minds of men' (Beccaria 1767: 31), positivism proscribes 'treatment', for mental illness, drug addiction, family disruption, social deprivation and so forth. The extent to which one is privileged over the other is both a practical matter and a theoretical construct.

The same is true of place-based strategies. Just as central concepts of punishment and justice influence penal policies directed at reducing crime and reoffending, understandings of space, place and the related concept of community inform strategies of crime prevention, reduction, risk and public safety (e.g. Crawford 1997; Garland 2001; Hughes 2007). There are two basic approaches, one which treats the offender as a rational actor and aims to reduce criminal opportunities through preventative measures of spatial management, and another which addresses the environmental and social characteristics supposed to be linked to criminal motivation such as poverty, unemployment, poor housing and peer pressure. Although different in approach, situational and social crime-prevention measures are targeted at reducing crime in specific localities, as well as responding to wider issues of community safety (Crawford 1998).

Of course, all of this is also inextricably bound up with the way criminals are viewed generally by the public and in the media. In crucial respects, the social meaning of crime – how criminals are responded to along a continuum at one end of which criminality is considered to be a product of social circumstance and at the other end, a predatory, self-willed act – shapes policy responses to social control, and more so today than ever before, since the control of crime is now predicated on informal social interaction, rather than mechanisms of criminal justice and the law. Collective action centred on the community has become the guiding principle of all government policy – social, spatial and penal. Commonly thought of as a 'promiscuous' term (Worrall and Hoy 2005: 57), 'an aerosol can to be sprayed on to any social programme, giving it a more progressive and sympathetic cachet' (Cochrane 1986: 51), the concept of community has become so central to the traditional institutions of policing, probation and punishment, it is now considered 'the all-purpose solution to every criminal justice problem' (Garland 2001: 123). But what does it mean? Although, as defined in the symbolic sense of shared values, interests or culture, a community need not be coterminous with a discrete place, it is commonly understood to be 'a social network of interacting individuals, usually concentrated in a defined territory' (Johnston *et al.* 2000: 101). Within policymaking circles especially, the community is commonly identified as the primary solution to various social problems within specific settings (Low 1999). According to Nelken (1994: 249), local communities are commonly targeted and utilised as 'the agents, *locus* or beneficiaries of crime control'. In other words, they are treated as a repository of social ties and informal voluntary cooperation harnessed by the state to supplement formal criminal justice measures, as well as a setting to be monitored and controlled through strategies of crime prevention and/or punishment (Worrall and Hoy 2005).

Much of the remainder of this chapter is concerned with the way places and communities are conceived economically, socially, culturally and politically. In presenting general theories on the formation of patterns of socio-spatial differentiation, it assesses five broad geographical and criminological accounts of criminal behaviour thought to explain the spatial distribution of offenders. It begins by considering individual perspectives based on strictly environmental understandings of overt spatial behaviour such as perception, cognition and decision making. Psychological theoretical positions on the relationship between the mind, the environment, and behaviour continue to drive criminological spatial analysis as well as the policy responses which emanate from it. Alternative perspectives are then assessed which suggest that criminal behaviour, rather than being determined by the environment or individual factors *per se*, is always an outcome of the particular social context in which it occurs.

Place, rationality, behaviour

It is a key and abiding tradition of geography to understand the relationship between the individual, space and place. The sub-discipline of behavioural geography in particular has explored the mental impressions, environmental perceptions, and cognitive representations of individuals in order to explain spatial patterns of behaviour. An important methodological approach within this overall perspective is to consider behaviour as a product of the cognitive images and maps people assemble, organise and employ during everyday life to make sense of the world around them (e.g. Lynch 1960; Golledge *et al*. 1972; Walmsley and Lewis 1984). Although the role of 'covert' mental processes such as motivation, emotion and attitude to predispose individuals to behave in certain ways is also accepted, according to Pile (1996: 31) this was never fully elucidated during the period behavioural geography was most prominent during the 1960s and 1970s. In privileging strictly rational, economic and empirical understandings of spatial behaviour, behavioural geography 'failed to do justice to social behaviour – and therefore could not explain overt spatial patterns' (*ibid.*).

Today, although largely superseded within the field of geography by social and human understandings of spatial behaviour, the underpinning principles of behavioural geography continue to influence criminology. Drawing on the study of decision-making processes pioneered by behavioural geographers, since the 1970s the sub-branch of environmental criminology in particular has continued to assess crime as an outcome of environmental stimuli and the perceptions of offenders within given situations (e.g. Brantingham and Brantingham 1984). Based on classical control theory – the idea that human behaviour is governed by the economic concept of expected utility (Hollin 1992) – 'opportunity theories' of crime contend that environmental cues trigger purposive criminal behaviour (Cornish and Clarke 1986). Therefore, because people act out of self-interest, crime does not require a particular motivation or pathology to explain it. Essentially, it is a mundane decision made voluntarily by 'normal' people during the course of everyday life. As calculating individuals, criminals routinely utilise the spatial distribution of opportunity in order to maximise economic well-being. The geographical distribution of criminal offences is explained simply by the availability of crime targets and the absence of measures to block criminal opportunities (Clarke 1992). 'Target attractiveness', the availability of items that are 'CRAVED' – 'concealable, removable, available, valuable, enjoyable and disposable', in combination with 'accessibility' – the ease by which items may be obtained without risk of being caught, explains why some locations are more attractive than others (Clarke 1999). Although mostly associated with acquisitive crime such as burglary and robbery, the purview of 'rational choice theory' extends to so called 'expressive crime' – crimes committed for the express purpose of relieving frustration, maximising pleasure, achieving status among peers, and so on (Cornish and Clarke 2008). As we saw in Chapter 1, it also extends to explanations of criminal desistance.

Measures taken to defend high-crime neighbourhoods draw mostly on understandings of the offender's relationship to structural particularities: for example, the physicality and functionality of buildings, housing type, street layout, traffic flows, land use, shopping and leisure spaces, and so forth (Felson 1994). Based on an assessment of the way societal changes in energy, transportation systems and patterns of consumption, such as the availability of lightweight electronic goods, have affected crime patterns across urban space

(Cohen and Felson 1979), 'routine activity theory' focuses primarily on 'common-sense' principles of environmental design (Felson 1994: 116). Because crime rates fluctuate in line with changing patterns of routine activities, to understand spatial distributions of criminal behaviour, it is necessary to find out how 'people and goods move about in the course of a day' (Felson 1994: 46). The link with rational choice theory is clearly made. Most crime is ordinary and undramatic, and is 'committed mainly by people who are tempted more and controlled less' (Felson 1998: 23). For crime to occur regularly in a place, three basic conditions must be met. First, there must be a sufficient number of motivated offenders; second, a ready supply of desirable targets; and third, an absence of capable guardians – parents, teachers, police, security guards and so on (Cohen and Felson 1979). As cognitive awareness of these conditions is likely to be most acute close to home, offenders deliberately choose targets in or near to the places they live (Brantingham and Brantingham 1981). Informed by a geographical perspective that spatial behaviour conforms to networks, nodes, paths, edges and other environmental features which structure the movements of people within and across urban space (Lynch 1960), awareness of criminal opportunity is circumscribed by the immediate environment (Brantingham and Brantingham 1984). Through day-to-day movement in and around a restricted number of 'anchor points' – home, school, work, socialising with friends and so on – offenders learn that some places offer greater criminal opportunities than others. Therefore, although crime occurs as a matter of routine in all parts of cities, high-crime locations correlate closely with residential areas which contain large numbers of offenders (Mawby 1979).

As useful as this schema is for focusing on the geographical distribution of criminal offences, it is a partial construct because its conceptual framework accepts criminal motivation as pre-given. Routine activity theory has been commended by its advocates for opening up the reality of everyday life to criminological scrutiny (Felson 2008). But its notion of behavioural geography – environmental perception coupled to the routinisation of individual practice – allows no acknowledgement of the multiplicity of roles played out in everyday social settings (Mawby 1977). As argued by Taylor (1999: 124), the offender is envisaged as living 'in a historical, cultural and social vacuum, without any particular identifiable personal biography or identity'. Similarly, rational choice theory fails to account for the complexity of the human condition; for instance, for behaviours which are 'irrational, arational, or rational; and when rational, are more likely to be affectually rather than instrumentally rational' (Bottoms and Wiles 2002: 631). Because space is conceptualised in straightforwardly Euclidian terms – as a neutral, bounded container of human activity (Cloke *et al.* 1991) – the theory ignores the extent to which individuals are predisposed to act unconsciously, a consequence of thoughtlessness of habit rather than rational calculation (Bourdieu 1977).

Overall, rational choice theory fails to acknowledge affective dimensions of place: the historical, cultural, emotional and expressive characteristics that influence interpersonal relations and individual decision making. Place is important not simply because of the way physical characteristics are perceived. As Goffman (1968: 104) has observed, individuals regularly divide social space 'into different regions according to the contingencies embedded in them for the management of social and personal identity'. Places may be civil and 'provide an atmosphere of special piquancy' (*ibid.*: 103). Alternatively, they may be forbidden or out of bounds 'where exposure means expulsion' (*ibid.*: 102). As Hägerstrand (1982) has found, in crucial respects places constrain movement. For instance, 'capability constraints' – planning and architectural rules, poor transport networks, a lack of employment opportunities, inadequate public services – physically limit what it is possible to do in certain locations, while 'authority constraints' – the *de jure* policing of movement within protected and exclusionary spaces marked out by class, ethnicity, culture or gender – narrow social horizons, reinforce cultural divides, immobilise dysfunctional groups, stigmatise neighbourhoods, and generate inward-looking attitudes, territorialism, insecurity, fatalism, and even agoraphobia (Young 1990).

Because it is an abiding feature of social life continually to transform itself, it is necessary to analyse how individuals arrive at an understanding of who they are and their place in the world over time; for instance, how behaviour develops in relation to the interplay of continually changing social expectations, interpersonal contexts, and wider social environments. Since the 1980s, in critiquing the central assumptions of behavioural geography, human geographical perspectives have re-conceptualised the subject as a product of the meanings, values, expectations and goals that individuals develop in relation to the social world around them. Referring to the limitations of environmental criminology specifically, Ley (2002 [1978]: 69; emphasis in the original) has written that in prioritising the map and the mathematical modelling of spatial distributions, research on the geography of crime:

always overidentifies local variables at the expense of overarching ones. The demonstrable map correlation between the incidence of crime and the distribution of group X is used to make the inferential transition from r-value to causal reasoning with distressing ease. But if group X 'causes' crime here, why is it that they do not 'cause' crime in other locations? Why is it that the same urban neighbourhoods now occupied by group X also tended to be high crime areas a generation ago, when they were occupied by group Y? Clearly statistical or cartographic analysis alone is not sufficient to provide an understanding of the social action behind the map of crime, though it may well be a useful first step.... What is lacking is a sense of history, or at least of biography, and a sense also of the tiers of social context ranging from the innermost and immediate linkages of family and peer group to the outermost but no less pervasive realms of ideology and *Weltanschauung*, the global outlook and dominant ideas of the period.

To sum up this section, in drawing on strictly behaviourist notions of stimulus and response, or rational, logical functioning, environmental criminology presents what Pile (1996) has dubbed a 'ratomorphic' or 'robomorphic' model of the human condition. In ignoring or discounting social characteristics or elements of the mind which are not conditioned, rational or logical, it therefore fails to find any purchase on the finding that prisoners are drawn from and return to certain urban neighbourhoods. As we will see later in the chapter, it also has little or nothing to offer investigations which seek to understand processes of narrative change in relation to spatial dimensions of criminal desistance. When assessed against wider historical and socio-economic perspectives, as well as the fundamentally messy issue of human intention and motivation, strictly environmental perspectives on people–place relationships are simplistic at best (Canter 1977), and environmentally determinist at worst (Broady 1968). Other forms of spatial analysis are now considered.

Social disorganisation

The first systematic understandings of crime, criminality and place are commonly thought to have originated at the Chicago School of Sociology – a consequence of early research carried out into processes of urbanisation and social and economic inequality. During the first half of the twentieth century, the investigation of common psychological responses to the alienating effects of metropolitan life (Simmel 1969 [1903]) became a founding academic pursuit of a then nascent sociology. The idea that 'mind takes form in the city and in turn urban form conditions mind' (Mumford 1938: 5) informed a variety of critical approaches to industrial change and urban expansion. Researchers demonstrated that American cities expanded outwards in concentric circles as rapid influxes of urban migrants replaced established residents at the central core, who, once they had the means to, relocated to more desirable and affluent areas further out towards the commuter belt. On the premise that urban development is an ecological process, just as plant and animal species adapt to changing environmental circumstances or perish and die, it was proposed that peasant immigrant communities, unable to cope with alien urban environments, formed a 'purgatory of "lost souls"' (Burgess 1925: 56) within 'a zone of transition' surrounding the inner city. Using ethnographic research to explain the statistical finding that criminals were disproportionately concentrated in this area scholars suggested that previously strong communal bonds loosened and eventually broke down. The result was 'social disorganisation', a process by which the rules that normally govern behaviour are relaxed (Thomas and Znaniecki 1920). Under these conditions, criminal behaviour was assessed as a product of the way normal people attempt to satisfy 'certain felt needs within the limits of a particular social and economic framework' (Shaw and McKay 1942: 320):

> In some parts of the city attitudes which support and sanction delinquency are, it seems, sufficiently extensive and dynamic to become the controlling forces in the development of delinquent careers among a relatively large number of boys and young men. These are the low-income areas, where delinquency has developed in the form of a social tradition, inseparable from the life of the local community. (*ibid.*: 315–16)

Advancing as it did 'the first systematic challenge to the dominance of psychology and psychiatry in public and private programs for the prevention and treatment of juvenile delinquency' (Schlossman *et al.* 1984: 2), the key legacy of the Chicago School has been the study of local environmental processes. Ever since, however, the conclusions drawn from this large body of work have been the subject of sometimes trenchant critical reanalysis. For example, it was pointed out early on that 'delinquency areas' are not necessarily socially disorganised. Indeed, delinquents frequently act according to an alternative set of highly organised values and concerns (Whyte 1943). Furthermore, social disorganisation theory neglected to specify which factors within the total social and economic framework predict which outcomes. By linking criminal outcomes solely to a lack of social cohesion, it failed, for instance, to recognise the degree to which city populations consist of 'relatively homogeneous groups, with social and cultural moorings that shield it fairly effectively from the suggested consequences of number, density and heterogeneity' (Gans 1968: 99). A tendency to fetishise place – to assume that social environments directly determine human action – served to stigmatise deprived communities as socially disorganised and deficient (Perlman 1976) when in reality they are often characterised by dense family networks and close kinship ties (Bottoms and Wiles 1997). In overextending the relationship between community deprivation, ethnic heterogeneity and economic segregation, the theory privileged 'mechanisms of disorganization led by discontent', negating 'opportunities arising from urban aggregations' (Ruggiero 2001: 16). Most troublingly of all, social disorganisation theory perpetuated the idea that crime is a consequence of cultural inferiority. 'Influenced by both the salubrious and the toxic aspects of early twentieth-century culture' (Musolf 2003: 60), it assumed that criminality is a group pathology caused by a failure of immigrant communities to learn core American values.

Nevertheless, the idea that places exert 'neighbourhood effects' on individuals and place-based communities constructed around key social and institutional processes – social structure, social organisation, culture – continues to inform criminological spatial analysis, not least because distinct spatial concentrations of crime and criminality strongly correlated to indices of deprivation continue to be revealed (e.g. Wilson 1997; Hope 2001; Dorling 2004; Johnston *et al.* 2004). Predominately concerned with the internal dynamics of social life within small geographical areas, researchers have recently revisited the underlying assumption of social disorganisation theory that crime increases in areas where economic conditions reduce the capacity of local people to demonstrate non-criminal values (Rose *et al.* 1999). Employing quantitative analysis, social survey and ethnographic research to assess the effect of spatial inequality and social deprivation on a range of outcomes, including employment, health and crime, this approach has highlighted social and economic differences between deprived and non-deprived areas (e.g. Jencks and Mayer 1990; Brooks-Gunn *et al.* 1993; Elliot *et al.* 1996; Atkinson and Kintrea 2001; Buck 2001; Kearns and Parkinson 2001). Commenting on the spatial correspondence between inequality, health and violence, for example, Wilkinson (2005: 146–147) has written that

> there are now at least fifty papers showing that violence is more common in societies with bigger income differences. This relationship holds up both when we compare different societies internationally and when looking at regions or small areas within them … normally violence is concentrated among the poor themselves: the poorer neighbourhoods of most cities are well known to be the most dangerous.

In terms of crime specifically, the research has applied multi-level modes of analysis to assess various neighbourhood characteristics such as housing, unemployment, peer group influence and social networks; while controlling for individual risk factors such as heritable genetic effects, hyperactivity-impulsivity-attention problems, and parenting (e.g. Wikström and Loeber 2000; Weatherburn and Lind 2001; Oberwittler 2004). Rather than assume a direct causal link between social variables, it has been proposed that various 'bundles of spatially-based attributes' (Galster 2001) are highly correlated and together reinforce one another to indirectly produce outcomes amenable to crime (Wikström and Loeber 2000; Sampson 2006). For example, an increase in abandoned buildings (Skogan 1990), together with changes in owner to rental or single to multiple housing accommodation (Schuerman and Kobrin 1986), engenders fear, stimulates out-migration and, in turn, reduces 'the capacity of a neighbourhood to regulate itself through formal and informal processes of social control' (Bursik 1988: 526). The result is a compound loss in what has been termed 'collective efficacy'. Defined as 'the willingness of local residents to intervene for the common good' (Sampson *et al.* 1997: 919), collective efficacy focuses specifically on 'soft' outcomes such as mutual trust, solidarity, and the capacity to organise social networks, supervise teenage delinquents and access institutional resources and social support.

Neighbourhood effects research is in its infancy. As noted in Chapter 1, in relation to the 'Moving to Opportunity' project, most of the disagreements concerning it turn on the extent to which it is possible to isolate unmeasured individual or family factors from local, communal and wider socio-economic factors (Atkinson *et al.* 2005). According to Lupton (2003: 20), neighbourhood effects matter only if the methodologies employed are sophisticated enough to overcome selection bias and individual processes of residential sorting and thereby 'accurately reflect the concept of neighbourhood'. Overall, the results are not convincing. Generally, it has been concluded that after age, gender, class, ethnicity and other background factors are taken into account the effect of place as an independent variable is either non-existent or very small (Jencks and Mayer 1990; Brooks-Gunn *et al.* 1993). And yet, more specifically, it has been shown that neighbourhood deprivation does have an effect on physical and mental health (Ellaway *et al.* 2001) as well as rates of crime committed by individuals and groups who in individual respects have a low risk of offending (Wikström and Loeber 2000).

Institutional malfunction

Another qualification subsequently made to the work of the Chicago School is that, although concentric patterns of urban development were found in a total of 16 cities within the United States, including Philadelphia, Boston, Cincinnati, Cleveland and Richmond (Shaw and McKay 1942), and later in Baltimore (Lander 1954) and Seattle (Schmid 1960), subsequent analysis has shown that criminal communities do not conform necessarily to natural processes of economic competition, and the social and cultural characteristics thought to derive from these. Instead, they are socially constructed by institutional processes administered by the state, in particular local housing markets (Murie 1998). For example, in contrast to the United States, where, historically, homeownership has been particularly pronounced, the social geography of the UK is a legacy of public housing policies which spatially have organised the population principally on the basis of social class (Harrison 1983). During the 1950s, as families were relocated to peripheral housing estates from war-damaged inner cities, metropolitan areas were spatially reordered along socio-economic lines (Pahl 1969). Analysis undertaken to assess the effect this had on patterns of offender residence found that 'criminal areas' were a product of the decision of local authorities deliberately to assign tenants to housing vacancies according to 'worthiness'; thereby 'localising' problem families, and generally ensuring the social classes were kept apart (e.g. Morris 1957, on Croydon; Jones 1958, on Leicester; Bagley 1965, on Exeter; Davidson 1975, on Hull; Baldwin and Bottoms 1976, on Sheffield all in Evans 1980).

Today, 'dump estates' comprised of families with the severest social needs, including family size and low socio-economic status, are considered to be the outcome of divisive and exclusionary local zoning policies intended to spatially reorganise the problems of the poor (see Bottoms and Wiles 1992, 1997, on Sheffield). Subsequently neglected by public authorities, subjected to rigorous attention by the police, and stigmatised by outsiders, these 'communities of fate' (Jordan 1996) over time have developed 'community crime careers': specific neighbourhood identities characterised by alienated social networks, distorted reputations and labels, mistrust between neighbours, and antisocial attitudes and criminal behaviours (Bottoms *et al.* 1992: 97). Firmly based on social class and status, deeply ingrained community identities are established early on, even as neighbourhoods are constructed, such that they remain extremely resilient to change (Robertson *et al.* 2008). Forrest and Kearns (2001: 2134) explain how deliberate policies of residential sorting engender neighbourhood identities which over time become labelled and stigmatised in relation to the areas around them:

> Residential identities are embedded in a strongly comparative psychological landscape in which each neighbourhood is known primarily as a counterpart to some of the others, and relative differences are probably more important than any single and widely shared social characteristic.... These reputations may cling to some neighbourhoods longer than others. Moreover, the external perceptions of areas impact on the behaviour and attitudes of residents in ways which may reinforce cohesive groupings and further consolidate reputations.

Focusing on the housing market in this way helps to explain how and why it is that some residents come to live in specific urban neighbourhoods in the first place (Bottoms *et al.* 1992: 122). However, while it is generally accepted that 'what happens within neighborhoods is in part shaped by socioeconomic and housing factors linked to the wider political economy' (Sampson *et al.* 1997: 922), relationships between local neighbourhoods and the 'larger social system of cities, regions, and indeed the national or global economy are not well understood' (Sampson 2006: 43). It is to these wider social processes we now turn.

Structural inequality and racial segregation

During the 1970s, the idea that residential areas are socially constructed by local housing markets was taken a good deal further when urban sociologists and social geographers began to document the extent to which macro-economic processes reconfigured urban space. Heeding much wider processes than those contained within specific neighbourhoods, they critiqued global economic structures of power and uneven development between places. Marxist perspectives especially focused on processes of deindustrialisation, global consumerism, and the transition to a service economy, as well as the political ideologies which serve to maintain power relations and create institutional violations of justice directed at particular groups of people. In assessing the effects of dominant economic and cultural forces within the late modern world, it was argued that a fundamental restructuring of domestic and international economies had resulted in changes to the geographical location of production systems, causing extreme geographical differentiation. Driven by processes of individualism, competition and consumerism, spatial inequality is an inevitable outcome of the capital investment in land (Harvey 1973). Places either regenerate or degenerate depending on whether 'the landscape shaped in relation to a certain phase of development (capitalist or pre-capitalist) becomes a barrier to further accumulation' (Harvey 1996: 296). No longer centred on sites of production and administration, residential areas are reordered and rearranged by property markets – building societies and estate agents – sometimes as a result of discriminatory barriers erected specifically to prevent occupation by certain minority groups (Sarre *et al.* 1989). As there is always a limit to which property investment may be absorbed and made profitable within uncertain and fragile markets, urban development is epitomised by 'a perpetual struggle in which capital builds a physical landscape appropriate to its own condition at a particular moment in time, only to destroy it, usually in the course of a crisis, at a subsequent point in time' (Harvey 1981: 113). As a consequence, while some places are turned into 'citadels of power' others are 'singled out for stagnation, deterioration, and a return to "nature"' (Lefebvre 2003 [1970]: 80).

As this perspective shifted the focus away from specific modes of cultural adaptation within urban neighbourhoods to the global capitalist system and the economic reproduction of class conflict, the analysis of place-based factors and bounded social context was deprioritised. When, during the 1980s, it was rekindled, primarily as a result of the emergence of distinct concentrations of poverty and social deprivation within inner-city American 'ghettos', the agenda was set to investigate neighbourhood dynamics within a multidisciplinary framework encompassing processes occurring outside delimited areas: the role of the state, the world economy, and public policy.

For instance, according to Castells (1977), the emergence of extreme geographical differentiation and social deterioration is constitutive not only of economic competition and urban restructuring, but also of an overall tendency within capitalist societies to reorganise patterns of 'collective consumption' in housing, education, transport, health services and so on. It was also argued that fiscal constraints, and the rise of New Right political ideologies had downgraded the role of the state and reduced the provision of welfare services. As a consequence, the availability of goods and services funded by the public purse varies considerably across urban space. The result is a 'planet of slums' (Davis 2006) – American ghettos, French *banlieues*, Brazilian *favelas*, Japanese *yoseba*, Asian shanty towns and English sink estates. A global geography of social exclusion marked out by 'ungovernable spaces' (Lash and Urry 1994) populated by 'homeless, incarcerated, prostituted, criminalised, brutalised, stigmatised, sick and illiterate persons' (Castells 1998: 165).

Mirroring this analysis, criminologists also began to draw connections between wider economic and social forces, social injustice, and a range of individual outcomes including crime. Initially, 'strain theory' (Merton 1938) drew attention to the lack of legitimate means available to the poorest sections of society to achieve socially approved goals, while the various subcultural theories which followed attempted to explain why delinquency appeared to be concentrated within deprived inner-city areas. For instance, it was suggested that criminality was a product of the 'focal concerns' prevalent in working-class communities (Miller 1962), or of 'reaction-formation' – a psychodynamic mechanism which caused adolescents not equipped to meet expected standards of academic achievement to behave in ways diametrically opposed to the dominant value system (Cohen 1966). It was also suggested that different criminal subcultures developed according to the pattern of social relations prevalent within different urban neighbourhoods. Whereas income-producing crimes such as theft and burglary occurred predominately in relatively organised neighbourhoods, where older criminals acted as role models, conflict activity, 'bopping, street fighting, "rumbling" and the like … represent an alternative means by which adolescents in many disorganized urban areas may acquire status' (Cloward and Ohlin 1960: 183), as they lack the means to gain recognition in any other way. Later, rejecting these subcultural positions for ignoring the role of the state, and failing to explain the reasons for residential inequality, Marxist theory focused on class conflict, and the way in which the powerful in society maintain positions of dominance by labelling some actions criminal while leaving others alone (Chambliss 1975; Quinney 1977). Since then, new critical perspectives have investigated structural relations thought to determine crime in all its forms. As a corrective to the idealistic and oppositional stance of much radical Marxist theory, 'Left realist' criminology in particular has investigated 'the social context of crime, the shape of crime, its trajectory through time, and its enactment in space', including how it is experienced on a day-to-day basis by victims and offenders alike within the most vulnerable sections of the community (Young 1992: 26). We will consider 'Right realist' criminology presently, but first there is another critical issue to consider: race and ethnicity.

As previously noted, criminological research has continued to reveal micro-economies of subsistence and survival based on acquisitive forms of crime such as car theft, burglary and drug dealing (Taylor 1999), as well as deeply embedded informal social networks which engage in instrumental forms of criminal activity as a legitimate response to local economic disadvantage (Hagan 1993). Whereas in the UK causal explanations have tended to focus on the effects of class inequality, analysis undertaken in the United States has revealed a significant racial dimension to the spatial distribution of poverty and crime. Disqualified from new service sector employment opportunities due to a lack of education and relevant work experience, black populations, research has shown, have been forced to remain immobile, unable to move out of decaying and abandoned neighbourhoods within the older industrial cities (Dahrendorf 1987; Wilson 1987, 1997; Massey and Denton 1993). As the local tax base has eroded, 'ghetto-related behaviors' have developed which 'increase the likelihood that the residents will rely on illegitimate sources of income, thereby further weakening their attachment to the legitimate labor market' (Wilson 1997: 53). Unreported employment, 'hustling', drug dealing and other acquisitive forms of crime are justified and condoned given the abject social circumstances residents are forced to endure in these deracinated urban wastelands. According to Wilson (1997: 70):

> the more often certain behavior ... is manifested in a community, the greater will be the readiness on the part of some residents of the community to find that behavior not only convenient but also morally appropriate. They may endorse mainstream norms against this behavior in the abstract but then provide compelling reasons and justifications for this behavior, given the circumstances in their community.

Similarly, Anderson (1999) has revealed how interpersonal, often violent behaviours have emerged, founded on a 'code of the streets'. Acts of tactical resistance are perpetrated on a daily basis in response to the racism and contempt black residents feel is institutionalised within the police and judicial system. Oppositional cultures are legitimised by racism both real and perceived. Indeed, being seen to consciously oppose mainstream society attracts deference, affirms status and enables those who exert physical and psychological control over their local communities to dominate public space. The result is a street culture founded on drug-related crime and violence. In a series of readings of black urban marginality, Wacquant (2008: 4), has argued that 'hyperghettoisation' is primarily a consequence of deliberate 'market orientated state policies that have aggravated, packed and trapped poor blacks at the bottom of the spatial order of the polarizing city'. Cordoned off from the rest of society by a set of rigid structural, institutional and political constraints, micro-economies of subsistence have become deeply embedded which reinforce the idea that crime is natural within its environmental context. Crime control and penal policies deliberately targeted at racial groups have engendered distinctive forms of criminal culture which are ethnically homogeneous. While, on the face of it, black urban culture might appear uniformly destructive and violent, closer inspection reveals it to be organised according to an alternative set of highly ordered values and concerns (Wacquant 1997).

A primary objection often made to structural interpretations of social marginalisation and crime is that, in reading off 'the specifics of places through the general laws or tendencies of capitalism' (Thrift 2002 [1983]: 106), they contend that the social characteristics of places simply reflect the overall political and economic structure. More reductionist still, they suggest that macro-economic forces, industrial restructuring, and institutional disadvantage are responsible for engendering distinct behavioural responses. In conceptualising the capitalist world as having a unidirectional impact on human beings, structural accounts negate the extent to which individuals might defer the constraining effects of place-based variables on them, or even deliberately appropriate material goods in order to satisfy certain felt needs. Massey (1997: 321) speculates that given that the borders and peripheries of places today are so often crossed by global economic forces, personal and social identities are 'constructed on a far larger scale than what we happen to define for that moment as the place itself, whether that be a street, or a region or even a continent'. Places are an amalgam of processes defined by complex and constantly evolving entanglements of global processes and local situations. Comprised of porous networks differentiated by social class certainly, but also race, gender and sexuality, places are not fixed by global transformations in capital. And neither are the values and beliefs expressed by marginalised urban populations simply a product of spatial, social or racial exclusion. As Left realist criminologists have argued, it is necessary to understand the grounded reality of everyday life in high-crime communities – a reality which encompasses diverse populations of working people, the unemployed, single parents, nuclear families, young people, and old people, people who commit crime, victims of crime, people fearful of crime, as well as people just as likely to attempt to move out of an area or improve the quality of life through legitimate means as they are to resort to crime. Therefore, as critiqued by Newman (2002: 1595), ghetto culture in the United States

> cannot be explained solely by a unitary logic of oppression and exclusion... Political-economic forces create the structure within which the ghetto exists.... but ghetto dwellers are not simply bearers of social relations or victims of social structure. Understanding life in the ghetto requires granting its residents far more agency ... and being prepared to accept an understanding of causation more varied and less deterministic than a single uniform logic of racial exclusion that sweeps all in its path.

Moreover, for those who do embrace criminal culture, this is not indicative necessarily of moral values at odds with broader society. In the UK it has been argued for some time that high-crime communities are characterised predominantly by mainstream cultural elements, especially core values and beliefs promoted within consumerist society – self-realisation, lifestyle choice, fashion, enjoyment through leisure, hedonism and so on (Downes 1966). And as Young (1999: 86) has articulated more recently in relation to the United States, crime, gangs and criminal ghetto cultures are not 'somehow alien to the wider culture'. Achieving wealth through individual initiative and private entrepreneurship is common to both. As such, there is simply no evidence that:

> people in the inner city have an entirely different value system. What is so striking is that despite the overwhelming joblessness and poverty, black residents in inner-city ghetto neighborhoods actually verbally endorse, rather than undermine, the basic

American values concerning individual initiative. (Wilson 1997: 179)

And yet we must be careful here. To go too far with this line of argument leads to the opposite view entirely: that people always act voluntarily, and are free to exercise unfettered human agency and choice. Taken to an extreme, this suggests that the emergence of 'unruly cities' (Pile *et al.* 1999) and 'disorderly places' (Cochrane 2007) within them is the product of a dependency culture characterised by a purposeful decision not to work, and that criminal and other antisocial conduct is freely embraced and transmitted from one generation to the next. It is to this perspective we now turn.

Culture and dependency

Ever since the latter half of the previous century, a particularly dominant and controversial discourse has continued to inform explanations of distinct concentrations of urban poverty, and the social policies implemented to address them. It is that key characteristics of social deprivation – long-term unemployment, welfare dependency and a preponderance of female-headed households – are the products of an innate 'culture of poverty' (Lewis 1967) which revels in labour market inactivity and crime (Murray 1984). There has emerged a mono-culture, an 'urban underclass', early on defined as 'an unprivileged class of unemployed unemployables and underemployed who are more and more hopelessly set apart from the nation at large and do not share in its life, its ambitions and its achievements' (Myrdal 1962). Fusing individual trait and personality theories of criminal behaviour with broader cultural ones, conservative 'right realist' criminologies have advanced the view that 'pathological' criminal communities are the result of a self-sustaining condition endemic to the poor (e.g. Wilson and Herrnstein 1985; Gottfredson and Hirschi 1990). Embracing a set of moral values at odds with mainstream society, criminal behaviour is taken to be constitutive of a collective decision to remain jobless through voluntary withdrawal from the labour market. Unwilling to 'sacrifice immediate gratifications in favor of future ones' (Banfield 1974: 126), the 'self-defeating actions by poor people themselves' (Mead 1997: 13) result in no work, unwed child rearing, poor parenting, and a tendency to indulge in criminal acts (Murray 1984). Most controversial of all, the explanation given for disproportionate numbers of African-Americans within underclass communities is their inherent cultural inferiority: a below-average intelligence and propensity to criminality (Herrnstein and Murray 1994).

The co-location of poverty and criminality in urban space is considered simply to be a numbers game: either a reflection of random 'underlying distributions of constitutional factors' (Wilson and Herrnstein 1985: 103), or a mere aggregation of like-minded and similarly motivated individuals. It is advanced that spatial concentrations of criminals develop in the following way. Ever since the middle of the nineteenth century, regardless of efforts to promote social integration – be it on class, race or religious lines – people in different income and cultural groups have chosen to live apart for reasons of economic incentive and rational self-interest (Ormerod 2005). History shows that throughout periods of full employment and adequate levels of welfare, spatial patterns of social segregation have remained constant (Murray 1984). While the rich have prospered, the internal deficiencies of the poor have been transmitted from one generation to the next, establishing ever more deeply embedded concentrations of spatial disadvantage.

This is not to say that criminal behaviour is thought to develop entirely separately from social context. But it is within micro-level contexts such as the family home and the bringing up of children that the major failings and inadequacies are to be found. Based on the premise that a lack of self-control is internalised early in life and then becomes a permanent trait throughout the life course, efforts to change criminal behaviour after childhood are generally considered futile (Gottfredson and Hirschi 1990). Dismissing the link between neighbourhood factors and criminal development, these theories consider poor parenting and dysfunctional and disrupted family backgrounds to be the primary signifiers of criminal motivation. According to Hirschi (1969), close supervision by the mother and meaningful communication with the father, alleviate the risk of juvenile involvement in crime. Children who benefit from good standards of parental supervision are inculcated with pro-social values and as a consequence develop the self-control necessary to avoid criminal temptation. Children who are brought up by 'bad parents', on the other hand, 'tend to be impulsive, insensitive, physical (as opposed to mental), risk taking, short-sighted, and non-verbal, and they will tend therefore to engage in criminal and analogous acts' (Gottfredson and Hirschi 1990: 90).

As detailed in Chapter 1, it is common in theories of delinquent development to suggest that the early onset of offending is a precursor to persistent criminality, the causes of which may be discerned by the presence of various risk factors located within the family. While it is generally accepted that the concentration of crime within certain families is a characteristic of the general population (Farrington *et al.* 2001), the assumption that poor parenting or disrupted and abusive family relationships inculcate antisocial behaviour detached from wider spheres of social life is difficult to countenance. Individual, family, community, and wider spheres of social life are not separate constructs. They interact in ways which generate and reinforce behavioural responses. Elliot (2001: 10) has written that 'selfhood' is never completely self-contained, impervious to 'the multifarious cultural links between people, and the impact of social context'. To argue otherwise – that criminal behaviour develops in a vacuum – commits what Currie (1985: 185) has termed 'the fallacy of autonomy – the belief that what goes on inside the family can usefully be separated from the forces that affect it outside: the larger social context in which families are embedded for better or for worse'. For instance, the pressures of economic disadvantage – unemployment, or working long hours for little pay – can reduce the capacity of parents to maintain effective standards of discipline and supervision (Sampson and Laub 1994).

Unsurprisingly, given the controversial and extreme positions adopted in much conservative underclass theory, it has been vigorously contested; most obviously for making the blatantly false assertion that social conditions are unaffected by economic change, and that wider occupational structures do not impact on poverty (Katz 1989). Moreover, arguments asserting the voluntary basis of residential location have been invalidated for failing to acknowledge the differential constraints placed on people of different class and race. As recently pointed out by Cheshire (2007: ix), there is a long-established pattern to spatial segregation in which the social characteristics of poor neighbourhoods are

> effectively capitalised in house prices and rents. It costs more to live in nicer neighbourhoods. The poor do not choose to live in areas with higher crime rates and worse pollution: they cannot afford not to.

Underclass theories also reify high-crime communities as socially, culturally and behaviourally homogeneous; a failing they share with some structural accounts. Indeed, when personal and social outcomes of spatial segregation are assessed, the differences between these divergent perspectives often resolve into similarities. Although they differ fundamentally over whether it is a function of market economies to divide landscapes of consumption from landscapes of devastation (Zukin 1991), they tend to agree that criminality and poverty are directly linked to social marginalisation from mainstream society (for example, compare Dahrendorf 1987; Feeley and Simon 1992 with Murray 1984, 1990, 1994; Mead 1997). Essentially, 'the underclass' is an American term. Both perspectives have largely been dismissed in the UK, where, to the extent it exists at all (Macnicol 1994), the underclass is considered to comprise a small group of people, who, rather than being permanently excluded from mainstream society, slip in and out of employment, unemployment and underemployment (Morris 1993). Moreover, no evidence has been found in the UK that the long-term unemployed display cultural characteristics which 'separate them off as having a fundamentally different style of living' (*ibid.*: 410). After carrying out research on a deprived estate in Teesside in northeast England specifically to test the proposition that the underclass is a deeply embedded, within-group identification, MacDonald and Marsh (2005: 199–200; emphasis in the original) concluded that:

> conservative underclass theory fails to appreciate that individuals can react quite differently to apparently similar events *and* that this reaction is not fixed, clear or predictable (across cases or within individual biographies). A static view of 'underclass culture' ignores the complexity and changing life experiences of young people who find themselves in difficult circumstances. As such, this approach fails to grasp that experiences beyond individual control or the orbit of personal morality can impact severely on young lives.

Neither one thing nor the other: the criminal and the community

So far, different conceptions of the relationship between crime and place have been presented, each underscored by a rigid theoretical perspective. Although offering only a partial reading of the relationship between crime, criminality and place, to a greater or lesser extent and at different times and in different situations, each of these broad approaches has resulted in distinct forms of government action intended to reduce crime and improve community safety. In one, places contain environmental cues which trigger criminal behaviours in people already motivated to offend. The policy response in this case is to inhibit such behaviours through situational crime-prevention strategies. In another, the social characteristics of urban neighbourhoods influence whole communities to seek illegitimate solutions to personal and social problems caused by social and economic segregation and a reduction in social cohesion. The policy response in this case is to implement area-based interventions designed to reorganise community resources of social control. In another, criminal communities are socially constructed by the housing market. The policy response in this case is to develop sustainable and entrepreneurial communities through local housing strategies and urban regeneration. In another, the wider social, economic and political forces inherent in the capitalist system cause extreme geographical differentiation. The policy response in this case is macro-economic and macro-social change. And finally in another, places contain aggregate groups who are considered to be essentially different from other people, and are bound together by a unified collective consciousness, a common criminal culture. The policy response in this case is remoralisation through social education or, failing that, containment and incarceration.

It is a feature of these divergent policy approaches that, at one time or another, crime and penal policies have tended to focus on individuals, communities or places. As argued throughout this book, people and place are not mutually exclusive. Yet, rarely have policies been adopted which aim to improve outcomes for people and places together. Academically, each approach has been criticised: individual solutions, for denying that crime has a social dimension (Currie 1985); 'administrative' solutions, for applying a 'cosmetic' fix to a 'chronic ailment of society as a whole' (Young 1999: 130); and social solutions, for believing the utopian dream that it is possible to eradicate poverty (Wilson 1975). Nevertheless, depending on which perspective has been in the ascendancy at the time, different penal strategies have been adopted by governments across the world to control crime (Garland 2001). Today, three broad strategies are privileged: incarceration, social education, and 'administrative' measures designed to prevent crime in specific locations. It is argued that informed much less by a 'logic of wealth distribution in a society of scarcity' and far more by a 'logic of risk distribution' (Beck 1992: 19), policies to alleviate social inequality have been replaced by a 'culture of control' (Garland 2001). Rather than emphasise reform and rehabilitation, penal policies are directed at controlling the perceived risk presented by aggregate groups of people. No longer represented in official discourse as socially deprived citizens in need of welfare support, potential offenders must be carefully managed in ways that maximise security and minimise costs (*ibid*.: 175).

Yet, penal welfare measures have not disappeared entirely. As detailed in Chapter 2, rising rates of reoffending committed by former prisoners have recently refocused attention on rehabilitation and reintegration. Rehabilitation remains a fundamental aim of imprisonment and an important component of prison regimes. 'Treatment' programmes continue to be advocated, designed and implemented to address psychological deficits, and instigate changes in thinking and attitudes (Andrews 1995). Moreover, new, desistance-focused approaches and initiatives have been developed as both a supplement and alternative to these (Petersilia 2003; Maruna and Immarigeon 2004; McNeill 2006; Ward and Maruna 2007). In the light of these developments, given that it remains a central dilemma of the state to balance public protection, justice for victims, and the civil right of offenders to re-enter society as full and active citizens, this chapter concludes by assessing whether punishment, prevention and rehabilitation are spatially reconcilable. Various policy responses are assessed under the following headings: area-based social rehabilitation, ordering devices and prevention techniques, morals and responsibilities, and fortress cities and warehouse prisons.

Area-based social rehabilitation

An enduring legacy of the Chicago School of Sociology has been a tradition of attending to the internal dynamics of disorganised neighbourhoods through programmes of community organisation and development. Inaugurated in 1934, and still prevalent today, the 'Chicago Area Project' (CAP) pioneered a range of welfare strategies intended to physically restore the housing stock in high-crime urban neighbourhoods, provide vocational training, engage with juvenile gangs, and enhance local community relations (Marris and Rein 1972). Early evaluations of the CAP suggested that the various measures adopted had 'probably reduced delinquency in the program areas' (Kobrin 1959: 19), and 'that some lower-class, minority neighborhoods still retain a remarkable capacity for pride, civility, and the exercise of a modicum of self-governance' (Schlossman *et al*. 1984: 47). However, more recent commentaries have been less positive. The CAP was most effective in neighbourhoods which already had a semblance of organisational structure, but it has been shown that the various interventions introduced have failed to address the problems of the communities most in need of public support. Overall, the CAP has been unsuccessful in controlling crime rates, or rehabilitating offenders, largely because it targeted areas in which substantial numbers of residents do not require public assistance (Hope 1995).

More recent work, based on a similarly broad perspective on the link between social disorganisation and crime, has focused specifically on improving levels of informal social control in high-crime neighbourhoods. For example, the much vaunted 'broken windows' thesis suggests that obvious signs of social malaise – abandonment, graffiti and vandalism – encourage the commission of low-level incivilities which escalate into more serious forms of crime when criminals perceive that 'potential victims are already intimidated by prevailing conditions' (Wilson and Kelling 1982: 34). It follows that relatively minor disorders should be dealt with as soon as they become evident through 'zero tolerance policing'; or the imposition of 'child curfews' and 'Anti-Social Behaviour Orders' (ASBOs), for example.

This approach has been challenged for failing to acknowledge that disorder in an area does not necessarily lead to an escalation in crime; in fact, the causal relationship in reverse is just as likely to be true (Sampson and Raudenbush 1999). As we saw earlier in this chapter, it has been argued that both disorder and crime are a product of weak 'collective efficacy', the willingness and capacity of residents to intervene for the common good. Structural characteristics impact on crime problems, but the effect is indirect, mediated by a strong or weak sense of community (Sampson *et al.* 1997). However, this idea has also been challenged. As pointed out by Weatherburn and Lind (2001), the main problem is that the hypothesis remains elusive. To date, evaluations have failed to isolate the impact of informal social control from other factors such as a lack of resources, economic stress, socialisation processes, or, indeed, more formal mechanisms of control such as policing *(ibid)*. Informal social control on crime is likely to be limited by the effects of capital disinvestment in social and local community structures such as employment and housing, or more generally a failure to fundamentally regenerate local environments and secure their future economic and social development (Hagan 1997). Moreover, as we shall see presently, the evidence for a correlation between high levels of social cohesion and low crime is ambivalent when assessed across areas of different economic and social status. While collective efficacy is taken to explain the existence of areas that suffer equally high levels of social deprivation but differential rates of crime (Sampson *et al.* 1997), it has been found that affluent areas often display a distinct lack of mutual support and connectedness, and yet are characterised by negligible levels of crime and disorder (Baumgartner 1988).

Area-based urban regeneration, which on both sides of the Atlantic over the past thirty years has been introduced to reorder the structure of cities, as well as aid community organisation and combat crime (Graham and Bennett 1995), is similarly contested. For example, in the United Kingdom between 1988 and 1998 the Safer Cities programme promoted economic enterprise, and aimed to reduce crime and the fear of crime in local areas by drawing together different partners in multi-agency arrangements. Beset by various organisational problems, such as a reluctance of agencies to participate, and conflicting interests and priorities, area-based partnerships generally have failed to engage local populations, improve community cohesion, and encourage pro-social relationships of control. Indeed, mainly as a consequence of rigid management criteria, they often undermine local trust formation (Hughes 2007) to the extent that some local urban regeneration partnerships have been criticised for actually creating, rather than rehabilitating, local criminogenic environments (Hancock 2007).

Urban policy responses which focus on particular places raise a number of dilemmas. A crucial one is that, in prioritising social problems as they are experienced in local areas, wider structural inequalities are ignored. It is a feature of area-based initiatives that they tend to deal with the symptoms rather than the causes of spatial inequality. In focusing intently on internal neighbourhood dynamics, economic and social issues are marginalised; most importantly, in the lack of 'vertical connections that residents of localities have to extracommunal resources' (Hope 1995: 24). Overall, area-based initiatives are founded on a false assumption: that poor communities can be regenerated and recreated 'through particular forms of development or urban design, rather than any engagement with the social processes of segregation and exclusion that produce them' (Cochrane 2007: 54). Despite the insistence of neo-liberal commentators that the reconfiguration of urban space is an economic necessity, or that stimulating local economies through 'place marketing' improves welfare outcomes for the poorest sections of the community, the evidence shows that area-based policies have failed to alleviate the social consequences of uneven economic development. Commenting on the British experience specifically, Atkinson and Moon (1994: 271) note how, ever since its emergence as the primary response to social deprivation, area-based urban policy has failed comprehensively to combat the effects of the capital disinvestment in land and reverse the spread of spatial inequality. They conclude that

> there has been a failure to conceptualise the nature of the problem, political support has been half-hearted, organisational structures and interests have obstructed the development of coherent policy, and resource availability has been minimal. Government-led strategies have failed as have the so-called private-led strategies of the 1980s.

A more specific criticism of neighbourhood-effects research and the urban regeneration policy responses that emanate from it, is that the primary focus on spatially delimited areas obscures the fact that all areas, particularly within contemporary cities, are interrelated. A useful illustration of this is the recent UK government response to the spatial concentration of social and 'short-stay' rented housing. This has attempted to change the occupational structure of socially deprived residential areas by reordering them into mixed-income and mixed-tenure communities (Office of the Deputy Prime Minister 2005). In part, it has been successful (Holmes 2006). However, research has revealed that higher-income residents are often unwilling to move to areas they know contain pockets of social housing, and that poorer residents are prone to move out of less deprived neighbourhoods once they have the means to do so. There is also little evidence that local gentrification schemes have fostered meaningful social relationships between older and newer residents. In fact, the reverse is true. Rather than improve community relations and networks of loyalty, trust and support, lower- and higher-income residents have tended to keep their distance and live apart, so weakening previous reciprocal social relationships between similarly placed friends and relations (Cheshire 2007).

Acknowledging such criticisms, Sampson (2006) has emphasised the need to improve social relationships and informal social control across, as well as within, urban neighbourhoods – for instance, to help residents access services and opportunities, and extend social cohesion and community participation, beyond the confines of places of residence, or, indeed, satisfy a frequently expressed desire to move to a more desirable and safer residential area (Atkinson *et al.* 2005). Repeated face-to-face interaction in an immediate physical locale with the same group of friends and acquaintances is thought to restrict life chances and experiences. This is borne out by social network analysis that has mapped the daily reality of interpersonal relationships empirically in terms of both proximity and range (see Wellman 1987). In keeping with geographical behavioural analysis (see Lynch 1960), it has been found that, whereas wealth confers mobility and extends self-help networks, poverty results in stasis, defensive withdrawal, and restricted understandings of the wider urban environment. The policy response is clear. City environments which encourage mobility, diversity and difference convey benefits especially for social order (Jacobs 1961; Sennett 1990).

Ordering devices and prevention techniques

The overall failure to revitalise disordered spaces and recreate them as home environments in which the quality of life improves for the people who live there needs to be seen within the broader context of the 'aetiological crisis' afflicting capitalist society generally throughout the latter part of the previous century. In fundamental respects, this has drawn attention away from the structural antecedents of spatial and social segregation, and towards the more limited aim of managing and controlling the problems associated with poor living environments. As crime rates have increased since the 1960s and criminal justice systems have been put under added strain, despite publicly funded programmes of social assistance, confidence in penal welfarism has waned. Abandoning previous attempts to investigate the causes of crime according to 'a vocabulary of motives' (Downes 1988: 177), high crime rates have come to be accepted as a given. A loss of faith in the rehabilitative ideal to change offending behaviour has led to the prioritisation of what are now considered more realistic and moderate crime reduction policies. The 'nothing works' (Martinson 1974) consensus that programmes of offender rehabilitation and reintegration are generally ineffective has 'precipitated a criminological shift away from the offender as the object of knowledge towards the offence – its situational and spatial characteristics – as well as the place and role of the victim' (Crawford 1998: 35).

According to Garland (2001), this fundamental shift in the way the criminal subject is conceived is today made manifest in new criminologies, a key component of which distinguishes between offenders who commit crime because they are pathologically predisposed to do so (Wilson 1975), and those who simply perceive that the benefits of crime outweigh the potential costs (Cohen and Felson 1979). Everyday crimes are normal, rational and commonplace, 'a generalized form of behaviour, routinely produced by the normal patterns of social and economic life in contemporary society' (Garland 2001: 128). As a consequence, they cannot be eliminated, but only deterred, controlled and prevented through administrative techniques. Pathological crimes of 'the Other', on the other hand, are abnormal. Indeed, they are 'a catastrophe ... intrinsically evil or wicked' (ibid.: 184). Beyond understanding, they must be eradicated through deliberate strategies of protection, separation and incarceration. As a result, new community typologies have emerged.

A pervasive one is the 'territorial' or 'defended' community. Employing computerised geographical information systems to geocode address data at increasing levels of resolution, criminological spatial analysis has documented the geographical distribution of specific offences, the various methods employed during their commission, and patterns of repeat victimisation. It has been shown that the distribution of crime conforms to three basic characteristics: a small number of offenders commit a large number of crimes, a small number of victims suffer a large number of crimes, and a small number of areas suffer a disproportionate amount of crime (Trickett et al. 1995). Crime clusters in 'criminal hot spots', defined as locations which experience a heightened risk of crime compared to similar locations (Eck 2005): for instance, street corners and street networks (Taylor and Gottfredson 1986), rundown urban neighbourhoods (Brantingham and Brantingham 1991), city centres (Wikström 1991), and shopping and entertainment complexes (Wiles and Costello 2000).

The 'everydayness' of criminal behaviour is most effectively controlled by manipulating the environmental contexts in which it occurs. National and local government, as well as private interests, attempt to 'defend' (Newman 1972) places against the threat of potential criminal activity. For example, they do this by helping local residents assume 'responsibility for insuring a safe, productive and well maintained living space' (ibid.: 3); ensuring that planning applications conform to crime-prevention building and planning standards and are secured by design principles; installing sophisticated surveillance systems such as CCTV; and partitioning public space into privately controlled 'gated communities'. Such situational measures are commonly allied to psychological perspectives which analyse the purposive use of place for criminal gain. For example, the notion that housing estates comprising multi-storey buildings, overhead walkways and dark underpasses 'can teach children to adopt criminal decisions, and this learned disposition can then cause them to see all situational weaknesses as rational opportunities for crime' (Coleman 1989: 109–110) has led to practical redesign measures such as reducing the number of public entrances to high-rise flats and turning residential blocks into self-contained units.

The environmental determinism intrinsic in such perspectives has been criticised already, and this criticism will not be repeated here. In fact, more positively, it should be noted that evaluations show that situational crime-prevention measures have made a significant contribution to the reduction of crime in specific locations (Kershaw *et al.* 2008). Nevertheless, it is also important to note that, more generally, the narrow focus of much situational crime prevention, based as it is on evidence-based empirical analysis of 'what works' and 'actuarial' techniques of controlling risk, has served to deprioritise 'more ambitious social programmes of prevention and safety' (Hughes 2007: 61). Situational crime prevention is also closely harnessed to instrumental strategies of penal incapacitation and containment, as well as approaches to community safety based on authoritarian 'geographies of responsibility' (*ibid.*: 190). It is to these we now turn.

Morals and responsibilities

Another community typology to have emerged in recent years draws on the notion that safe and crime-free communities are a consequence of shared moral values. Based on the assumption that moral authority is a prerequisite of civilised society, it advocates responsibilising individuals, families and communities through programmes of social education (Wilson and Herrnstein 1985). It follows that resources should be provided to enhance self-control through reformative practices of good parenting, as well as provide instruction on moral and social responsibility in schools, workplaces and the wider community. This is a social, political, but above all moral, response to what are understood to be the competitive excesses of market liberalism. It is thought that by 'gently prodding kin, friends, neighbors, and other community members, rather than building on government controls or fear of authorities' (Etzioni 1995: 15), a range of social ills may be countered: crime, drug taking, the collapse of the nuclear family, welfare dependency and so on. The watchwords are 'debts, inheritances, rightful expectations and obligations' (MacIntyre 1985: 220), emblematic of the moral bonds thought to bind local communities together. Community itself is taken to be a sort of 'moral compass' which can be used to plot a return to traditional human values. So, according to Etzioni (1995: 191), community works 'not merely or even mainly to fight crime, but to sustain civility and values in general. Prevention of crime is a bonus of a moral and civil society'.

Despite its apparent concern for the corrupting influence of individualism within neo-liberal capitalist society, there are two major assumptions underpinning the 'communitarian' response to social disorder which mark it out as an essentially conservative social movement. First, in downplaying the role of the state, it remains unconcerned with political and economic issues such as resource distribution or unemployment. It is predicated on a 'community deficit' model (Taylor 2003), and moral and civil conduct is divorced from economic deprivation (Byrne 2005) and social justice (Young 1999). Second, like social disorganisation theory, it assumes that crime is caused by a lack of social ties and mutual trust. To an extent, this is countered by research which has shown that relatively wealthy suburban communities which experience low levels of crime tend to be characterised by distanciated, anonymous social relations – what Baumgartner (1988) has termed 'moral minimalism'. The 'moral order of the suburb' 'does not arise from intimacy and connectedness, but rather from some of the very things more often presumed to bring about conflict and violence – transiency, fragmentation, isolation, atomization, and indifference among people' *(ibid.*: 134). Of course, neither are suburbs marginal or isolated places which suffer high levels of economic stress. According to Baumgartner *(ibid.*: 93), the loosely woven texture of life there

> with most families segregated on their private lots makes avoidance easy. If tensions escalate, the parties can simply ignore one another without disrupting a larger network of associates. In many cases, their avoidance will not even be noticed.

To bring this section to a close, if it is the case that social order is not necessarily a product of close social networks, mutual support and intimacy – communal characteristics which in fact tend to be rejected by mainstream society – communitarianism as a social movement has no option but to seal a commitment to communal responsibilisation through authoritarian strategies of social control (Levitas 2005). By ignoring power relations and access to resources in the wider environment, it must promote moral conformity in high-crime communities through a zero-tolerance approach to antisocial behaviour (Hughes 1996).

Fortress cities and warehouse prisons

This leads us finally to a particularly dystopian view of contemporary society. Encapsulated in the notion of the 'punishing community', in its most extreme form as practised in the United States, this justifies the control and incapacitation of 'dangerous populations' considered beyond reform and rehabilitation. The belief that social inequality is legitimate, an inevitable outcome of the differential distribution of power and resources within market economies (Murray 1984), has encouraged policymakers to focus on the problems of inner-city neighbourhoods specifically through the lens of the criminal justice system (Feeley and Simon 1992). The widespread acceptance that 'wicked people exist [and therefore] nothing avails except to set them apart from innocent people' (Wilson 1975: 235), has justified a dramatic rise in the use of imprisonment (Herrnstein and Murray 1994). Targeted at aggregate groups of people 'rejected by the depleted institutions of family, work and welfare' (Garland 2001: 135), upfront strategies of coercive responsibilisation are advocated such as the forcible removal of rights-based public spending on unemployment benefit (Murray 1984). If this strategy fails, the legitimacy of social inequality must be upheld by deliberate urban abandonment and strategies of outright social and spatial exclusion. For instance, Davis (1990) has documented how new, coercive, zero-tolerance policing tactics have resulted in the mass arrest of ethnic populations for minor public disorder offences. Those not removed to prison are held in a 'scanscape' of constant surveillance, bunker architecture and CCTV. Subject to restrictive urban planning policies and deliberate acts of discrimination, black populations in particular have been excluded from taking up residence in 'white only' residential areas. If all else fails, there is one fail-safe measure to fall back on: 'the undeserving poor' should be confined within a 'high-tech and more lavish version of the Indian reservation ... while the rest of America tries to go about its business' (Herrnstein and Murray 1994: 523).

Although most evident in the United States, the use of space to protect the interests of the powerful in society, and its role in the formation of culture and identity are characteristic of contemporary cities generally. In the UK, revanchist processes of privatisation and deregulation, such as those described above, are not as prominent. Nevertheless, the benefits which have accrued in recent years from the 'free market' gentrification of public space have not been distributed equally. As we saw in Chapter 2 in relation to London, while the developers and owners of property derive profits from rehabilitating rundown inner-city areas, residents unable to pay rising occupancy costs have been forced to move, or are evicted. As Coleman *et al.* (2005) point out, an important component of this overall urban regeneration strategy is the governance of crime. A crucial attraction of newly gentrified areas is their perceived security. As such, they are marketed to high-income, professional people as safe and free from visible forms of crime. The result is new urban spaces created around crime-prevention initiatives such as gated communities and CCTV, which guarantee to regulate and control the poor and keep marginalised 'others' out. Meanwhile new social housing estates populated by residents displaced from newly gentrified neighbourhoods are effectively 'criminalised' (Johnston and Mooney 2007: 139), subject to increasingly punitive strategies such as zero-tolerance community policing, electronic tagging, ASBOs and imprisonment.

The consequence of this is that the crime-reduction and community safety agenda, linked as it is to urban and social policy, is imbued with particular notions of morality and responsibilisation which exclude difference. Over the past ten years or so, the Labour government has introduced measures intended to tackle social exclusion, and reintegrate marginalised people into the economic and social mainstream. As we have seen, community programmes of support have also been introduced to reintegrate ex-prisoners back into society (SEU 2002). But the responsibilisation strategies that have been adopted to achieve crime reduction and community safety are highly ambivalent. Founded on communitarian principles of remoralisation, these strategies assume that low-income housing estates may be recreated as places 'where order, respect and responsibility prevail' (Johnston and Mooney 2007: 139). Although this conception of community is intended to promote inclusion, in reality it is 'exclusive'. Appeals to self-help and community are often perceived by marginalised communities simply as a form of abandonment by official state agencies. In pandering to local concerns about difference, they also engender a 'criminology of intolerance' (Young 1999). It is a characteristic of 'punishing communities' that they remain disinclined to develop positive and participatory approaches to addressing crime or facilitating offender reintegration (Worrall and Hoy 2005). Indeed, far from encouraging inclusion, reintegration and conformity, they create a 'parallel universe', reinforcing for some offenders 'an embeddedness which takes for granted that the only way to behave is criminally' (*ibid.*: 70). Worrall and Hoy lay out the matter-of-fact consequences of this:

We are engaged in a 'war' against crime, where there are two clear sides: the respectable law-abiding citizen and the feckless outsider. *This* sense of community reflects an insecure society, suspicious of, and hostile towards, anything and anyone who is different. Community means segregation, prejudice and the desire for revenge. (*ibid.*: 69; emphasis in the original)

Conclusion

As others have argued, what is needed is a pluralist response which contextualises crime and criminality socially, economically, culturally, politically and spatially (Hughes 2007). This is a response that, by seeking to resolve class, racial and gender conflicts, often intensified in local community contexts, affirms the rights of different marginalised groups, including ex-offenders, to full and active citizenship. That is, people have the right to a minimum level of personal security, as well as 'the resources that would allow them to participate as a full citizen of their society' (Scott 1994: 150), or, as Lefebvre (1976 [1973]: 35) would have it, 'the right not to be "colonized": not to be classified forcibly into categories which have been determined by the necessarily homogenizing powers'.

Taken to its logical conclusion, this suggests that it is a responsibility of the state to make good to those who suffer the effects of inequality and social exclusion. Retributive forms of punishment may be deserved for the crimes offenders commit, and utilitarian responses justified on the basis that the public has a right to be protected from future crimes, but the state is also obliged to provide rehabilitation to offenders in order to offset the effects of punishment on them (Carlen 1989). Particular attention should be paid to the 'counterproductive effects of punitive sanctions, such as incarceration, when considered in the long run of individual lives' (Laub and Sampson 2003: 291). Furthermore, ex-prisoners should be supported to access housing, work and welfare in order to ensure they re-enter society as full and active citizens (Rotman 1990). This is both a right and a necessity. In order to protect the public, a primary objective of prisoner resettlement is to control and risk-manage offenders, but unless targeted programmes of social rehabilitation are also implemented in the places prisoners return to, a lack of legitimate opportunities to support their resettlement back into society is likely to frustrate efforts to maintain criminal desistance and reinforce justifications for continuing to offend.

As argued throughout this book so far, the failure to address the causes of crime and its consequences for victims and offenders alike is a consequence of the limited frames of reference commonly employed in single-factor explanations of criminality. Crucial tiers of explanation have been neglected in the criminological analysis of crime, criminality and place. Behavioural explanations in particular have ignored the affective or emotional relationships that exist between people and place, and the role of place to engender diversity of feeling, experience and consciousness, as well as the impact of the unconscious on perception and thinking. Primarily concerned with arranging behaviour empirically into observable spatial patterns, these explanations have marginalised subjective meanings, values and goals – such as understanding how constraints on movement shape the meaning and value derived from everyday activities, such as spending time at home, working, being a parent and socialising with friends, and how these vary over the life course. These are all mundane occupations, which, nevertheless, can strengthen residential stability and friendship ties and so act as significant turning points in the lives of offenders contemplating desistance (Sampson and Laub 1993). The next chapter discusses crime and criminal desistance in relation to the way time, space, human agency and behavioural change play out in specific localities and engender such everyday experiences. Referring to human geographic and social scientific literature, which considers space and place as affective milieu, constitutive of rational and non-rational elements, subjectivity and social context together, it assesses the extent to which offenders affect, and at the same time are affected by, the places they inhabit.

Chapter 4

The hidden limitations and possibilities of everyday life

Introduction

Throughout the previous chapters, the term 'everyday life' has been used a number of times; for instance, in reference to routine activities and the spatial distribution of criminal offences (Cohen and Felson 1979), as well as offences viewed as normal and commonplace within modern society (Garland 2001). This chapter broadens the definition to focus on the lived world. It conceives of the everyday in terms of social practice – the things people do, their dispositions – habits, propensities and inclinations, and subjective experience – of consumption, meaning and emotion. This ubiquitous, but ultimately imprecise notion of everyday life is drawn upon to investigate the spaces and places routinely inhabited by persistent offenders – the home, the street, the neighbourhood, the shopping precinct, and the prison – and their role in both enabling and constraining human agency (Dear and Flusty 2002). In reviewing the work of four writers – Anthony Giddens, Pierre Bourdieu, Michel de Certeau, and Henri Lefebvre, as well as sociological literature on the impact of imprisonment – the chapter considers the commonly held view that daily existence is repetitively mundane and banal, and that a sense of alienation and disidentification stems from it. In the conclusion, these ideas inform some general observations about the significance of theoretical perspectives on 'social work' and 'social capital' for offender rehabilitation and reintegration methods and practice.

Social practice

It is commonly asserted in recent urban geographical discourse that merging macro-, meso- and micro-levels of analysis – global and national influence, social and environmental context, and local and indigenous interpretation (Soja 1995) – focuses attention on how, at different spatial scales, the physical, social and economic environment structures social relations and, in return, is modified by them. Dear and Wolch (1989) identify three fundamental facets of this 'sociospatial dialectic' (Soja 1980). Social relations are *constituted* in space, as, for example, by patterns of *de jure* settlement and industrial organisation and production; *constrained* in space by physical, social and economic characteristics which limit human activity, and *mediated* in space by cultural values and belief systems and the reflexive practice of everyday negotiation and resistance. Rather than space being a neutral geometric container of material, social and economic features – as in 'positivist' spatial science (Cloke *et al.* 1991) – it is important in its own right. Space is a 'mental thing' or 'mental place' (Lefebvre 1991 [1974]: 3) which has symbolic, cultural and religious significance. It is also socially constructed. As noted by Massey (1984: 52), 'just as there are no purely spatial processes, neither are there any non-spatial social processes.' Therefore, fluid and psychodynamic as it is, space can only be understood in relation to everyday human experience and activity.

The importance of space and place in the structuring and reproduction of everyday human experience is central to 'structuration theory' (Giddens 1976, 1984, 1990), an attempt to articulate the relationship between social structure and individuals in shaping institutions and everyday life. Structuration theory has been applied widely within criminology. For example, it has informed work on crime and place (Bottoms and Wiles 1992), social order in prisons (Sparks *et al.* 1996), and criminal desistance (Farrall and Bowling 1999; Farrall and Calverley 2006). Briefly, it contends that social structure is not autonomous; it is maintained and changed by what people do during the course of everyday social practice and routine. As a key structural component, place influences and, in turn, is influenced by human action. As knowledgeable actors, human beings retain the ability to construct how and when they behave in particular situations. According to Giddens (1984: 102):

The fact that a human path in the time-geographic notation seems to represent nothing more than a point on the move should not lead us to forget that at its tip – as it were – in the persistent present, stands a living body-subject, endowed with memories, feelings, knowledge, information and goals – in other words capabilities too rich for a conceivable kind of symbolic representation but decisive for the direction of paths.

So, places are active milieu made meaningful by the way they both enable and constrain movement and social interaction. In order to embrace the complications inherent in the interplay, it is necessary to allow each perspective to bear upon the other. In so doing, it is revealed that 'structures are constituted through action' and 'action is constituted structurally' (Giddens 1976: 161). 'Knowledgeable' human agency is gained through the competence of individuals to describe and 'rationalise' the situations they find themselves in, and to 'monitor reflexively' what happens to them in those situations. The 'discursive consciousness' which arises from this reiterative process is built around 'a sense of continuity and order in events' (Giddens 1991: 243). But while this provides 'ontological security' – 'confidence or trust that the natural and social worlds are as they appear to be' (Giddens 1984: 375) – human agency is never completely voluntary. Choice and change are bounded by routine, convention and repetitive practice, as well as the unintended consequences of routine, convention and repetitive practice.

The relevance of this thinking to the geographical distribution of crime is that spatial practice shapes criminal activities through repetition. Through the routine carrying out of the same actions in the same social and spatial circumstances, crime becomes unreflective, a taken-for-granted practice mutually accepted as a conventional feature of everyday human experience. According to Bottoms and Wiles (1992: 20), place reproduces certain social practices, rules and resources over time. The conventional regularity of these eventually shapes 'understandings of the nature of particular areas and, within them, of specific locations – and those understandings are undoubtedly important in shaping the geographical distribution of offending behaviour.' Its relevance to criminal desistance is the importance it accords to the 'reflexive monitoring' of conduct, and how the interaction of structural constraints and individual decision making impacts on the timing and pace by which offenders eventually give up crime over the life course (Farrall and Bowling 1999). For instance, as offenders age, maturational reform, arising from an unconscious need for security within stable family and work relationships, reproduces these social institutions as important behavioural constraints. A consequence of adhering to the conventional regularity of marriage and work practices, for example, is that offenders consciously or unconsciously make progress towards criminal desistance (Farrall and Calverley 2006). The relevance of structuration theory to prisons is referred to later in the chapter.

Although Giddens accepts the possibility that in some social contexts individuals are likely to respond to structural constraints beyond their control, his work has been criticised for negating the influence of key structural regularities such as class, culture, gender and ethnicity. In particular, structuration theory ignores the extent to which the ability of individuals to resist structural forces is limited by the position they occupy in relation to these forces (Bauman 1989). In assuming an equal relationship of power between structure and agency, the theory fails to recognise that 'social structures, such as economic and social institutions, value and cultural systems have a relative autonomy from the situated activity which they in part govern' (Layder 1981: 132). In focusing exclusively on social practice, the theory negates the existence of forces outside individuals which determine or condition the way they act; for instance, the extent to which reflexive monitoring is a human attribute exercised mostly by the economically privileged (Lash and Urry 1994), and therefore of limited utility when assessed in relation to the social circumstances of most offenders, who possess neither the capital nor the resources to engage in critical self-reflection. Most importantly perhaps, structuration theory is 'poor at addressing motivational issues' (Farrall and Calverley 2006: 177). The reality of social life is not simply an aggregate of individual behaviour centred on a set of everyday, routine activities. Options available to individuals are limited by physical constraints, cultural norms and historical precedents which structure practice and strategies of action. In reducing social relations to 'an almost cybernetic-like "monitoring" of conduct' (Lash and Urry 1994: 44), structuration theory disregards the impact of the unconscious, 'the emotional or feeling side of our nature [which] goes hand in hand with our reflective, intelligent and calculating side' (Layder 2004: 12). Therefore, in assuming that the relationship between people and place may be reduced to a tacit awareness of social practice, the theory ignores the extent to which people are emotionally affected by the places they inhabit – for instance, how places in which people are born, grow up and live for long periods of time trigger collective feelings of desire, excitement, drudgery or boredom – in other words, all of the personal, subjective and affective dimensions of place (Tuan 1977).

Cultural dispositions

We will return to the notion of reflexive monitoring in the conclusion, but, for now, the criticism that structuration theory artificially separates practical consciousness from the macro-economic forces which spatially determine economic position and access to capital and resources is assessed. The problematic that everyday experience and practice are at once individually and collectively felt and also structured by rules and conventions deeply embedded within the organised system of production (Williams 1973) has been addressed generally in cultural political theory and in particular by Bourdieu's 'theory of practice' (1977, 1988, 1990a), another attempt to transcend the opposition between the individual and society. It contends that social practice is a response, on the one hand, to structural situation – income and employment, for example – and, on the other hand to dominant cultural forms – beliefs, meanings and values; as well as competencies, skills, manners, knowledge, expertise – and the different social circumstances of class, race, gender and place in which such forms predominate. In an attempt to straddle both these dimensions, Bourdieu argues that everyday routines are contained within prior cultural dispositions (termed 'habitus'), which engender intersubjective categories of thought and appreciation (Bourdieu 1990a). Individuals and groups actively seek 'social and cultural capital' according to the 'practical logic' of their particular life worlds within a structured social space (termed 'field'), such as a family or a class. Throughout the life course, respect or cultural 'distinction' is achieved through adhering to particular patterns of leisure and consumption – styles of dress, speech, taste in music and literature, food, bodily comportment and so on. Accordingly, class location is betrayed and differential material circumstances of social location are reproduced. In contrast to Giddens' concept of reflexive monitoring, social practice is never a consequence of conscious deliberation or rational choice. A product of both thinking and feeling, it is mostly unconscious and therefore unreflexive. Because access to particular forms of social and cultural capital is always limited by class, race gender and place, individuals and groups 'appropriate as voluntary choices and preferences, lifestyles which are actually rooted in material constraints' (Shilling 1993: 129). Bourdieu (1990a: 54) explains the differential distribution of social and cultural capital as follows:

> being the product of a particular class of objective regularities
> the habitus tends to generate all the reasonable common

sense behaviours which are possible within the limits of these regularities and which are likely to be positively sanctioned because they are objectively adjusted to the logic characteristics of a particular field whose objective future they anticipate. At the same time it tends to exclude all extravagances – behaviours that would be negatively sanctioned because they are incompatible with the objective conditions.

Critiques of this approach have suggested that, in approving the unconscious character of social practice, and denying the possibility of rational decision making, it fails to explain decisions freely made and creatively acted upon (Jenkins 2002). While some individuals may be constrained in the choices they make, some of the time, others retain the power of self-conscious deliberation and intervention in their own histories. As such, the attempt to transcend the divide between objectivism and subjectivism, structure and agency, habitus and field, downplays conscious reflexive resistance and wavers towards determinism (Mouzelis 1995). In suggesting that the internalisation of past experience predisposes individuals to think and act in certain ways, it promotes the idea that 'social stability is the product of the internalisation of shared values, beliefs and norms' (Jenkins 2002: 81).

Despite these criticisms, Bourdieu's work has been applied extensively, most notably to critiques of neo-liberalism, cultural politics, social capital and the sociology of education. Primarily because the concept of habitus has been taken to explain why some people engage in specific everyday social practices while others do not, Bourdieu's ideas have also been taken up within criminology (for example, see MacLeod 1995 on street gangs, Barry 2006 on criminal desistance, Allen 2007 on crime and drugs, and Hall *et al.* 2008 on crime and consumption). Generally, it is argued that, while the educated and the wealthy retain the capital to define themselves in consumer culture relative to a shared aesthetics of elegance, refinement and taste, less dominant groups are prone to legitimise alternative means of achieving positions of social distinction including through criminal behaviour. Rather than consider crime as a routine, voluntary social practice, as in the case of structuration theory, it is considered a product of objective factors: economic planning, neo-liberal modes of consumption, and the class differences these tend to perpetuate. In specific application to the geography of crime, it has been observed that, while certain forms of middle-class 'gentrification habitus' develop in so-called metropolitan 'status areas' – 'dormitory developments', 'gated communities', 'new urban colonies' and the like (Webber 2007), micro-communities imbued with a deep sense of educational and occupational failure become firmly established in deprived (formerly working-class) urban areas (Allen 2007). Unable to achieve money, wealth and status through legitimate means, but just as susceptible to the enticements of advanced capitalist culture as everyone else, the poor and marginalised are exhorted to consume (Hall *et al.* 2008). As such, the spatial distribution of consumption mirrors the spatial distribution of crime. It is time to assess the influence of consumption in everyday life in a little more detail.

Consumption

Another way of analysing everyday social practice is to divide geographic locations into different but dialectically related elements. Employing personal and public frames of analysis, this approach has attempted to 'bring together levels and terms which are isolated by existing spatial practice and by the ideologies underpinning it' (Lefebvre 1991 [1974]: 64). The purpose of doing this is to distinguish subjective meaning from the way places are conceived and represented objectively, as, for example, by urban planning practices. In the latter sense, places are real, material and empirically measurable; in the former, they are mental and imagined, foci of affective meaning. Beyond the material conditions of existence and the sway of cognition, there is always an 'affective bond between people and place', constitutive of what it means to be human (Tuan 1974: 4).

For instance, it has been suggested that cities are both 'hard' and 'soft': 'hard' because they are socially constructed by functional rational planning strategies, and 'soft' because they are moulded by individuals, who, engaged in a 'continual creative play of urban living', occupy different roles and identities within them (Raban 1974: 10). Cities may be distinguished by architecture, stratified by class, and regulated by bureaucracy; but they are made meaningful by the way they are perceived individually through 'illusion, myth, aspiration [and] nightmare' (*ibid.*). As a consequence, although power and authority flow from the top down, people are never completely passive in the way they relate to the places they inhabit. Because power is always in tension and never omnipotent, there is always resistance (Foucault 1982). By engaging in reiterative social and cultural practice, people deliberately intervene in their individual and collective destinies (de Certeau 1984). Everyday life might be 'framed within a grid of socio-economic restraints', but it is comprised of 'tactics, creations and initiatives' (*ibid*.: ix) used intentionally to 'manipulate the mechanisms of discipline and conform to them only in order to evade them' (*ibid*.: xiv). According to de Certeau, opposition is embodied mostly in a personalised logic of creative consumption – cooking, shopping, reading, decorating – all of which subtly delineate the context of the home from the outside order of the city. The main site of resistance, however, is the street. Pedestrians move about the city – talking, walking, shopping, dwelling – but these are not automatic practices. Pedestrians occupy the streets 'with the forests of their desires and goals' (*ibid*: xxi). Urban planners employ panoptic mapping 'strategies' and other actuarial logics of discipline and surveillance to define and demarcate the boundaries of place and fix and control movement, but these are never perfect. Eluding such 'micro-physics of power' (Foucault 1977: 26), people often deviate from predetermined spatial discipline 'through hit-and-run tactics of spatial occupation' (Dear and Flusty 2002: 303).

As others have noticed, there is a large dollop of romanticism pervading the view that everyday acts embody resistance; a sense in which ordinary people have been elevated to the status of heroes, creative artists free to indulge a passion for resistance in imagined and idealistic representations of reality (Massey 2005). For example, Ross (1996: 71) has insisted, 'resistance to what' exactly? Everyday space has been reified, turned into a realm of liberation and revolution, when in fact it is characterised by puerile, infantile acts of transgression performed for no other reason than to outwit the 'master planners' (*ibid*.). In some respects, this idea mirrors recent cultural understandings of criminal behaviour as often sensual and seductive (Katz 1988) – a form of leisure and popular resistance which offers 'a frequent delight in excess, a glee in breaking the rules, a reassertion of dignity and identity' (Young 2003: 408). Rather than being the outcome of rational decision making, it is an expressive act intended to subvert the conformity of everyday life with a 'stylish counterpunch to the belly of authority' (Ferrell 1996: 195). Hayward (2004) in particular has argued that 'parafunctional spaces' – dilapidated playgrounds, abandoned car parks, poorly lit subways and so forth – should be considered not as deficient exactly, but as sites of cultural resistance: 'zones in which creative, informal and unintended uses overtake the officially designated functions' (Papastergiadis 2002: 45 in *ibid*.: 143).

This view has been criticised for 'a reluctance to confront squarely the bleak reality of advanced capitalist culture' (Hall *et al*. 2008: 157). For instance, the argument that consumerism exhibits 'both progressive and regressive features' (Kellner 1992: 174) is often made. It suggests that, while consumerism 'can lead to a totally fragmented, disjointed life, subject to the whims of fashion and the subtle indoctrinations of advertising and popular culture', it also provides opportunities 'to play with one's identity and to change one's life dramatically' (*ibid.*). Everyday consumer capitalism is an 'emporium of styles' (Raban 1974) or 'a game' (de Certeau 1984) in which to explore new opportunities for creative freedom and reproductive self-expression. It is the means by which individuals may reconstruct themselves symbolically, and give form to particular narratives of self-identity and lifestyle (Giddens 1991). In important respects, this idea returns us to a consideration of the relative impact on identity of unequal distributions of power and resources (Castells 2004). While those with financial capabilities might be free to reinvent themselves symbolically through the purchase of particular consumer goods and lifestyles, the rest must contend with the mundane realities of work and controlled consumption. Indeed, according to Bauman (1998), those unable to consume, so-called 'flawed consumers' who survive at 'the lower-most regions of the power hierarchy', are simply relegated to the status of non-persons, and 'cast outside the social space in which identities are sought, chosen, constructed, evaluated, confirmed or refuted' (Bauman 2004: 39).

To some, the outcome of this is disturbing at both social and personal levels of enquiry. Unequal power relationships between production and consumer processes within capitalist society have induced deep human suffering masked as passivity and complacency (see Adorno 1991). Saturated as it is with commodities, advanced capitalist culture uniformly levels individuality and debilitates subjectivity (Jameson 1984). For instance, oriented solely towards pleasure, hedonism and lifestyle, it engenders a condition of permanent 'pathological narcissism', an antisocial preoccupation with fantasy, self-image, pornography and appearance (Lasch 1980). According to Hall *et al.* (2008: 13), the implications of this for the (re)construction of criminal identities are extreme. Rather than provide opportunities for pro-social personal growth, consumerism engenders new forms of infantilism which embrace crime as the primary means of 'achieving fantasised positions of social distinction and "respect"'. Ethnographic research carried out in north-east England has found that the lives of young criminals today are increasingly characterised by:

> an almost childlike fascination with youth-oriented clothes, gadgets and media productions. For those we spoke to, life was

understood as a constant battle for cultural significance in the
locale and in a fantasised version of the broader culture, a battle
that could be fought only with an armoury well stocked with the
weapons of consumer symbolism, a battle in which involvement
was compulsory and the perceived benefits of triumph massively
outweighed the potential pitfalls. (*ibid*: 29–30)

What is missing in accounts of productive consumption is 'any
structural engagement with the problems of material distribution and
economic justice' (Roberts 1999: 28). These are considered next.

Boredom and desire

Although it might be assumed that the trivial and repetitive nature
of everyday life is unavoidably boring and humdrum, there is a
tradition of social scientific enquiry that has sought to reveal the
extraordinariness within everyday lived experience (for a review,
see Highmore 2002). It suggests that, after all the 'distinct, superior,
specialized, structured activities have been singled out by analysis'
(Lefebvre 2008 [1947]: 97) – political, institutional and artistic – it is in
daily life that the essence of human existence is to be found. Through
subjective experience of the everyday, individuals develop a sense of
who they are and their social standing in the world. According to
Lefebvre (2003 [1970]: 118), it is urbanisation, the city itself, which
'constructs, identifies, and sets free the essence of social relationships'.
Connecting the binaries of objectivity and subjectivity, materiality and
mentality, reality and imagination, the theory conceptualises everyday
life according to three spatial elements. 'Conceived space' is physical,
objective and empirical, and is represented by models, images,
maps and coordinates. 'Perceived space' is social and comprised of
mundane and common-sense actions, reactions and relations. And
'lived space' is mental, subjective and imagined, and is distinguished
by emotional attachment. These processes interact so that real and
objective practicalities combine with trivial and commonplace activity,
which combine with imagined and subjective meanings (Lefebvre
1991 [1974]).

Lefebvre maintains that everyday life is bland, boring and mundane
essentially because it has been 'colonised' by the state. Space has been
commodified and impoverished by abstract economic relations and
consumer processes. In both 'real' and 'ideal' terms (Lefebvre 1991
[1974]), 'the commodity, the market, money, with their implacable

logic, seize everyday life' (Lefebvre 1988: 79). The daily round of existence is endlessly repetitive, characterised by 'gestures of labour and leisure, mechanical movements both human and properly mechanic, hours, days, weeks, months, years, linear and cyclical repetitions, natural and rational time' (Lefebvre 1984 [1968]: 18). Space has been commodified, constrained by the unequal distribution of opportunities, services and resources. As a consequence, individuals are denied 'the right to the city'. In order to overcome these geographies of power, resistance and control, which have resulted in seclusion, segregation and criminalisation, they must (re)appropriate a multiplicity of everyday contexts and situations. These include routinised, private, public and social spaces: homes, streets, schools, meeting points, leisure spaces, shopping centres, community support agencies, including 'the use of the center, a privileged place, instead of being dispersed and stuck in ghettos' (Lefebvre 1996: 170).

The difference in this respect, to the notion of tactical resistance suggested by de Certeau (1984) is that, because daily life is completely 'colonised' by modernity, and in particular the 'capitalist logic' of consumption (Highmore 2002), evading it simply is not possible through stylistic tactics of deviation. Resistance occurs, if at all, as a 'moment' of transformation. Everyday life is distinguished by all the emotions: boredom, inertia and depression certainly, but also more extreme moments 'of delight, surrender, disgust, surprise, horror, or outrage' (Harvey, afterword in Lefebvre 1991 [1974]: 429). No matter how fleetingly experienced, it is in the sensual realm of 'lived space' that people may 'attempt to achieve the total realization of a possibility' (Lefebvre 2008 [1961]: 348), break free from routine and deadening practice, resist the alienating effects of capitalism, and determine their own lives. Crucially, it is through 'desire', needing and wanting what we do not have, which motivates resistance and engenders change. There is little in this to suggest instrumentality. Desire takes many forms: it can have a purpose: 'a love, a being, or a work'; but it can also be 'discharged explosively, with no definite object, in violent and destructive or self-destructive ways' (Lefebvre 1991 [1974]: 394). Yet, even the most mundane event reverberates with social and psychic desire; such that without it 'everydayness would become hopelessly uniform' (Lefebvre 2003 [1970]: 86).

Owing to the mixture of romantic, radical and revolutionary thinking that informs these ideas, they have been dismissed as anti-structuralist (Castells 1977). They have also been criticised for lacking clarity and offering no clear, practical methods or tools to transcend everyday reality. For instance, although Lefebvre argues persuasively against the homogenisation of capitalist space, no understanding is given for how diversity and difference will emerge, other than that, somehow, naturally, the constraints and contradictions of everyday life will one day spawn challenging oppositional and ultimately revolutionary cultures (Shmuely 2008). Nevertheless, Lefebvre's influence on urban social geography is widespread and increasing; and recently has begun to also inform criminological analysis of the foreground, experiential nature of much criminal behaviour. For instance, how it is bound up with 'the gritty particularities of everyday existence' (Ferrell *et al*. 2004: 2), and the fact that it is 'as much about emotions – hatred, anger, frustration, excitement and love – as it is about poverty, possessing and wealth' (Presdee 2000: 4).

The concluding sections of this chapter explore the relevance of paying close attention to problems of material distribution as well as the trivial details of everyday experience as they impact on actions and decision-making involved in criminal desistance; most importantly, the capacity of offenders to envisage new possibilities and futures, and thereby transcend familiar notions of space and place in which they live out daily life. As Farrall (2005: 371) has argued, it is only at this micro-level of analysis that it is possible to capture 'the total person'... 'the fusion of the rational and irrational, the heady mix of emotional states (sometimes intense, sometimes mundane), the specific locating of individuals in particular times and spaces, the uniqueness of their experiences and the desire to combine both "the human" and "the social" in one account'. But for now it is necessary to return to a particular physical and social environment in which everyday existence is at once mundane and trivial, and, at the same time, 'extraordinarily' acute: prison.

Everyday life in prison

Subject to the disciplinary power of constant surveillance – recording, monitoring, observing, training (Foucault 1977) – prisons are social institutions in which the minds and actions of the people held in them are shaped in rigid, blunt, but also subtle and complex ways. Punishment is justified in law because human beings are self-determining and therefore offenders choose to commit crime freely. However, it is also a fundamental aim of imprisonment to reform offenders; to address the causes of their criminal behaviour – be they psychological, behavioural, structural, social or cultural. Yet, even though the relationship between the environment and the self is central to the everyday experience of imprisonment, in terms of both punishment and rehabilitation, the social and psychological impact of incarceration remains poorly understood (Toch 1992).

Throughout the last two centuries, during which time imprisonment has been the keystone of the modern penal system, there has been fundamental disagreement over its purpose and value. Ever since the second half of the eighteenth century, when prisons ceased to be places of incarceration for people awaiting trial, execution, deportation, or payment of debts, and became places of punishment in their own right, they have had a dual purpose (Ignatieff 1978). It is a fundamental principle of Western democracies that punishment is justified on retributivist grounds that it is deserved for the crimes offenders have committed in the past, and also on the utilitarian principle that it reduces the incidence of crime in the future (Walker 1991). Punishment is delivered by confining offenders against their will; reductions in crime are facilitated through incapacitation, deterrence and rehabilitating offenders to behave as law-abiding citizens after their release. Yet the objectives of punishment, security, deterrence and reform are never held in balance.

Traditionally, prisons are understood as monolithic places, self-regulating and securely insulated from the outside world. They are 'capsule environments' (Wortley 2008) specifically structured and organised spatially and temporally to enforce 'disciplinary monotony' and render prisoners 'docile' (Foucault 1977: 141). Given that the social, cultural and economic circumstances of everyday life in prison are highly regulated, dimensions of space – size, proximity, distance, density – exert powerful influences on how social interaction is sensed, felt and experienced. Partitioning and compartmentalisation determine social networks, movement, boundary, location and territoriality. More than this, spatial arrangements in prison have a significant impact on physical and psychological well-being. For example, population density is associated with poor health (Baum and Paulus 1987), and more frequent requests for medical attention (Wener and Keys 1988). It is also associated with aggression (Cox et al. 1984; Pontell and Welsh 1994), and increases in disciplinary infractions (Paulus et al. 1981). According to Matthews (2009: 26), space in prison is never neutral:

> It establishes social divisions. It defines and redefines behaviour. It sends out messages. It provides the basis for the construction and dissemination of ideologies. It is a mechanism through which the distribution and circulation of bodies is achieved. It

reflects and defines social relations and finally, it is a mechanism through which order is realised.

All of this suggests that the way space deliberately and unknowingly imposes authority, routine, order and discipline makes prison an obvious context in which to study the dialectical relationship between structure and agency. To the extent that prisoners are laid low and conditioned by it (Foucault 1977), or able to overcome its privations and exercise self-determination (Giddens 1984), imprisonment would appear to offer a unique opportunity to analyse the contradictory, lived experiences of individuals who find themselves in similar environmental situations. However, notwithstanding the significant impact that the rise in incarceration rates has had on prison conditions and regimes over recent years, little new research has been carried out on either individual or collective behavioural responses to differential prison environments (Wacquant 2002). Much of the extant literature on adaptive modes of prisoner behaviour dates from the last century and was carried out mostly in high-security prisons in the United States (Morgan 2002). While a few studies in the UK have focused on the impact of imprisonment on specific 'problem behaviours' such as violence (Sim 1994), and suicide and self-harm (Liebling 1999), in more general terms little is known about 'the uniqueness and variability of response to the same setting or about differential impacts of settings on the same person' (Toch 1992: 3).

There are two traditional schools of thought on how prisoners respond to the conditions of their confinement. Imprisonment imposes an 'indigenous' subculture; or prisoners 'import' into prison the behavioural characteristics of the particular culture to which they belonged on the outside. The 'indigenous' model conceptualises prisons as 'people processing factories'; their *raison d'être* is to mortify and humiliate prisoners by subjecting them to a series of deprivations: of liberty, goods and services, heterosexual relationships, autonomy and personal security (Sykes 1958). Deprivation is 'symbolized by the barrier to social intercourse with the outside and to departure that is often built right into the physical plant, such as locked doors, high walls, barbed wire, cliffs, water, forests, or moors' (Goffman 1961: 15–16). The level of separation from the outside world is made more extreme by strictly enforced mechanisms of interior discipline and control, intended to bring about 'a series of abasements, degradations, humiliations, and profanations of self' (*ibid.*: 24). These include 'batch living', the categorisation and segregation of prisoners into relatively undifferentiated groups; a lack of privacy and security; a strict timetable of routines and activities; a code of discipline based on privileges, sanctions and rewards; and the stripping away of personal identities through the compulsory allocation of prison numbers and clothes. Prisoners respond to the rigidity of prison life in set ways. Some keep themselves to themselves; others confront prison authority by remaining defiant. Some stoically endure their captivity or form relationships with other prisoners in order to present a united front; others become mentally depressed; some commit suicide (Sykes 1958). However, pervading all of these responses is a uniform sense of defeat. 'Prisonization' (Clemmer 1940) – the degree to which prisoners are 'invaded' by imprisonment at a deep psychological level – has a deleterious effect on behaviour. Most prisoners are marked by 'personal failure', 'self-pity' and 'time wasted or destroyed' (Goffman 1961: 66). They become 'lonely individuals', totally reliant on the distribution of privileges, and constantly fearful of the imposition of sanctions (Mathiesen 1965: 12).

In contrast, the 'importation' model suggests that prisoners respond to everyday life in prison in ways that are an extension of the 'type of experiences a man has had with other persons before he came to prison' (Clemmer 1940: 1). A common reaction is to adhere to an 'inmate code' which derives from their predominately poorly educated backgrounds within working-class urban neighbourhoods. While this provides a sense of cohesion and community, it can also harden into a 'criminal code' or 'thief subculture' characterised by a tough and intransigent approach to prison life and a determination to return to crime after release (Irwin and Cressey 1962). Rather than being brought low by imprisonment, such prisoners are largely unaffected by it. By affecting a state of 'cryogenic suspension', many wait out their time until release (Sapsford 1983: 76). Although some may find assurance, comfort and ontological security (Giddens 1991) in the routine and habitual banality of everyday life in prison, even many long-term prisoners do not lose 'their identities as a result of being processed through the prison system' (Cohen and Taylor 1972: 148). They remain consistent as individuals and retain the capacity to resist by asserting 'superiority over their guards, and [developing] ways of dealing with attacks upon their self-conceptions' (*ibid.*).

Prisons have changed, of course, since the publication of this early sociological literature. Conditions and regimes have modernised and improved, and prison management has been reprioritised as different perspectives on the effectiveness of prison to deter crime and reform offenders have held sway. Society has also changed. As noted in Chapter 2, in the United States especially, the racial composition of the prison population has changed in recent years. As documented by Jacobs (1979), a manifestation of this has been a growing sense of solidarity among black prisoners based on ethnic origin, but also the formation of violent street gangs, many of which pledge allegiance to a shared residential location. Today, according to Wacquant (2001: 110), this has transformed the culture of American prisons:

> the predatory culture of the street ... has entered into and transfigured the social structure and culture of jails and prisons ... 'the old hero' of the prison world – the 'right guy' – has been replaced by outlaws and gang members. These two types have raised toughness and mercilessness to the top of the prisoners' value systems.

Yet, prison is not a uniform experience. Although sometimes considered as alternatives, it is increasingly accepted that the traditional modes of prisoner adaptation outlined above are not mutually exclusive (Thomas 1977). Instead, collective experiences prior to imprisonment mediate individual perceptions and responses in prison (Toch 1992). Prisoner culture is an amalgam of both institutional structure (the indigenous model) and personal agency (the importation model). In reality, power relations vary considerably in prisons, as do the ways prisoners respond to the various restrictions placed upon them. Depending on age, gender, race, length of sentence, their psychological profile, and ability to cope, the circumstances of their lives prior to imprisonment, the number of times they have been to prison, and their experiences afterwards, different prisoners respond to different prisons in different ways (Liebling 1999). As such, everyday life in prison is not uniform; it is 'both patterned and ordered and at the same time, dynamic and changing' (Jewkes 2005: 377). In fact, prisons should be considered 'less as prior, stable, fixed entities, and more as made, dynamic, fluid achievements' (Philo and Parr 2000: 513). Drawing on structuration theory, Sparks *et al.* have observed that, although the spatial and temporal restrictions placed on prisoners limit opportunities for resistance, 'prisons quite commonly seethe and boil with human agency, passion and conflict – in ways that are not infrequently magnified and rendered more intense precisely by the constraints and frustrations encountered there' (1996: 68). For example, illicit trading networks, gang allegiance, violence, bullying and racism (King and McDermott 1995) are characteristics of everyday life in prison which routinely challenge the capacity of prison officials and officers to maintain normal standards of security and control. While some prisoners may be rendered docile and choose to remain in their cells all day long, others spend the majority of their time on the landings, playing head games of 'cat and mouse' with staff (McDermott and King 1988), or engaged in prohibited trading networks involving drugs and mobile phones (Valentine and Longstaff 1998).

The diversity of prisoner response stems in large part from the different prisons and prison contexts they are held within. Prisons retain different categories of prisoners, and are run according to different protocols of security and surveillance. In the UK, some prisons date from medieval times; others are positively futuristic in design. Some, especially Victorian-built prisons, are situated in densely populated urban areas, whereas most of the 'new generation' prisons are situated in rural areas. Some prisons are relatively safe; others are rife with racism, bullying and theft. Some prisoners are held close to their homes; others are sent to prisons hundreds of miles away. While local prisons tend to suffer from high levels of overcrowding, training prisons and the highest security dispersal prisons remain relatively unaffected by increases in the prison population. All of these differences have important implications for the levels of security and control exercised over prisoners, and the capacity of prisons to provide effective regimes and programmes intended to reform offending behaviour.

Reform and rehabilitation

The difficulties involved in reforming prisoners under these different physical and social circumstances have been recognised throughout the history of imprisonment (Morris 1974). Prison encourages some offenders to re-evaluate their lives, take stock of current circumstances, and reflect on the future consequences of persistent criminality (Hood and Sparks 1970). But it is generally accepted that efforts to rehabilitate prisoners under conditions of captivity have failed. Indeed, the possibility of changing people through punishment, treatment or (re)education is simply 'a noble lie' (Rothman 1980). Rather than reform offenders, imprisonment often engenders aversive behaviours, not least because of the way the meaning of existence is hollowed out by the everyday cycle of enforced inactivity and wasted time. Referring to Lefebvre's distinction between physical, mental and social time, Matthews (2009: 38) asserts that

> The process of imprisonment, rather than channelling and redistributing time, involves the negation of time.... Thus, although imprisonment is in essence about time, it is experienced as a form of timelessness, with prison terms often described as 'doing' or 'killing' time.

'Doing time' stifles self-awareness and the awareness of others. Moreover, because it is a central feature of imprisonment to uphold 'impenetrable barriers in the way of introducing within the prison, accounts of the prisoner's identity and prospects which derive from his or her life outside' (Roberts 1994: 232), freedom of self-expression is rigorously controlled and meaningful social contact further curtailed. By treating prisoners, not as subjects – 'as bad and as dangerous and as irresponsible as they may be, and as good, and reliable and responsible as they might be' (Pryor 2001: 1) – but as objects, whose individuality is held to be subservient to the larger needs of the prison, the capacity of prisoners to demonstrate autonomy, and reflect authentically on their past, present and future lives, is significantly reduced (Duguid 2000: 57).

It has been observed that lengthy spells of inactivity inculcate a high degree of passivity, indolence and irresponsibility, such that many prisoners treat life as a party and are unable, or unwilling, to form meaningful and lasting attachments to friends and/or marriage partners after release (Shover 1996). Moreover, some are also more likely to resort to interpersonal violence, a hangover from the routine confrontational relationships which are typical of everyday control problems in prison (Sparks *et al*. 1996). The necessity of demonstrating power and masculinity to deflect victimisation and gain respect becomes part of the personal arsenal necessary to survive in both prison and the wider community (Crewe 2006). And, in a more practical sense, long periods of idleness and separation from the outside world affect various post-release outcomes such as education, employment, and housing, as well as physical and mental health (Richards and Jones 2004).

As a consequence, prisoners motivated to give up crime must transcend the 'penal harm' (Clear 1994) caused them both physically and psychologically, and in so doing overcome a set of personal and social barriers to reintegration specifically related to their new identity and self-image as an ex-prisoner (Becker 1963). This illustrates the value of rehabilitative and reintegrative approaches which address individual factors in order both to increase internal motivation, and improve upon the personal and social circumstances of offenders' lives (Rotman 1990; Raynor and Vanstone 1994). 'State-obligated rehabilitation' is justified given that the effects of poverty, social inequality, drug addiction and physical abuse can lead many people into crime, and that the experience of imprisonment often results in a loss of responsibility, family ties, housing and employability (Gallo and Ruggiero 1991). However, whether it also justifies attempting to rehabilitate offenders not motivated to give up crime remains something of an institutional dilemma. While some offenders may be encouraged, even coerced into accepting rehabilitation interventions, others are likely to actively resist the attempt to re-educate and change them (Robinson and Crow 2009). Furthermore, most offenders are unlikely to engage meaningfully in rehabilitation programmes unless they recognise the advantages to be gained from them. The following and concluding sections of this chapter discuss the application of practical interventions which seek to empower offenders to make their own decisions in life, irrespective of whether they are prepared to participate in proscribed rehabilitation programmes or not. Informed by the commonly held belief that social, economic and political policies are more effective than penal responses to crime and recidivism (Young and Matthews 1992), they assess two comprehensive and wide-ranging interventions which attempt to effect positive change in people's lives at the level of everyday social existence: social work and social capital.

Social work

Although in offender rehabilitation practice changes in mood and feeling are regularly attended to on an individual basis – for instance, in relation to frustration and anger in the management and treatment of violent offenders (McMurran 2002) – the emotional responses, commitments and readjustments associated with the maintenance of a crime-free lifestyle for offenders generally are poorly understood. This is surprising given the primacy accorded to emotion within social psychology – the context of cognition, subjective experience, interpersonal relations, and motivational change in particular. In fact, emotion is commonly linked to attitude change (Breckler 1993) and the development of pro-social behaviour (Davis 1994). For example, positive emotional states, such as the desire for meaningful human contact with a friend, and pride in a new role at work or as a parent, are intimately involved in the processes by which people interrupt the repetition of everyday human experience and reinvent themselves socially (Gottman 1993).

Recently, writers on criminal desistance have begun to respond to these ideas and consider the reactions of offenders to given situations and roles, 'and their associated emotional commitments and readjustments' (Bottoms 2006: 267). It has been observed that, just as negative emotional states and mood changes are linked to the development of criminal motivation (Caspi and Silva 1995; Zamble and Quinsey 1997), the regulation of emotion and its transformation into new pro-social and law-abiding ways of being is an important component of the internal change processes which can lead to criminal desistance (Farrall and Calverley 2006). How offenders respond to the informal order of their lives within everyday personal and interpersonal contexts – what has been referred to as 'the "blood and guts code" of families, groups and neighbourhoods' (Jordan and Jordan 2000: 10) – is crucial to understanding why it is that some offenders successfully give up crime, while others struggle to do so. For example, as Bottoms has observed (2006: 268), persistent offenders may continue to seek instant gratification through crime 'precisely because the demands of daily living in a relatively unstructured environment impose a preoccupation with short-term needs which tends to be accompanied by the insistent "pushes and pulls" of reactive emotions'.

The methodological problem this presents is how to analyse individual offenders in relation to the myriad personal and social contexts which impact emotionally on them throughout the course of everyday life. Aside from the acute micro-levels of analysis required, reconciling conflicting physical, social and mental relationships between individuals and everyday environmental circumstances is far from straightforward. Yet, there is a practical tool which aims to explore individual processes of behavioural change in relation to wider social contexts, albeit one which has become unfashionable in recent years. It is social work. As an instrument of welfare which aims to promote collective services for citizens, social work is intrinsically concerned with understanding how individual and social situations play out in relation to physical and social contexts. There is a crucially important proviso to this however. Premised on the interpretation of singular events, routines, relationships and responses, social work, in terms of practice requires the establishment of close emotional communication between professionals and service users based on mutual trust, empathy and equality.

Mutuality and partnership have particular significance to social work with offenders. Despite the move away from welfare and social inclusion, and the shift towards supervision and public protection in probation policy and practice in recent years, social work approaches continue to be advocated as an effective form of intervention and engagement with offenders. According to McNeill (2006: 49), offenders' commitment to desist from crime 'is generated by the personal and professional commitment shown by their probation officers, whose reasonableness, fairness and encouragement [engender] a sense of personal loyalty and accountability'. A guiding principle of the approach is that through forging a therapeutic alliance (Ward and Brown 2004) between offenders and practitioners based on a firm foundation of mutual trust and professional support (Rex 1999) it is possible to explore needs, frustrations and desires normally hidden from view. Furthermore, it is possible to explore everyday living arrangements, such as leisure pursuits, drug and alcohol consumption, family arguments, and peer influence, as well as the measures that may be taken to help offenders negate or dissociate themselves from the determining and structuring effects of what are often short-term and transient, local life circumstances (Horney *et al.* 1995). In short, good relationships foster individual choice.

In important respects, this returns us to Giddens' notion of self-responsibility; that purposeful life planning and biographical development entail the critical and reflexive examination of social practices 'reformed in the light of incoming information about those very practices, thus constitutively altering their character' (1990: 38). In applying structuration theory to social work theory and practice, Ferguson (2009) has commented on the benefits that accrue to service users when social workers respond differently to the structures imposed upon them. While rules and procedures provide consistency of practice, they are also 'given meaning through human action and how they are mobilized by the creative practices of lay people, service users and professionals who, together, co-construct what social work is' (*ibid.*: 28). For example, in relation to marital separation and divorce, Giddens (1991) has observed how individuals may incorporate psychological and emotional upset in novel and unexpected ways, leading to emotional growth and strengthened intimacies. In relation to offenders, this may also apply to 'strengths-based' rehabilitation, an approach which attempts to build on the contributions offenders can make to society through reparative work in the community in order to support processes of de-stigmatisation and de-labelling (Maruna and LeBel 2003). In nurturing the ability of offenders to plot a new autobiographical path based on emotional commitment and a sense of hope, such interventions represent a significant departure from more traditional models of offender rehabilitation based on the interrogation of past behaviour and the management of risk.

However, much more than this is required if social work is to become a force for good in the lives of offenders. Because the capacity to effect behavioural change in people's lives is influenced by the wider economic and social context, creative social work practice does not result simply from the routine actions of professionals going about their daily business. For real progress to be made, social workers must understand the habitus of their profession; they must challenge what they do and why on a daily basis (Garrett 2009). For instance, unless social workers consider not only the methods and procedures they employ, but also the style and morality of the overall approach they are asked to take on as agents of the state, instead of empowering service users they are more likely to cause them what Bourdieu and Passeron have termed 'symbolic violence': 'the imposition of a cultural arbitrary by an arbitrary power' (1977: xiii). This observation is particularly relevant to social work practice with offenders, which, as Raynor (2007) has pointed out, lacks overall clarity of purpose and has become increasingly entangled in the wider crime reduction strategies described in detail throughout the previous chapter. Welfarist rehabilitation has not disappeared, but the privileging of one-dimensional crime-preventative measures as the primary policy response to crime reduction and community safety has repositioned probation work with offenders contextually to prioritise short-term control over longer-term behavioural change.

Social capital

A growing response to these wider structural issues has been to call for the renewal and reproduction of 'social capital' (Bourdieu 1986b), a contested theoretical concept which has been defined in a variety of ways, and continues to provoke considerable dispute and controversy. Compared to 'human capital' – the productive capacities of the self such as skills, knowledge and education – social capital is generally considered to be a productive effect of group social relations (see also Coleman 1988; Putnam 2000). As constitutive of well-being and civil engagement, Bourdieu (1986b: 248) has defined it as 'the aggregate of the actual or potential resources which are linked to possession of a durable network of more or less institutionalized relationships of mutual acquaintance and recognition'. In fact, Bourdieu (*ibid.*) distinguishes between four types of capital, which, depending on physical and social location, together shape everyday social relations and behaviour: economic capital (goods and monetary resources, land, housing, employment and so on), social capital (valued and meaningful relationships), cultural capital (lifestyle and knowledge), and symbolic capital (class, distinction, respect and prestige). There are not mutually exclusive. For instance, cultural capital is accumulated through upbringing and education. It helps to optimise economic capital, and it is communicated within social capital, which, in providing connections and networks between people, prevents the social order from falling into anomie. According to Bourdieu (1986b: 241):

> The social world is accumulated history, and if it is not to be reduced to a discontinuous series of instantaneous mechanical equilibria between agents who are treated as interchangeable particles, one must reintroduce into it the notion of capital and with it, accumulation and all of its effects.

Despite its lack of clarity, social capital is commonly linked to crime because it is thought that a deterioration in 'system capital' (Esser 2000), the collective social relations and involvement in community life, affects levels of public spiritedness, cooperation and trust, thereby allowing crime, particularly violent crime, to rise unchecked (Lee and Bankston 1999). As we saw in the discussion of collective efficacy and communitarianism presented in the previous chapter, this makes it particularly relevant to understandings of neighbourhood effects on crime and levels of victimisation (Sampson *et al.* 1997). The emphasis it places on 'relational capital' (Esser 2000) – the individual resources and relationships which, accessed through participation in social networks, enhance personal capabilities – also makes it applicable to criminal desistance and offender reintegration. As noted by Farrall (2002: 218), it is through relationships with others that offenders are able to achieve civic engagement, participation and inclusion in society: 'as some forms of social capital are eroded ... so behaviours are altered, and ... this frequently has implications for some people's involvement in crime.' The obvious question arising from this is the practical one of how ex-prisoners might gain the social capital necessary to support their efforts to reintegrate and desist from crime. Bourdieu suggests that by following 'the leanings of their habitus' individuals and groups 'find an activity which is entirely *them* and with it, kindred spirits' (1986b: 223; emphasis in the original). Social capital accrues to an individual or a group 'by virtue of possessing a durable network of more or less institutionalised relationships of mutual acquaintance and recognition' (Bourdieu and Wacquant 1992: 119).

It follows that resources and services should be provided to strengthen family and social relationships in the communities prisoners return to after release (Travis and Petersilia 2001; Farrall 2002). As we have seen, it is commonly asserted that close family ties and friend networks provide significant levels of support for offenders contemplating desistance (Sampson and Laub 1993). But because the distribution of social capital is uneven, 'material capital' is also required (Jordan 2008). To rectify the balance, social capital should be created in specific residential areas through improving life chances, better governance, overcoming market failure, promoting equity, managing externalities, and stemming decline (Lowndes and Pratchett 2008). So, in terms of the reintegration of offenders, this might involve the co-location of agencies providing housing services, for example, to ensure ease of access and encourage offenders to make collective use of the resources and services on offer (Millie and Erol 2006). Local employment opportunities are equally important. Given the difficulties offenders face in obtaining work in today's labour market, particularly in areas where economic disinvestment has resulted in long term if not generational unemployment, Farrall (2004: 73) has recommended that probation services attempt to create jobs locally for their caseloads, the aim being to 'get people to the first rung of the employment ladder.... Employment provides a record of "employability" in the form of people who can be approached to provide references and, as such, may well provide the basis for further jobs in other occupations.'

But facilitating pathways in to work for offenders is only part of the response required, and it is perhaps not as important a part of offender reintegration as is often cited (see SEU 2002). It has been found, on average, in Britain that the population spends only 15 per cent of their time in work, compared to 40 per cent in voluntary leisure activities (Henley Centre 1994 in Mowl 2001). Contextually, this emphasises the importance of the everyday as a form of recreation or productive consumption (de Certeau 1984) and is immediately suggestive of a rehabilitative approach which prioritises leisure time, activity and experience at least as much as interventions intended to improve local employment opportunities. As Rojek (1995) has shown, the social and cultural relations played out in informal leisure pursuits are important constituents of both personal and place identity. Locating everyday leisure and recreational facilities in deprived urban communities contributes to their regeneration, promotes social cohesion, and results in new behaviour patterns. It also constitutes an inclusive, rather than an exclusionary, response to crime and antisocial behaviour. Given that the majority of ex-prisoners are unemployed and spend large amounts of time involved in mostly informal and unstructured activities, many of which involve 'illegal forms of leisure' (Parker *et al*. 1998) such as recreational drug use or vandalism, there would appear to be every reason to improve the quality and context of local discretionary service facilities – shopping centres, parks, play areas, learning facilities, meeting places, community centres, youth services, sports clubs, tourist facilities and so on. By prioritising process as much as product, leisure activities may be delivered in such a way, as to cultivate meaningful social interaction and provide offenders with the practical and social skills necessary to manage risk, and play a full and active role in local community life. The extent to which it is possible to introduce housing, employment and leisure services within social spaces 'determined economically by capital, dominated socially by the bourgeoisie, and ruled politically by the state' (Lefebvre 1991 [1974]: 227) is assessed in the final chapter. To conclude this chapter however, a negative effect of area-based policies limited to the promotion of social capital *in situ* is considered.

In the context of risk decisions relating to crime, social capital has been critiqued recently by Boeck *et al*. (2006) on the grounds that reoffending is affected by the type of social capital to which offenders have access. The conclusion drawn is that social capital is not always benign. Two types of social capital, 'bonding' (exclusive) and 'bridging' (inclusive), have been identified (Putnam 2000). While bridging social capital establishes relationships between and across communities, which may open up extensive and diverse social networks, so increasing opportunity and facilitating citizenship and social mobility, bonding social capital is restricted to an immediate locality containing a homogeneous circle of family and friends. Although social networks based around family and friends can engender informal bonds of trust and cooperation, as referred to in the previous chapter, depending on the way spatial boundaries are constructed and controlled, they can also shape inward-looking territorial attitudes and behaviour. Spatial segregation limits social horizons and restricts meaningful integration across urban boundaries. For instance, it can encourage permanent inward-looking and exclusive responses, drawing people into dependent, proximal networks which serve to embed crime and unemployment as a way of life (MacDonald and Marsh 2005). To address this, Kintrea *et al.* (2008: 52) have suggested that 'interventions such as diversion, education and association with young people ... act in different ways to change the perceptions that young people have about both their own neighbourhoods and other locations within the cities where they live.' Similarly, Amin and Thrift (2002: 150; emphasis in the original) have stressed that

> in order to encourage citizenship as an everyday practice, people need to experience negotiating diversity and difference. Yet this is exactly what has been put to the test in our times of associating with only those like you or whom you like. Citizenship has to develop through its *practice*, perhaps by taking individuals out of their daily communities.

The next three chapters assess the life-course experiences of prisoners, including the extent to which the perceptions and feelings they have about their home neighbourhoods and prison shape meaning and identity. In referring back to theoretical positions on everyday life, together they describe how, to date, the past lives of prisoners have been circumscribed along a pathway characterised by limited choice and opportunity.

Chapter 5

'On the up': pre-prison experiences

Introduction

This chapter focuses on the circumstances, experiences and under-standings of the interview participants up until the point they experienced a first prison sentence. It is necessary to emphasise at the outset that the qualitative element of the research programme was not designed to identify or assess specific individual personality traits linked to criminal behaviour (Eysenck 1964). Any information of a psychological nature was provided voluntarily by the participants during the course of the interviews. For example, many admitted to being arrogant, greedy, impatient, anti-authoritarian and enjoying violence. However, while some were willing to admit that these traits characterised them as individuals, only a few believed they predisposed them to commit crime. Similarly, while some thought that a shared experience of economic and social disadvantage and/or an unstable family background (Walmsley et al. 1992) explained, and in some cases excused, even justified, their criminal behaviour (Sykes and Matza 1957), most recalled how the propensity to commit crime developed gradually, naturally, unthinkingly, during childhood and adolescence.

Although early life was generally characterised by poverty, family instability, and lack of achievement at school, as well as exposure to criminogenic environments, the influence of these factors on them was variable. Initially, crime was embraced as a form of play, a means of alleviating the boredom and frustration of life in the family home. The active city streets surrounding their homes offered the possibility of truancy from school, autonomous mobility, and adventure. Through engaging in high-adrenalin, but low-level, criminal activities such as vandalism, drug misuse, theft and violence, they achieved status and respect among a close circle of friends and acquaintances. As such, public space was intrinsic to self-actualisation, the negotiation of key life transitions, and the construction of personal identity. For some, a sense of 'super place attachment' (Kintrea *et al.* 2008) habituated and normalised risky activities, and inculcated a high degree of collective territorial behaviour. Time spent 'hanging around' specific 'anchor points' – stairwells, street corners, shopping precincts, recreation areas and so forth – initiated shared patterns of consumption based on clothing, music, drugs and cars. To the extent these formative experiences initiate a social and spatial trajectory which reinforces crime as a key determinant of status and identity, they are predictive of recidivism. The means by which it is possible to reverse these associations are assessed in the chapters which follow.

The family home

The family home is a primary determinant of security, autonomy, well-being and status, a place which sustains self-image and self-expression. As affirmed by Stretton, 'people are produced there and endowed with the values and capacities which will determine most of the quality of their social life' (1976: 183). The design of our homes – detached or high-rise flat, where they are situated, whether we are owner occupiers or tenants, the stored wealth they represent, and the possessions we keep there – influences how we feel towards them. Simply put, they are valuable, 'a form of stored wealth … the point from which the user relates to every other aspect of the urban scene' (Harvey 1972: 16).

However, home and family life is characterised by diversity. While for some it is private and secure, an intimate place of rest (Seamon 1979), for others it is chaotic, constraining, even threatening. For most of the participants the latter was true. Most had grown up in cramped, overcrowded, public-sector or rented housing, and a few had spent long periods of childhood sleeping in makeshift conditions – for example, on the living-room sofa, or at the homes of friends or relations. Home was not a sanctuary, a place where they could be by themselves. For instance, rather than providing a sense of personal autonomy, everyday life was 'like living in a goldfish bowl', a place in which 'the front door was always open, and people would just come and go all day long.'

More insidious than this, the family home is also often an environment in which domestic abuse and violence occur as a matter of everyday routine behind closed doors (Duncan 1996). As discussed in Chapter 3, persistent criminality is commonly associated with low self-control brought about by dysfunctional, unstable, disrupted and abusive family backgrounds; ineffective child rearing (Hirschi 1969); and criminal siblings and/or parents (Farrington and West 1993; Farrington *et al.* 2001). Gordon (2002: 194) has argued that 'social class and the influence of peer groups … pale in comparison to family factors', the latter being generally accepted to be the most important risk factor in the early development of criminal behaviour. It is also commonly argued that criminal desistance is supported when offenders are able to maintain stable family relationships during periods of imprisonment, and so have a degree of informal support to fall back upon after release (Ditchfield 1994). Alternatively, returning to damaged and destructive family relationships can make prisoners vulnerable to relapse.

Farrington (2002) has identified criminal and antisocial parents; large family size; poor parental supervision and discipline; abuse, both physical and sexual; and parental conflict as the most important early-life predictors of criminal behaviour. In some of these respects, and in a few cases all of them, unstable family experiences characterised the early lives of the participants. For instance, a few of the participants had grown up in overtly criminal families in which the influence of parents and/or siblings on them had been invasive and insistent. In such cases, because crime was openly and routinely discussed, as children, they had become aware of the criminal activities of older family members, which they grew to accept as a natural and everyday occurrence. Soon enough they were recruited to sell drugs or keep lookout during raids on shops or domestic burglaries, for example. In time this would lead to a fully committed life of professional crime (Hobbs 1995). Theo described how as a young child he had been inculcated into a life of professional drug dealing and armed robbery:

> It was through my older brothers, yeh. 'Cause they had to do crime to survive. 'Cause they weren't settled at foster care and whatnot. And they were rebelling, you get me. And they had to fend for their selves. I was the youngest one and my brothers took care of me. My brothers are like my dad to me, you get me… Yeh, my brothers are like hard core, you get me, hard core. Big amounts of drugs coming in, guns getting moved from

Manchester to London. That's what I watched going on around me as a child.

In other cases, although criminal behaviour was not actively encouraged within the family home, neither was it wholeheartedly disapproved of. Mika explained that, while his mother did not condone or excuse his crimes, she was prepared to accept them for the financial support they provided the family.

> Another thing that's attractive to a lot of criminals' mothers is that no matter how much they try to stop them, it starts to get attractive when they realise they're struggling to pay the bills. And you come in the front door, 'Ah, Mum, there you go, Mum, no worries.' 'Where did you get this from?' 'Does it really matter?' 'No, it doesn't, I'll pay the bills with it' [laughs]. You know what I mean?

For a significant number of the participants, an insidious characteristic of family life was routine, everyday physical abuse. In keeping with research which has found that children who are physically abused, or have suffered serious neglect, are prone to become offenders later in life (Malinosky-Rummell and Hansen 1993), just under half of the participants said they had been the victim of some form of abuse as children. For most, this was habitual and routine, meted out as a matter of course by alcoholic, drug-influenced and violent parents or older brothers. In some cases, the abuse was random, an everyday, matter-of-fact occurrence. In others, it was systematic, ritualistic and disguised as family discipline (Duncan 1996). Either way, the outcome was the same: regular beatings which often resulted in serious injury. Some described how they had been 'hammered every day', 'beaten to a pulp' and 'in and out of hospital with broken arms and that'. Theo explained how behind closed doors, violent abuse was sanctioned by his father as a means of instilling discipline. Along with his brothers, he was regularly locked in the house all day and made to do homework his father had personally set for them. If they failed to achieve the standards expected,

> My father used to make me and my brothers kneel down in a row and place family albums, like big albums ... and me and my brothers used to hold two albums on each arm and he'd go out for at least an hour or so. And by the time he comes back, if we'd dropped any of the albums, he'd beat us up. It sent him crazy.

117

Undoubtedly, abusive family relationships affected some of the participants greatly. Research has found that child abuse is particularly prevalent in poor and socially deprived neighbourhoods, a consequence partly, as noted in Chapter 3, of long working hours and financial hardship reducing the capacity of parents to supervise their children (Straus *et al.* 1980). Together, such factors are thought to influence the development of various problem behaviours associated with crime, such as failing at school and running away from home (Graham and Bowling 1995). Paul explained that because his father was 'a crack addict and was very violent', and his mother had 'rent arrears problems and things like that', he had experienced problems confronting authority at school.

> If I tried to concentrate on something it would go out the window, because I wouldn't have the mind or the time to concentrate. And then I would be sitting there thinking about how's my mum, or what's going on, or things like that. And, you know, because I was trying to be so close to her, and she was sharing a lot of things with me, and it was kind of hurtful. So if someone said the slightest thing to me at school, I would flip, go off the handle, and I would be just unstable really.

Some of the participants explained that they put up with the beatings and abuse until they reached an age they were able to fight back. For example, once John realised he was no longer afraid of his parents, 'then the tables turned and that's when they definitely had enough.' In a small number of cases when this happened, the family member responsible for the abuse left the family home. In most cases, however, the participants themselves escaped by sleeping rough or in night shelters, living with friends or relations, or putting themselves into a children's home or living with foster parents. Thus was established a pattern of intermittent, and for some permanent, spatial and social disaffiliation. Just under a third of the participants had spent time 'in care' as a result of disrupted and abusive family life. However, although the abuse necessitated they leave home, in most cases the living arrangements they made, or had made for them, were just as, if not more, erratic and dangerous than those they had left behind. In some cases, a major reason for this was the inappropriateness of the foster families they had been sent to. At an early age, Tim, a black participant, had been placed into foster care with a white family in a predominately white town outside London. He described the problems this clash of 'habitus' caused:

I don't think the woman really understood what pressures she was bringing on herself. The father of the family worked long hours. He worked in London and he commuted every day. So basically she had two kids and I don't think she was really prepared for what that entailed. And she just didn't handle it very well. She had an anger management problem, and she just took it out on me and my sister. Maybe it was a lack of support and other people's judgements. I remember her getting names called in the street and for a white person that's like new. For a black person it's different. She was being racially abused in the street and I think that was probably a shock for her.

Later, Tim was sent to a children's home. Here the environment was more in line with a habitus which disposed him to behave in ways he accepted unconsciously as a matter of routine. With others, he formed a gang with whom he regularly broke out of the home at night to commit violent street robbery. In a telling description of how social interaction, and the perceptions of others, can engender criminal responses (Becker 1963), he described how he and his new friends assumed the behavioural characteristics they thought were expected of them as problem children:

Sometimes with children – I know this now right – you attach a label to them, or a stigma to them and they will tend to act up to it. And so we were the bad kids from the children's home. We must of done something bad, 'cause we were in a children's home. It couldn't be anybody else's fault but ours, could it? It couldn't be circumstances that put us there, or somebody else, like irresponsible adults. So, obviously, you're bad, you go to a children's home. So at certain times we'd go out and we'd know that we were from the children's home, and it was just like how people would treat you. I suppose sometimes you call a dog a dog enough, it's going to bark, innit.

Joshua had a different story to tell but with a similar outcome. Having grown up in Ladbroke Grove in north-west London, he was placed at the age of 15 in a children's home in Streatham in south-west London. He described how this had brought him into contact with rival criminal gangs, and the personal danger he was placed in:

This is going into a dangerous area, but I'll explain some stuff to you. Going there first of all was all right. They wanted to get to know me. They wanted to know who I was. But I didn't know what was behind that, and when I found out I was actually in danger being up there. It was kind of dealt with every day as it came. They tried to get me to nick stuff, go out there and rob things for them. And I was like, 'What, I ain't doing that for you lot.' And soon as the morning comes, whoosh I was gone... I told my social worker I didn't want to live up there no more. And I got into a big fight. And I also started stabbing guys up there, you know while they was sleeping in the dormitories and stuff like that. So I had to come out. Otherwise I would be doing life, put it that way. So from there I stayed in hotels all over the place.

It should not be assumed from this that all the participants came from families or 'care' homes that were criminogenic, abusive or unstable. Cutting across class, culture, ethnic and spatial lines, as is the case with people generally, the everyday contexts of family interactions and relationships were variable. Indeed, given the hardships and difficult social circumstances they experienced as children, a significant number thought their parents had been extremely supportive and had done the best they possibly could to raise them properly. In fact, nearly half described their parents as 'loving', 'decent people', 'law-abiding and hard working', and 'strict but fair' towards them during childhood. Peter thought his father was exemplary:

My dad is the type of man, he can't read or write, he can read a little bit, but he's not good at spelling and things like that. And he's a contract cleaner, which is a person that cleans carpets and toilets... He's done nothing but work his whole life and never asked for nothing back. He hasn't got any friends he goes out drinking with, he doesn't smoke, he doesn't even ... probably has the same pair of slippers for the next ten years. I can't fault him in any way. I've never known anyone like it. He just does everything for the family.

In several cases the participants explained how, once they had begun to get into trouble, their parents had intervened and tried to steer them away from crime. They had been 'upset' and 'disgusted' when they found out they had been arrested for the first time. While some responded with violence or indifference, others attempted to confront the problems they thought had influenced their children to become criminals. For example, they had attempted to find them employment, sent them to new schools or to stay with relatives, or moved the family to different parts of London, away from children they considered to be a bad influence. Stuart explained:

> My parents certainly didn't agree with me when I first got into trouble with the police when I was about 14. All hell broke loose in the house. I remember my mum coming down to the police station. There was a bit of a riot down there because, you know, no son of hers gets into trouble with the police, and things like that. So my parents and my family did not have any influence on the fact that I started to offend, simply because they done all that they could to try and prevent it, and didn't influence me in any way by way of example.

Interestingly, many of the participants claimed they understood and sympathised with the hardships their parents faced, and the sacrifices they had made, to support them. As referred to in Chapter 3, research has shown that 'economic stress' has a detrimental effect on the capacity of parents to supervise childrens' leisure time, and that, in turn, creates conditions for uninhibited and pervasive delinquent peer influence. It suggests that 'conditions … central to the prevention of delinquency (i.e. strong emotional attachment to parents, parental supervision of children, consistent discipline) are precisely those which economic stress in the absence of social supports appears prone to disrupt' (Weatherburn and Lind 2001: 51). In recent years, owing to the restructuring of the UK labour market, such conditions have become more prevalent, and family relationships generally have been put under greater strain. Faced with an employment market polarised at one end by high levels of education and skill attainment, and low-paid and low-skill casualised labour at the other, many young people today have had the period of family dependency extended (Furlong and Cartmel 1997). Due to reduced parental supervision, single-parent families in particular face severe difficulty in supervising children, thereby doubling the likelihood that they will develop offending behaviours in later life (Kolvin *et al.* 1988). Just under half the participants had been brought up by a single parent or step-parents. While some who had personally experienced the separation of their mothers and fathers had become withdrawn and depressed, others felt relieved that violent and abusive family relationships had come to an end. However, most understood the pressures their mothers now faced in providing for the family on their own. Hari explained:

It was hard for my mum bringing up all of us 'cause we was all boys. But she done her best and she did do good. But it was just me. I wasn't listening. I'd get beat from my older brother, but my mum would just tell me off. She wouldn't beat me. The love was always there for me. I ran away from home for a few days and said fuck it. And then I'd go back. And yeh, my mum always loved me.

The tendency of parents to work long, unsocial hours in poorly paid jobs was mentioned by most of the participants from single-parent families. The impact of divorce and separation, combined with increased economic hardship, weakened family relationships and resulted in participants spending more time unsupervised. Joshua explained why he rarely saw his mother after the break-up of her marriage:

I hardly ever saw my mum, and if I did it was to make her a cup of tea. Because she was always working, secretarial jobs during the day and cleaning jobs at night and stuff like that. But she's a strong woman. My mum was just looking out for herself and her children. 'Cause if you've been in a relationship and you've just split up, you don't get over that person straightaway. So my mum was going through a form of depression as well because like, you know, she didn't have that person to lie down next to at night with, and someone to confer with, and, you know, that had all gone out the window. So now she was doing it all herself.

It also meant they had to assume more responsibility for taking care of family matters. For some this had been beneficial. It had set them a good example, and encouraged them to be self-reliant, and responsible adults. Freddie explained:

We were always taught from an early age how to cook, how to take care of one another. We learned how to be fathers and mothers, yeh, from a very early age. 'Cause if you're looking after your younger brother and sisters and then gradually that same kind of looking after you do later in life with your children so ... we got taught well.

However, while some accepted the added responsibility of looking after siblings as an inevitable consequence of family break-up, others admitted to feeling unloved and unwanted, abandoned to the reality of self-sufficiency too early in their lives, and frustrated at not having had the opportunity to experience a more supportive and happy childhood. Some felt constrained by the need to look after domestic arrangements – 'you know, rent's got to be paid, food's got to be put on the table, you know, stuff like that' – when what they really wanted to do was experience freedom and adventure away from the family home, a quality of life a few readily identified with the lifestyles of their absent fathers, whom they thought of as 'on a level, you know', 'good to be with', and 'not as strict' as their mothers. Dalmar described the frustration he felt at being housebound because his mother worked every day and night:

> My mum was living by herself and it was like a hectic time. She'd be going to work and I'd have to look after my little brother because I've got a little brother, so I had to be man of the house. All the duties what my mum was supposed to do I had them. So maybe I had to grow up faster than the average 9-year-old and 10-year-old because, obviously, when my mum goes out I've got to watch over my little brother and settle things in the house that have to get done before my mum comes back.

Neighbourhood

As discussed in Chapters 2 and 3, it is commonplace to find that poverty during childhood and adolescence impacts significantly on family life, health and well-being, as well as different forms of criminal behaviour (Taylor 1999), and that prison populations are characterised by poverty and social exclusion. Nearly all the participants recalled the places in which they had grown up as being poor and socially deprived. For example, they were places where there 'was nothing to do' and 'no jobs and no training programmes or support'. More emotively than this, they were also 'filthy', 'a shit hole, 'a dive', 'poor and racist', and 'full of druggies, muggings and crime'. Stuart offered the following description of the area in which he had been living prior to going to prison for the first time:

> It was one of those areas where the local authority would house people with issues, I guess, who had problems of one type or another. They couldn't afford to accommodate themselves, so

they would get cheap council housing and there would be other issues relating to mental health, poor education, unemployment and stuff like this. It had all the sorts of problems that you get in any council estate.

Preoccupied with the realities and risks of life within severely disadvantaged communities, a few of the participants thought that growing up in social environments characterised by a lack of educational and training opportunities had from an early age conditioned them to behave criminally. Kev explained:

There was no such thing as a good education, or social services weren't going to do anything for me, or job seekers allowance where I lived. I was a young black kid. They would have carted me off and put me in some home. So in a raw sense I never had a mindset that I have to work, that I have to earn an honest buck, or be law-abiding.

Most of the participants referred to problems they had suffered at school. Like the family home, school is a primary influence on early identity, an essential constituent of sociability as well as human welfare in later adult life. Indeed, according to Unger (1998 in Amin and Thrift 2002: 145), the developmental and social aspects of education and learning are 'the most important enabler of individual and collective freedom'. According to some criminologists, it follows that criminal behaviour is closely associated with a restriction of life chances caused by lack of education and training in early life. For example, it is commonly found that truancy is closely linked to unemployment, social exclusion and criminality (SEU 1997), and that three-quarters of boys who are excluded from school are offenders (Graham and Bowling 1995). In keeping with the prison population in general, most of the participants had a history of poor educational achievement, a characteristic they shared with many people who, like them, grew up in deprived areas in which the quality of education was relatively poor (Dorling 1995). Most had truanted from school, nearly three quarters had no qualifications, and nearly a third had been expelled for fighting or being disruptive in class. Moreover, reflecting an educational ethos which tends to accord little worth generally to academic achievement within working-class families and communities (Willis 1977), most displayed a distinct lack of academic ambition in terms of both past experience and future career plans and prospects.

To a significant extent, a general lack of commitment to education and skills-based training is explained by the absence of good-quality employment prospects, and therefore a downgrading in the value of work in precarious local labour markets (Byrne 2005). It follows that, although persistent criminal behaviour throughout the life course is commonly associated with a lack of employment (Tarling 1982), and the value of a job to instil self-worth, provide social and economic resources, and structure everyday routine activities is often associated with criminal desistance (Sampson and Laub 1993, 2003), the possession of a job does not necessarily result in reduced offending (Henry 1978). Given widespread unemployment and a dearth of stable, well-paid jobs in deprived communities, the capacity of work to fundamentally change criminal identities is severely limited. Although unemployment, interspersed with periods of sporadic employment in a variety of unskilled and partially skilled occupations characterised the lives of nearly all the participants, because nearly half had been convicted of a first offence before the age of 16, it is unlikely that unemployment on its own had been a cause of their early offending. Moreover, the impact of employment on criminal desistance was not proven. Most expressed a general lack of commitment to the low-skill, insecure jobs on offer, which they described as 'dull', 'boring' and 'poorly paid'. Indeed, most had a dismissive, cynical attitude towards employment generally, which supported the belief that social and material success could only be achieved by criminal means (Box 1987).

It is sometimes argued that criminal behaviour is justified and accepted as normal by many people who live in socially deprived neighbourhoods. There are a number of reasons for this. First, social learning perspectives suggest that owing to the propinquity of social life in poor communities, various forms of criminal behaviour are copied by individuals after they have been observed directly within the family, or being carried out by friends and associates within the neighbourhood (Bandura 1977). Second, through a process of 'collective socialisation' (Crane 1991), behavioural norms are spread through social contact and relationships between people in close-knit urban communities, and transmitted from one generation to the next (Foster 1990). And third, Parker (1974) has observed how low-income neighbourhoods often become 'condoning communities' in which the value of legitimate forms of employment is negated, and a shared hatred of authority becomes a standard response. Certainly, many of the participants described how, as they got older, they became increasingly aware of pervasive criminal activity around them. Barry described how, in the area he had grown up, 'everyone was doing something on the side, you know, like getting by with stolen gear or selling drugs, or going out thieving or something like that.' And Keifer recalled that 'the people I grew up with were the first people I saw with guns, doing armed robberies and doing like syndicate crime.' Kev explained that a deeply ingrained and cohesive criminal culture within his local community accepted criminal activity as an alternative way of life which offered a source of income, as well as security, belonging and support.

> I just stayed within my own community and got involved with what was going on, the way everyone else was surviving, where like the police were them and we were us, and society was them and we were us, and as far as we were concerned we were quite organised within our social, you know, unit kind of thing. So obviously that was a mindset where we thought we were on top of the world. We can take care of ourselves.

It is noteworthy that many of the black participants referred to their home areas as 'the hood' or 'ghetto', an environment they implicitly understood to offer few prospects for social advancement, unless by criminal means. Criminal behaviour was embraced as being at odds with normal standards of living and was fuelled by a strong sense of resentment towards the wider society, especially the police. It was also highly organised, an alternative economy which offered rewards far beyond those likely to be gained through legitimate forms of employment. Dalmar justified drug dealing as follows:

> There's two different people in like life in the UK, because there's like the well-off people and then there's people from the hood and the ghetto, who are never like going to like leave the ghetto... They might work, work all their life, but they're never going to leave the ghetto because either they've got bills to pay, or some sort of problem. So that's why I feel – and a lot of people who I know probably say the same thing, right, they might explain it differently, but it's the best way I can explain it to you, Nick, yeh – that I feel society made me like this. Oh, people offer drugs to me to sell and bigger people would offer you drugs and it's a fucking tempting thing, get me, especially when you don't have no sort of income.

It is sometimes argued the most characteristic feature of criminality is that it is shared behaviour, that 'most delinquent conduct occurs in groups; the group nature of delinquent behavior is one of its most consistently documented features' (Warr 2002: 3). According to Thornberry and Krohn (1977), the effect of peer-group influence on criminal behaviour is greater than that of parental supervision and discipline. However, whereas some contend delinquent peer groups form as a consequence of random social interaction, others argue 'birds of a feather flock together', and therefore individuals who have a prior disposition to commit crime purposefully seek out similarly minded friends (Glueck and Glueck 1950). After this outline in broad terms of the personal and social characteristics of the neighbourhoods the participants grew up in, the next section explores the extent to which their early motivation to commit crime stemmed from close-knit social interaction (Blumer 1969).

'More like high jinks than crime'

All of the participants described how at an early age they had made the transition from the family home to the street and had become acquainted with large groups of friends from the local neighbourhood. As they had grown up in cramped, overcrowded houses and flats, the street provided freedom, a place to play. As such, the 'place they called home' was an important signifier of identity. It distinguished them as people and, in the company of friends, provided opportunities to test themselves, most commonly by engaging in activities which mixed trouble and fun. In contrast to the confinement and boredom of the family home, the streets provided a social arena in which 'juvenile offenders and the exuberant cameos of teenage life reverberate, alternate and sometimes they get crossed' (Hebdige 1988: 30). The spaces within and around their local neighbourhood were where the action was, a place where they could talk and share feelings in a way they never could at home (Corrigan 1979). Potential friends were everywhere – next door, in flats above and below, at school, and in local playgrounds, the precincts and estates across the road. They remembered stairwells, back gardens, car parks, public gardens, playing fields, and 'recs' where they congregated and through everyday, face-to-face interaction, became 'one of the crowd' (Goffman 1969). Recalling childhood activities evoked memories of finding their way in the world, developing competence and confidence, marking out territory, and resisting adult definitions of their lives (James 1993). Of course, social interaction in public space is an everyday characteristic of life for most people, young and old, in modern urban society, and there is absolutely nothing wrong with it. To quote Lefebvre again (2008 [1961]: 309–10):

> the places through which we pass and where we meet – the street, the café or the station – are more important and truly more interesting than our homes and our houses, the places which they link. ... the street represents the everyday in our social life. It embodies it almost completely, like a digest which is interesting because it is so condensed. And this is despite being external to individual and social existence, or because of it. A place of passage, of interaction, of movement and communication, it becomes, via an astonishing volte-face, the reflection of the things it links together, something with more life in it than those things themselves.

What a contrast this perspective is to the narrow conception of human spatial activity articulated by environmental geography and criminology. Rather than simply consider the way people behave in public space according to their perception of physical characteristics, space is imbued with meaning and value. As Berman (1983) has articulated, the street is important because it is the most obvious public space in which to express ourselves to others through shared characteristics of fashion and performance. It is also a place of independence, excitement and risk, to 'hang around' and socialise with others (Karsten 2005). However, it is a growing feature of contemporary urban life that the street is more important to some people than others. Compared to the suburbs, which, as we saw in Chapter 3, tend to be characterised by limited social interaction (Baumgartner 1988), many young people from working-class communities treat the streets as their place (Valentine and McKendrick 1997). Whereas wealthy children are more likely to use the parental home as a place of leisure and privacy in which to 'stay in', watch television, and play computer games (Silverstone and Hirsch 1992), for lower-class children growing up in small, crowded homes, the street is often the only autonomous space where they can play and socialise free from the restrictions of parental control (Corrigan 1979). To a significant extent, this common childhood experience was articulated in the testimonies of the participants. After they had reached an age at which their parents were no longer able to exert control over them, a clear line of demarcation opened up between life inside the family home and life on the street. Billy described this early life transition as being motivated by a wilful act of disobedience, a purposeful and deliberate decision to transgress family discipline:

> I wanted to be like my mates. I always wanted to go home late, you know, things like that. But I always got in trouble. I always got in trouble. My mum would say to me, 'Don't come in late', and I'd go and repeat the same thing over and over and over and over again... My mum was always... to really be honest, I used to hate going home.

The public spaces the participants routinely occupied defined them situationally; their growing sense of personal identity was buttressed by relationships of trust and reciprocity, 'generated by that attribute of local events which renders them interpretable by witnesses' (Goffman 1997: 23). A shared attachment to local space engendered mutual trust and respect which bound friendships together. Like children everywhere, they felt a particularly close attachment to friends who shared similar biographies and interests to themsleves. They associated selectively according to common social characteristics such as age, gender, ethnicity and social class, which became more meaningful when significant life experiences and events, as well as personal characteristics, such as aggression, humour, and similar interests in clothing or music, were also shared. Mika explained:

> My friends, they're like proper friends regardless you know. I've realised that we must have just liked each other from the beginning, before we started thieving. They lived close, they went to the same school, I know them and I can trust them 100 per cent. We got together because of the tragedies in our families. When we was sitting down and having a cry together, and that was when we realised this is the crowd here.

In recounting stories of early childhood, most of the participants conveyed a sense of nostalgia for the places where they grew up. They had felt comfortable there, at ease with themselves to engage in normal childhood pursuits collectively for pleasure and excitement; 'a good time', and 'fun and thrills'. Then, as they got older, having spent time together exploring, playing football, riding bikes and skateboarding, they gravitated to more youthful activities, such as drinking, taking drugs, and having sex (Parker *et al.* 1998), but also fighting, shoplifting, and vandalism. Hanging around on street corners, signing graffiti, and public displays of drinking and drug taking, cemented friendships and signalled a shared intent to resist adult power (Corrigan 1979). However, although everyday life on the streets often involved theft, vandalism and violence, at this stage in their lives this was not classified as crime as such. Rather, it was 'more like high jinks than crime', 'a way of exciting ourselves', 'a fun thing to do', 'just getting up to naughty things', and 'not going out to commit crime, going out to mess about'.

As we saw in the previous chapter, it has been suggested that much youthful, antisocial activity bordering on crime is motivated by a 'delight in being deviant'; 'a special attraction to excitement, trouble, tests of autonomy, and proofs of toughness; as well as an apparently romantic tendency to abandon life to fate' (Katz 1988: 117). High-adrenalin teenage acts are considered a primary means by which young people 'carnival' (Presdee 2000), party and have fun (Jacobs and Wright 1999). Such behaviours are particularly attractive to young people who do not have access to legitimate forms of leisure activity. Hayward (2002: 82) has written that acts of purposeless violence 'such as … theft and destruction of cars, firestarting, hoax emergency service call-outs, car "cruising", peer group violence and other forms of street delinquency have as much to do with youth expression and exerting control in neighbourhoods where, more often than not, traditional avenues of youthful stimulation and endeavour have long since evaporated'. John described a typical day out with his friends:

> We just lived our life for that day. See how far we could go. There was a group of us that used to live on the same road. And we used to hang around, do what we want, when we want. There were about 13 of us, maybe more. Hanging out, drinking, smoking, going round causing trouble, throwing things at people's doors, damaging people's cars and all that stuff. You damage someone's car and people come out of the house and start chasing you down the road, and it was just a laugh, just for fun, the buzz of someone chasing you. It's just like another drug. They used to try and find out where we was living and that. They used to drive round following us, but we used to disappear, go and jump over people's gardens, go through the churchyard, disappear.

The blurring of crime and play in the minds of the participants – the shared belief that crime is a matter of fact, an everyday life experience common to all children and therefore needs no explanation – also suggests that criminal behaviour is experienced unconsciously during childhood through social interaction and is passed on as a deeply internalised attitude (Bourdieu 1977). Rather than being learned, or a product of conscious rational decision making, it is a thoughtless disposition, 'placed beyond the grasp of consciousness, and hence cannot be touched by voluntary, deliberate transformation, cannot even be made explicit' (ibid.: 94). When asked why they had started to commit crime at such an early age, it was common for the participants to answer that they had never thought about it. It was 'just to be popular with my friends', 'just a way of life', 'just what we did', 'normal kids, up to fighting and burgling sheds, things like that'. Adusa explained:

> There was a group of us nicking clothes, shoplifting. It was like... people say its peer pressure. It's not peer pressure, it's adolescent, innit. I personally will say no one forced me into whatever I done, yeh. I'm... when I was doing it, I didn't, I didn't feel like, I didn't feel the, urm... how can I put this one?... I didn't feel no regrets or hurt that I'm hurting someone. Do you understand what I'm saying?

Moreover, most did not consider that their early crimes had been motivated by a lack of money. While a few had started to steal because their parents could not afford to buy them 'chopper bikes, trainers, things that I wanted and my mum couldn't give me', others explained their families had provided for them, and that 'within reason, they bought me pretty much what I asked for.' What they were stealing was not as important as the act of stealing itself. It was 'sweets and toys', 'video games and DVDs from Toys R Us, Star Wars action figures I already owned', 'clothes, trainers, you know, all sorts of silly things', 'tools, bikes and lawnmowers'; things that 'had no real value, and couldn't be sold on'. Jimmy described how crime was committed on a whim, as a normal everyday childhood prank, 'a spur of the moment thing'.

> Like we'd be walking along and say, 'Look Nick, come on, let's have it', done. It was a spur of the moment kind of thing. Don't forget I was only 14. I weren't involved in any major big things then... We'd go canoeing, we used to go to Shadwell Basin and do canoeing, sailing, all them kind of things, and we were just like a little gang. And if we'd go out and see something, we'd

nick it, but we weren't concentrating then on like wake up, one o' clock, 'OK, come on, we're going to work now', bang. It weren't that kind of scenario. It was just, if we see it, we take it. If it ain't bolted down, it's gone.

And Joshua recalled the fun he and his friends had trying to outwit store detectives in the local branch of Woolworths:

I never really looked at why. I think it was just to have things and having a laugh. It started that way. You could say it was like a little fun thing as well. 'Cause I wasn't really thinking how I was feeling at the time, 'cause I was young, you understand. It was just, go in there and see if we can outwit the security guards and that [laughs], or the undercovers that were in there, the store managers, the store undercover people. So it was ... that's what it was kinda like.

The importance of being violent

It should not be assumed from this that these were victimless crimes, or they had no social consequences for the communities in which they occurred. Exposed to risk as a routine part of daily experience, and also pursuing it to relieve everyday boredom, many of the participants began to indulge in more extreme forms of pleasure and entertainment. Increasingly, it is shown that young people unable to integrate into mainstream society through legitimate means escalate criminal activities to an extent that can have a devastating impact on local community life. Once infantile pranks lose their appeal, such is the way young men attain masculine status within peer groups (Collier 1998). As documented by Campbell (1993), the wanton and widespread destruction of homes and cars that took place on a number of peripheral housing estates throughout the UK during the summer of 1991 was an expression of out-of-control, 'lawless masculinity'. With no public status to affirm identity, or a recognised role to perform, groups of young people formed 'a cult of honour and loyalty which exempted them from everything that demanded responsibility' (ibid.: 170). And more recently, Hall and Winlow (2004: 277) have documented how within certain micro-communities groups of young people increasingly demonstrate, 'a novel and quite disturbing type of despair ... the presence of virtually total cynicism and nihilism: virtually no opinions, no realistic expectations, no hope and no fear of authority'. Barry recounted how he and his friends asserted power and authority over his neighbourhood through wanton vandalism and terrorising local residents:

> There was quite a few of us at one time, about 30, 40 kids all just milling about. Neighbours would come out, complain and we'd just terrorise 'em.... We used to go out and cane the shops you know. There used to be a big group of us, and it used to be called Moss Road, and we used to tear granny out of it. I mean like vandals, stairwells, terrorise people that was walking past. We'd go down the local shops, a whole group of us, just walk in there and just ruck up. You know, just take anything, and there was nothing they could have done. You know, they tried locking us in the shop, but we just picked up bins and threw them through the window and just walked out. So just take liberties with them.

For many of the participants, the highest-risk, most exciting activity was fighting. While most of the activities they engaged in were communal, living life as a physical challenge was also how they found out about themselves individually. Violence was engaged in for reasons defined by the social and cultural consensus; to achieve 'social distinction' (Bourdieu 1986a), as 'sanctioned within its own historical logic of working class "tough" masculinity' (Crawshaw 2004: 238; emphasis in the original). By confronting risk head on, they tested themselves in the presence of others. According to Goffman (1967), asserting status and commanding respect are achieved through engaging in 'character contests'. For the participants, these mostly involved fighting face to face; to find out 'who's bigger and best out of the lot of us. That's the way it used to go. I'm hard. Come and try it and see how far it goes.' Winning fights and injuring opponents showed others that they could handle themselves physically, and demonstrated 'true masculinity' (Connell 1995). However, as well as being a rite of passage to social acceptance and authority, violence was also engaged in for visceral, hedonistic reasons. Nige explained the thrill of fighting:

> It was something I enjoyed. Do you know what I mean? When I look back at it, sometimes it makes me laugh – not laughing at people laying there beaten up, or me laying there beaten up, or anything like that – but I thought it was a laugh when I was doing it so... It was just so much excitement in fighting. It was

like a big thing from where I was from, being able to fight, because everyone had to.

As well as one to one, fighting was staged in groups or gangs. Most of the participants described how as children they had joined gangs and fought with children from other neighbourhoods and schools. While public space is an obvious venue for youthful expression, it has the potential to be contradictory, unpredictable, dangerous; it is a space of 'provocation that comes in large part from experiences of the unexpected' (Sennett 1990: 152). The association of the urban street with territorial conflict is pervasive. According to Bauman (2001: 89), social networks span the contemporary city such that the borderlines between neighbourhoods are 'often blurred or poorly signposted; in most cases they are contested and in need of constant realignment through borderline skirmishes and reconnaissance forays.' Although most of the participants had been members of gangs, perhaps because race and gangs are closely associated in teenage black culture (Lucas 1998), it was more common for the black participants to speak of specific gang identities, and territories or 'turfs'. However, although the gangs they belonged to all had names – 'the Bloods', 'the 28s', 'the Untouchables', 'the Brixton Boys' – unlike the highly organised structure of street gangs in the United States (Sanchez-Jankowski 2003), gang membership was mostly age limited, small scale, and carried out more for the thrill of being deviant than control of rival neighbourhoods, or dominance over local drug markets. Hari explained he used to enjoy fighting the most when he knew the odds were stacked against him and he was going to lose:

We used to go, like 30 of us. Sometimes the whole school against 15 of us, and the whole school would come out and we would get battered… It's like, you know, football hooligans, the same sort of buzz, innit. We were young as well, so, you know, we used to go out with knives, go out with bars and that.

Recent research suggests that gang activity is increasing throughout the UK (Young *et al.* 2007), and that today gang members are more likely to be involved in organised criminal activity, especially drug dealing, and to carry guns and other weapons (Bennett and Holloway 2004). Many of the participants described how gang activity and violence had escalated throughout London in recent years, and some admitted to knowing gang members who had been killed or received life sentences for murder. Current research into spatial youth group activity and patterns of drug dealing has revealed the extent to which Greater London has become spatially divided into a mosaic of different gang areas, especially within the deprived inner city (GangsinLondon 2006). Gangs of different ethnic origin, with names taken from local streets or landmarks, have become associated with particular locales such as housing estates, public parks, street networks, car parks and shopping complexes; although not all of these are by any means cohesive or permanently based. Most of the participants were aware of the need to uphold the reputation of where they lived, and navigate public space, alert to the fact that 'one person's home ground is another person's hostile environment' (Bauman 2001: 89). Mika described how the area of south London in which he lived was clearly marked out, bounded, and defended according to who 'owned' specific neighbourhoods within it:

> Brixton's not just Brixton, there's territories. Brixton, going up north, we still owned Streatham, and Streatham even had its own gang that were overthrown by the Brixton Boys. Once Brixton arrives in Streatham, Streatham do not argue, they very much step aside. You know, sometimes you can ask someone from Streatham, 'Where you from?', and they'll say 'Brixton' and they hardly ever come to Brixton. They live in Streatham, work in Streatham, girlfriend in Streatham, but they consider themselves Brixton Boys. You know what I mean? You go to Camberwell, which is where Brixton stops, because after Camberwell is Peckham, and they're two separate gangs. We're friends, but there is rivalry with Peckham.

And Liam explained that in recent years gang rivalry between Hackney in the east of the city and Tottenham in the north had intensified into 'a war' in which murder and reprisal attacks had become commonplace.

> This Hackney and Tottenham thing is a big, big, big thing. If you're from south London, if you're from west London, if you're from north London, no matter where you're from, whether you're involved in it, you know about it. That's how big it is. Over the years I've lost about 10, 13 friends, shot in the head, shot all over the place. You hear what I'm saying, and I could say the same about the Tottenham side as well. They've lost a lot of friends on route as well, and it's still going on.

'What you need'

How does crime escalate from trying to outwit store detectives in the local branch of Woolworths to street robbery, burglary, armed robbery and murder? As we have seen, for most participants crime started as a normal childhood activity, committed mostly on a whim for fun and excitement in the company of friends, but soon intensified into a career, 'a way of life', which for some of them persisted into their forties despite the experience of repeat spells in prison. Crime began with shoplifting, vandalism and fighting, and progressed to more organised forms of criminal activity such as street robbery, drug dealing, burglary and armed robbery. A range of possible explanations, spanning psychological and sociological perspectives, have been presented to explain why criminal behaviour increases in seriousness, and is maintained into adulthood by a small number of life-course-persistent criminals. As referred to in Chapter 1, these include deep-seated individual risk factors such as a deficit in neuropsychological functioning associated with hyperactivity and impulsiveness (Caspi and Moffitt 1995). However, they also include the negative impact of criminal justice sanctions such as repeated spells of imprisonment (Loeber and Farrington 1998); involvement in delinquent peer groups including criminal gangs (Thornberry and Krohn 1977); failure to assume adult roles and responsibilities, exacerbated by drug addiction (Graham and Bowling 1995); and continued exposure to neighbourhood disadvantage and poverty (Sampson et al. 2002). It is common to present these explanations as independent variables, although it is also stressed that individual and environmental factors interact (Moffitt 1993).

A small number of the participants attributed the escalation in criminal activity to specific childhood experiences; for instance, losing a parent, growing up in a children's home, or being abused by foster parents. Considering themselves to be the victims of a deprived childhood, they felt that they were 'doomed to deviance' (Maruna 2001). Barry explained his life in the following way:

When I was growing up I never really had anyone to show me the right way, you know the way that I've gone. This is my excuse, I've done things the best I know how, and it's not the right way, but when you're growing up and no one is telling you it's right and wrong, you have your own perceptions of something, do you see what I'm saying? And my perception is that me committing crime back then, I had to do it to survive.

My father died when I was 16 and I was out on the streets when I was 14, in and out of children's homes, and so I never had anyone to really love me, or show me the way, to say this is the right way – don't do it like this, do it like that.

For others, the lapse into serious crime stemmed directly from 'the pressure of drugs'. Aware of how to obtain drugs easily from the places they lived – active local drug markets are a characteristic of socially deprived areas generally (Parker *et al.* 2001) – most of the participants were regular drug users. A third claimed to be recreational users of mostly 'leisure drugs' such as cannabis, amphetamines and Ecstasy, while over a half described their use of class A 'poverty drugs' such as crack cocaine and heroin as problematic. In most cases, criminal activity preceded drug use, but as drug taking became more serious, the maintenance of an expensive drug habit entailed moving on to more serious forms of acquisitive crime such as street robbery and burglary. As such, drug use and criminal behaviour became an inseparable, routine feature of everyday life (Zamble and Quinsey 1997). Hari explained:

My older brother, the one older than me, I think, yeh, I wanted to be like him, 'cause he was involved in gangs and all that. But I suppose when you're young you do them things, and I wanted to be like him, you know. But he grew out of it. He settled down and got a restaurant, his wife and kids. He only done it for a little bit, you know, when he was young. But I just went all the way in [laughs]. Fucked up and got into drugs really. That's what fucked me up. None of my brothers got into drugs.

However, the most consistent explanation given by the participants for increasing the amount and seriousness of the crime they committed was that it was a premeditated and deliberate lifestyle choice. While this often entailed the maintenance of a serious drug habit, many were inclined to describe the gravitation to more serious crime as a purposeful decision which gave them a sense of direction in life and defined them as individuals. Crime and drug taking were characteristic of their lifestyles, but one did not necessarily predict the other. Having enjoyed the thrill and excitement of crime as a childhood prank, they now wanted to up the ante, feed their greed, keep the party going. Crime was not the product of an unhappy childhood, poor parenting or poverty. Indeed, some of them did not feel the need to justify the escalation in criminal behaviour with a reason at all. When asked why, in his early twenties, he had begun to commit armed robberies, Keifer, who described himself as 'a recovering addict', responded:

> I got into crime because I wanted to get into crime. I hear people bang on about 'Oh, I started smoking drugs because and...' but, you see, I'm of the opinion that if you're ever talking to someone and they say, 'Oh, it's because of and but', everything after the 'because of' and 'but' is bollocks.

Many of the participants described how crime became an integral part of who they were and what they wanted to do and achieve in life. Initially, shoplifting had provided them with toys, sweets and video games; now as they grew older, they developed more adult, expensive tastes for cars, clothes and gold. Crime, they began to realise, was a means to an end, a way of achieving social distinction and material success. Living in neighbourhoods where crime was accepted by many of the people around them, there was no shortage of contacts with whom to form 'crews' or criminal gangs, sell drugs, or establish arrangements for 'fencing' stolen goods. As such, many became seamlessly embedded in organised adult criminal networks which engaged in crime as a lucrative source of income (Hagan 1993). Mika described the moment he recognised that crime could be more than a fun way to pass the time, it could be profitable as well:

> I started off with silly things, sweet shops, newsagents and chemists. And I think chemists funny enough... you'd go through the labour stage and the baby was actually born in chemists, because the money was slightly bigger. And even if you didn't get money, you got the pharmaceuticals off the shelf that you thought were worth nothing, and you were getting silly offers for them...We were stealing Anadin and people were showing an interest in buying Anadin at half the price off the shelf. And they started questioning you, 'Can you get this? Can you get that?' And you don't know what they're talking about. You've never seen it, but you're going to start investigating into it now, because you've been offered a bit of money.

It has been suggested that, whereas relatively poor people are defined by the subject positions they occupy, relatively affluent people have the means to choose lifestyles and emulate a range of subject positions which structure and change their individual identities (Kellner 1992). In contradiction to this, Giddens (1991: 6) has written that continually revised biographical narrative development does not apply only to people in positions of power: '"lifestyle" refers also to decisions taken and courses of action followed under conditions of severe material constraint; such lifestyle patterns may sometimes also involve the more or less deliberate rejection of more widely diffused forms of behaviour and consumption.' The testimonies of the participants reveal this to be only partly true. In deliberately constructing a new lifestyle for themselves, rather than reject the pleasures of contemporary consumer culture, they embraced them. Motivated by a desire to transform the personal, situational and social circumstances of their lives, they did not question the appropriateness of pursuing the gratifications and rewards a fully committed criminal lifestyle can bring. Although, for some, crime was a means to an end, a straightforward choice between making large amounts of money quickly or working long hours in arduous, poorly paid jobs, for others it was a physical demonstration of power and identity, a lifestyle symbolised by the conspicuous display of expensive consumer goods – goods which, given their situation in life, they were supposed not to be able to attain. As some began to make considerable amounts of money through crime, life was increasingly foregrounded by a desire to alleviate the effects of family instability and economic disadvantage. Assuming that what you buy is a visible expression of who you are (Lasch 1980), they attempted to break free from 'the degradation of locality' (Bauman 2001: 38). From stairwells, streets and public parks, they gravitated to new social spaces – pubs, clubs and raves – where they passed themselves off to others as young people of taste and sophistication. Jimmy explained:

> At one place I got 14 grand cash, you know what I mean? Fourteen grand for an hour's work, two hours' work. I went Egypt. Cor, mate, I was living it large, living it large. There used to be about at least 10 of us, 10 mates. We all had our nice cars, our nice clothes, our gold, our watches. 'Cause that's all it was, it was material things. You know, who had a Rolex on, and who had the thickest chain on, who had the thickest bracelet on.

Harvey, whose crimes mostly involved stealing and selling cars, itemised the luxury goods, designer clothes, and leisure pursuits he spent his money on.

Cocaine, cannabis, couple of pills here and there, never anything else. I had my own car. I had an RS Turbo, legal until I lost the licence, but I still carried on driving. Nice clothes, Versace suits, Gucci shoes, bling, things like that, what you need, walking around like you got a lot of money. Playstations, computers, things for my flat. Going to nice restaurants, going shopping with my girlfriend. I like splashing out on people I like. Take 'em away, they like it.

And, given the reduced circumstances of his upbringing, Sean considered the fact he had been able to buy expensive clothes, even for a short while, to be something of a personal achievement:

It started getting pretty wild. Good days. Yeh, I did have a lot of fun. For me growing up with absolutely nothing, and going out and having all that fun, that's good times for me, and not having no education like. Clothes, we used to go in some shops and spend like £2,000 each and you'd get like jeans, a shirt and a jumper for like £800 and a pair of shoes for £400 and you'd buy another couple of jumpers for £300 apiece.

Unsurprisingly some of the respondents considered this new lifestyle to be romantic, cool, fashionable, reflecting an image of the gangster as hero derived from popular culture (Hayward 2004). In this sense, crime may be considered an addiction, a powerful seductive influence on their lives. Offering freedom and adventure, it was a sign to others of their 'superior moral ability to transcend local communal boundaries and move in a spirit of freedom and emphatic self-respect without accepting social limitations' (Katz 1988: 116). The experiential nature of the offences they committed was perhaps summed up best by Theo. When asked why he and his crew regularly committed up to five armed robberies a night, when he admitted that they did not need the money and were mindful and often fearful of arrest, he responded:

I think it was a buzz, you know what I mean? It was like a gangster image. One time we had so much money round us. And I don't know, just robbing them places, it just seemed to be like a... I don't know, a fetish, do you know what I mean, yeh? 'Cause when I used to stay with like certain girls, I used to like go through my money stash and think ahead and try and humble myself and look forward and think about not doing crime no more, yeh. And I used to look at my money and think to myself, I could do things with this money, like invest in something. Do something and not get into crime no more and watch the money come back legitly. 'Cause it only takes a matter of time before the police start watching you, or people that are afraid of you start calling your name to the police, and then wherever you're staying gets kicked off. But everyone was always down for it. I don't know, man, it's just a way of life. Like if we weren't doing something dramatic like that, yeh, there weren't no point us being together.

Mika described how the thrill of committing crime, combined with the gratuitous consumption of fashion items and the enjoyment of basking in the status and respect accorded the successful criminal, were all an integral part of the total experience of carrying out bank robberies in central London. Of course, crime was committed for the money, but it was also important to derive the maximum amount of enjoyment possible from a day trip into the centre of town, involving a premeditated itinerary of unfettered excitement and desire.

It happened so many times. We'd go to West End, do a robbery in West End, an exchange bureau. The Abbey National was the prime target most of the time. From the robbery, jump in a getaway car, bus, taxi, we even took London Transport sometimes as getaways. And from there, from the robbery, we'd go straight to like Cecil Gee's, buy an outfit, take off the clothes that we'd done the robbery in, put them in the bag, so we can dump them when we walk out the shop. Walk out the shop in our brand new clothes and then just go and get high on our marijuana, cannabis or whatever you want to call it, for a few hours until the rave starts. And then it's the respect, 'Ah! You did the Abbey National today, yeh, wicked, mate, yeh, champagne's on me'… It was like scoring a goal, you felt like an England goal scorer. When you were running away, you'd start giggling. You'd be running down the street, money in your hands, looking at each other, 'ha ha ha ha' [laughs hysterically]. And then that night you'd go and get your prize, so to speak. The money was part of the prize, but there was still more prize to come. Women throw themselves at you. You'd look at pictures of how you were dressed the night before, thinking, yeh, I look like David Beckham there, I look like Puff Daddy there. It was crazy, man.

Leaving home

For most of the participants, as their criminal activities increased so did the desire to leave home. It has been suggested that, while the spatial activities of offenders who cease to offend relatively early in life tend to be routine and local (Wiles and Costello 2000), as they get older, life-course-persistent criminals become more mobile. Since the middle of the last century, when town planners separated residential areas from places of work and commerce, career offenders have travelled to find the greatest rewards, particularly when the local neighbourhoods they come from are blighted by poverty and neglect (Morris 1957). In search of new criminal opportunities and greater returns, 'criminal entrepreneurs' think about space and place instrumentally. According to Mack (1964: 43), professional criminals 'live in a neutral neighbourhood, or keep on the move. A criminal community may be predominately a network of communications over a wide region with some kind of foothold in various neighbourhoods but not tied to these neighbourhoods.'

More recent 'journey to crime literature' has cast doubt on this observation. It contends that the routine activities of offenders are restricted to paths and activity nodes near to, or surrounding, their immediate home areas. While there are variations in travel patterns according to offence and offender characteristics (Baldwin and Bottoms 1976), the majority of offender movements are relatively short and overwhelmingly local in nature. For example, quantitative analysis has found that offenders in the city of Sheffield travel only 1.93 miles, on average, to commit crime (Wiles and Costello 2000: 11). This finding is thought to be consistent throughout the UK. It is also thought to hold true in spite of the fact that travel has become easier and more fluid, and social networks more extensive and distanciated within contemporary society. This is thought to be because offenders generally 'are drawn from those groups in the population who lack the personal and material resources to learn to travel and sustain such travel thereafter' (*ibid.*: 44). As we saw in the introductory chapter, this is supported by geographical analysis, which has shown that, compared to wealthier areas, socially deprived urban communities have a fairly restricted activity space (Massey 1999), and that everyday life is characterised by short-range, routine journeys (Golledge and Stimson 1997). As Bauman (2001: 38) has observed generally, immobility remains 'the main measure of social deprivation and the principal dimension of unfreedom'.

However, as revealed in Chapter 2, unlike other parts of the country, London is not so divided into distinct zones of poverty and affluence that it allows no movement between one place and another, or across urban space generally. Nor are neighbourhoods so isolated that they develop separate 'territorial' identities. Most people of different social class and ethnicity live and work together in close proximity. The wealthy may assert a right to defend the places they live in and call their own; furthermore, location for the poor may be buttressed by unemployment and racial or ethnic segregation. But social relations within contemporary cities tend to be characterised by a maximal use of space, and as a consequence movement both out of and back into residential neighbourhoods varies enormously (Massey 1997; Amin and Thrift 2002).

To a significant extent, this was borne out by the narrative testimonies provided by some of the participants. As they got older and began to explore different parts of the city, they no longer felt constrained to stay within the places they had grown up in. Everyday experience and understanding began to encompass a wider world of routes across the city landscape, not roots within it (Massey 1998). It is common in much human geography to suggest that the attachment between people and place is most manifest in the family home, or the feeling of being at home within a specific neighbourhood or community. Home area is considered important because it conveys a sense of mutual identification, camaraderie and community (Young and Willmott 1962). According to Heidegger (1971), we belong in 'the place we call home', because it imparts territoriality, an awareness of value and esteem, and what we consider to be worth defending. This is contrasted with the sense of adventure and excitement to be derived from venturing into the unknown – from escaping mundanely familiar social situations, and meeting new people (Seamon 1979). As they got older, the participants became aware they lived in places that constrained them in important ways. As they were no longer inclined to demonstrate allegiance to areas of residence, Greater London presented a spatial mosaic of opportunity. As the seriousness of their crimes increased, the home neighbourhoods they previously had derived meaning and value from were supplanted by places which enabled them to establish a new identity for themselves as committed criminals. If circumstances had not already conspired to detach them from their home environments, they now became 'social nomads' (Foucault 1977).

For some, a purely practical reason for leaving home was they had begun to develop local reputations. Increasingly known to the people around them as 'little thieves and thugs', some had been banned from local shops, picked out at school as troublemakers, or targeted by the police. Home was where their families lived, and friends and neighbours were likely to know what they were up to. Paul, from Brixton, explained why he regularly travelled further south to commit crime:

> I was going to areas like Croydon, just out there areas, 'cause, obviously, living in the area and trying to thieve in the area, a lot of people saw me and knew me, knew what I got up to, so I couldn't really put myself in that position. But I did used to go to Croydon, Crystal Palace, just places away from where I lived.

And Joshua also explained:

> I have a philosophy, never dog on your own doorstep. So I'd go like Harrow on the Hill or Harrow and Wealdstone, which is like west London but far, far away. And I'd have my little gang up there. So I was far away from family like cousins and relatives, so they wouldn't see nothing that was going on. They couldn't tell my mum anything and basically I'd be down there doing what I want to do. It turned from shops to actually people and robberies, street robberies, you understand, and like very bad street robberies.

Furthermore, some of the participants, on realising that criminal opportunities in their home neighbourhoods were limited, began to seek out new crime locations where the rewards might be greater, locations which, as Keifer from Brixton disclosed, tended to be close by and offered relatively rich pickings:

> I was going Pimlico and the West End. I wasn't doing things on my manor, as it were, 'cause you're taught at a young age that you don't shit on your doorstep and basically the people that live where I live only had what I had really. You know, they didn't have much more than me, you know.

Another characteristic of contemporary cities is that, because they have dense, concentrated and heterogeneous populations, they offer numerous opportunities for criminals to live and work unnoticed in the close 'proximity with strangers' (Young 1990). Sennett has observed (1990: 127–7) that under these social circumstances 'deviance is the freedom made possible in a crowded city of lightly engaged people.' On a practical and instrumental level, this provides numerous opportunities for the professional criminal. For example, having decided it was too risky to remain in their home areas, some of the participants had set up home in one area, passing themselves off to their new neighbours as respectable, law-abiding citizens; while going out every day, as if to work, to commit crime in other areas. Kev described his double existence:

> What you have to understand is that I might live in Battersea or New Cross but my activity was in Brixton. Brixton was where I made my money. Obviously, as we started to gain notoriety for ourselves, people started to live double lives didn't they? Basically, you wanted to live, and be to neighbours that respectable person that was bringing their kids up and taking their kids to school and all that. But you know, on the other side of that, the house was stacked with gear [laughs]. It's the truth.

Similarly, others described how they had developed networks of associates and instrumental alliances in different parts of London based on certain types of crime committed in particular locations. In a few cases, these involved small, closely organised, business partnerships or syndicates, which – from the little information they were prepared to divulge about them – appeared mostly to involve drug dealing (Hobbs 1995). For others, however, it was simply a matter of forming loose, one-off and short-lived alliances, mostly as a consequence of chance meetings on the street. Having grown bored and frustrated with his immediate peer group, Harvey described how he 'bounced around', trying out different crimes with different gangs from other areas. Tim explained that joining different gangs for the day enabled him to 'run with the pack' and 'steam' through trains, buses and crowded shopping centres. And Mika described how he used to recruit 'loads of decoys' to 'bundle shops with loads of people':

> When we started getting more serious about the money and we couldn't afford to go on a robbery and come out unsuccessful, we would bundle the shop with loads of people. Sometimes we'd even go out of our way to find people that weren't interested in crime and say to them, 'Look, just go in there and pack out

the shop and be my decoy and meet me in half an hour and I'll sort you out for it.' So at that stage there was 15, 20, 25 people at a time.

Like-minded criminals appeared to be everywhere and were found relatively easily through normal everyday interaction on the street. Paul had joined a number of different gangs from different areas as a consequence of 'meeting girls from all over London'. Peter described how the highly visible nature of drug consumption made it possible to 'deal and take drugs wherever':

You just know how to find people; you just know where people are. That is their habitat and you get to know them. You just... if you've got drugs they'll speak to you – that's pretty much how it is.... When I first started, all this crack was up Brixton Hill and then the police raided these places up Brixton and it went back to Camberwell. So everyone kind of follows the crack. Now, when I went down to Camberwell, I got to know a whole new set of Camberwell people and then some of them took me round to Walworth Road. And it just goes on like that and you see the same people. You know, I see half of them in here [referring to Brixton prison].

Crime was committed casually, on the move with little planning or skill, wherever and whenever 'it seemed like a good idea at the time'. Rick explained:

No matter where I was, if I saw something that looked like it was worth taking, I would take it. I wouldn't travel out of my area specifically to go and rob, but I was always out of my area anyway, so if I was running a bit low on money and I was with like a couple of the lads, saw something, and then all right then here's some money.

Even commercial crime, such as armed robbery – crime which as a rule requires a much greater degree of care and sophistication than opportunistic crimes such as street robbery or car theft – was carried out with minimum preparation, organisation, or prior calculation of the risks involved (Matthews 2002). According to Hobbs (1995: 9), the lack of a rationale for where, when or how crime is committed is typical of much criminal activity today, which involves 'haphazard, essentially amateur excursions featuring minimal planning, a low level of competence, and a lack of commitment to specialized criminality'. Mika described the indiscriminate way his gang chose crime locations to carry out armed robberies outside London.

I've done robberies in places I wouldn't know how to get there or from there today. All I know, I would look on the train map, 'Anyone been there?' 'No.' 'All right, we're going there then', and we'd jump on the train for an hour there, pick somewhere at random.

Indeed, the participants who travelled regularly and far appeared to do so more for the fun, adventure and excitement of visiting new places than for the criminal opportunity it provided. Travel was engaged in for spontaneous reasons; for example, 'just to drive and get out of London'. Ian explained how learning to drive had resulted in a sudden and rapid escalation of criminal activity:

When I was a young teenager it was like pickpocketing, snatching people's change, snatching people's bags. Then gradually we started getting bigger. We had money, started driving. Yeh, I first started driving when I was 14, crashed my cousin's car [laughs] and, yeh, from then on it was just, I never looked back. We'd drive out to like Hertfordshire and places like that, Hatfield, Welwyn Garden City, Saint Albans, all round there. We just wanted to get out of London and we just happened to turn up there. Do post offices, smash and grabs, going into jewellery stores, smashing the windows, grabbing loads of things, running off.

And Sean recounted his experiences of committing crime in different locations as if they were simply a necessary feature of a continuous holiday excursion:

We used to go on the train up and down the country. Like we'd go to Scotland, Devon, Kent, Brighton way. We used to stay in hotels, like five-star hotels. We were having a good time. We was young, we was wild, really wild. Used to drink and have girls around us all the time. Smart clothes, nice cars and yeh… up and down the country. Manchester, we used to love Manchester, and then we'd go Bournemouth, then we'd go Dover, then we'd go Skegness. We used to be up and down all the time. Like we'd drive there, and then we'd start stealing cars out of showrooms.

Of course, persistent criminality is not without its downsides. For many offenders, it ultimately leads to prison, an experience which, for a time at least, puts an end to the material wealth, respect and social status crime can bring. Compared to the thrills and unfettered excitement of their lives up to this point, on being imprisoned, the participants were faced with a different spatial and social experience altogether: one that is strictly monitored, highly regimented, and deeply invasive. The effect of repeated spells of imprisonment on the participants is described in the following chapter.

Chapter 6

'On the in': the impact of imprisonment

Introduction

What little is known about the impact of imprisonment on prisoner behaviour is mainly derived from research which has sought to explain why prisoners, for the most part, remain compliant when they significantly outnumber their captors (Matthews 2009). Responses to this question have usually emphasised the controlling effects of imprisonment, in particular the security and surveillance methods employed, and how prison rules and regulations tend to institutionalise prisoners, causing them to behave submissively. However, indications that the age range, previous life experiences, social status and ethnic make-up of prisoners are changing suggest that imprisonment is a fluid, dynamic experience. As noted in Chapter 4, in the United States over the last 30 years or so, the incarceration of higher numbers of violent prisoners and increasing levels of racially motivated gang behaviour and conflict (Jacobs 1979; Wacquant 2001) have raised concerns about the effects of imprisonment, and prompted calls for the research literature on prisoner adaptation to be updated (Wacquant 2002).

As we have also seen, higher rates of reoffending and re-imprisonment have focused attention on the extent to which prisons function as agencies of reform (SEU 2002; Petersilia 2003). In the UK, although changing the behaviour of convicted criminals has been fundamental to the overall purpose of imprisonment since 1895, when the Parliamentary Committee on Prisons chaired by Herbert Gladstone endorsed the twin priorities of deterrence and rehabilitation, the dilemma of whether it is possible, in a practical sense, to balance punishment and reform has never been resolved. To an extent, gender differences between how men and women resist imprisonment (Bosworth 1999) and resettle back into society (Eaton 1993) have been addressed, but the research literature on how prisoners of different age, ethnicity, status, personality or sentence length, for example, respond to imprisonment generally, or to different prison contexts and regimes in particular, remains to be updated.

Most importantly perhaps, the extant research literature lacks a prisoner perspective. Aside from the autobiographical testimonies of a small number of 'celebrity' former prisoners (e.g. see Wilde 1898; Behan 1958; Boyle 1977; Leech 1992), there are few accounts of what prisoners themselves think about the impact of imprisonment, particularly on the decision-making processes involved in reoffending or criminal desistance. Given that 'imprisonment is ultimately an experience which only those who have been incarcerated can adequately relate' (Morgan 2002: 1160), this is a fundamental omission. Ever since the middle of the nineteenth century, during which time the prison as we know it today has been used as the dominant mode of punishment, we have never had 'a clear-headed understanding of what imprisonment means and what it does' (Pryor 2001: 1).

This chapter presents the views of the participants in relation to four major characteristics of imprisonment: initial prison experiences, relations with other prisoners, everyday life in prison, and preparations for release. For the most part, the views expressed have been assessed in relation to traditional accounts of imprisonment which emphasise its deterrent effect or the opposite view entirely, that prisons function as 'schools of crime' and impart criminogenic effects which influence offenders to reoffend after release (Maruna and Toch 2005). The impact of each of these characteristics on the offending outcomes of the participants, and their willingness to contemplate and work towards criminal desistance, is assessed throughout.

First-timers

Most of the participants had served time in a variety of prisons, first in a male local remand prison and then, depending on age, sentence length, and the period of time they had served, in a borstal, detention centre, young offender institution (YOI), or adult training prison. Given that most received their first sentence at a relatively young age – between the ages of 15 and 20 – it was common for them to react with a degree of apprehension, fear or alarm (Harvey 2005). Only a few claimed to have had no fear, or to have been indifferent to prison. Peter, who prior to his first sentence was homeless and had a serious drug problem, described it as 'just another shit thing in my life, if you haven't got anything anyway, what difference can prison make?' In contrast, John, was 'superstitious to see what gaol was like, get the feel of it'. However, in making the transition from 'street to prison', most admitted to feeling anxious, in view of popular perceptions of prison from films and television, and what they had heard colloquially about endemic bullying and rape. Concerned whether they would be able to adapt and survive, they had been 'shit scared of the way things were, doors banging all the time', 'nervous that I didn't know no one'. Sean admitted to having spent his first few days 'crying my eyes out'. Stuart described his first few weeks in a Victorian-built remand centre:

> It was one of the most mentally challenging experiences I'd had in my life. I remember spending one or two weeks in Rochester Prison and the cell was tiny, very little air coming in and out. It was hot summer and humid and I was locked up in that cell for at least seven days straight without ever coming out. I was allowed out twice for a shower and once to get my canteen. The food was brought to the cell door. There was no gymnasium and no reading material. And basically it was like laying on your bed staring at the ceiling literally for 24 hours a day. So it was tough. And at that point I really didn't think I was going to be able to make it through the sentence. Although it wasn't telling on my behaviour, I was really suffering.

Given the pleasure-seeking, hedonistic lifestyle of the participants prior to coming to prison, it is not surprising that the need to adjust to the cramped physical conditions of their confinement, and a strict ordered routine, initially had a 'mortifying' effect on them (Goffman 1961). Research has revealed that especially for young, first-time prisoners the reception period can be particularly distressing. Indeed, unless prisoners learn to cope and adapt, anxiety can lead to mental depression and suicide (Liebling 1999). However, for most of the participants, none of these outcomes applied. Rather than be seriously affected by the experience, they grew accustomed to it relatively quickly. Initial misgivings dissipated once they became familiarised to their new surroundings. Prison was not hard, threatening or claustrophobic, as they had been led to believe it would be (Jones and Schmid 2000). In fact, once processed into the system, most found it 'a laugh on the wings and that with a load of people'. Robert thought 'it was going to be a lot tougher but it wasn't ... it's like laughs and quite relaxed actually.' Joshua explained why he adjusted with relative ease:

> You get used to it. You get used to it within the first week. You have to, the first three weeks of being in prison is the worst time. After that, it's like everyday life. It becomes everyday life.

However, all of the participants agreed that surviving was crucially dependent on a facility to deal with high levels of interpersonal violence. Violence is a fact of life in prison generally where 'the acts of violent men ... sustained by a culture of masculinity, which idealises and equates personal power with physical dominance, reflects the world outside' (Scraton *et al.* 1991: 67). Although full-scale, front-stage, prison riots are rare, background violence and robbery are a daily occurrence (Edgar *et al.* 2003). Conflict problems, however, are most prevalent in YOIs (Sparks *et al.* 1996). As we saw in the previous chapter, having previously participated in gang attacks and fights in the streets, pubs and clubs near to where they lived, most of the participants had grown inured to violent confrontation. As such, they responded to bullying and intimidation in kind, with a marked degree of casualness. They had 'been around violence', and so knew 'what to do when push comes to shove'. Dealing with antagonism was simply a matter of living 'by the same rules inside as on the street'. John remarked:

> It was exactly the same. That's why it didn't bother me. I just kept myself to myself and when people come to me to cause trouble I dealt with it. I dealt with it my way. I'm quiet, but I'll flare up any time. The way I thought, the way I was brought up, it made me stronger. I just shut myself off.

The participants explained that; although much of the violence in YOIs is about 'mind games', and fuelled by mindless aggression, 'anger and madness', 'cussing people out the window', and 'stupidness, like insulting your family'; it also serves a purpose. It is the means by which young offenders achieve positions of power, authority and respect in relation to their peers. So, fights were provoked deliberately to 'make sure everyone knew I could, and was willing to fight'. They were staged in the open in front of witnesses, 'like some proving thing, to see who was badder than who, you get me'; and sometimes also in front of prison officers, 'so you know it's going to get split up, so you save face, but you don't actually get hurt.' Then, once a reputation for violence is established, prisoners are able to climb to the top of a hierarchy based on the monopolisation and control of illicit trading networks (Valentine and Longstaff 1998); that is, the supply of contraband such as phone cards, food, cigarettes, and, most important of all, drugs (Ruggiero 1995). Stuart described how, as a young offender, through demonstrating a capacity for intimidation and violence, he had coerced prisoners to work for him.

> You had to have, like they were called your boys. They would clean out your cell, they would give you their money, they would do anything you wanted them to do. And you might give them cigarettes, and you would send them out to go and sell cigarettes, and you would give them phone cards, and you'd send them out to go and sell them. And at the end of the day they would come back with a list of names of all the people they'd sold various products to. And at the end of the week they would go and collect it again. And if there was any problem with collection, then *you* would go and collect. But there never was any problem with collection, because they knew who *you* were.

It might be assumed from this that, in describing past experiences of violence, some of the participants glamorised their ability to fight. Only Raja admitted he was incapable of defending himself, and had been attacked repeatedly in prison. However, although most affirmed they could handle bullying and intimidation, any bluster on their part they were 'hard men' was tempered by the negative way they referred to prison violence generally. They had seen prisoners 'suffer some appalling beatings and injuries' including sexual abuse and stabbings. As a consequence, they had been pleased to leave YOIs behind, and move on to adult prisons where the threat of violence was not so intense, 'in your face'. They described how in YOIs, 'they will plunge you, they will leave you bleeding, so you'd better know what you're doing.' Young offenders were dismissed as 'disgusting', 'bitter and twisted', and having 'only one way of thinking'. Barry described how 'people were hanging theirselves in there, you couldn't relax, not a very nice place'. Adult prisons, on the other hand, were 'a different experience altogether. A lot more relaxed in terms of the actual regime, and the way people related to each other.' As John explained:

> because adult prisoners avoid trouble and do not draw
> attention to themselves, they are less against the system all the
> time. Adult gaols are more easy to get on. You got no young
> idiots running around doing stupid little things. Some of those
> you get in here, but it usually gets dealt with in the prison,
> not by the prisoners, who deal with it their way. In YOIs it
> got dealt with with razor blades and all that stuff. A lot of
> violence.

As recounted above, Stuart admitted to having been this way himself,
but now, looking back, he justified his behaviour as a defence
mechanism. Retrospectively neutralising his actions, he explained
why internalising hypermasculinity and enforcing status through
power and violent domination are necessary to survive in prison:

> Young people of that age group are terribly cruel and wicked to
> each other. Everyone was hyperactive and always had a point to
> prove. So in order to avoid becoming an outcast I found myself
> having to do things I never dreamed I would be doing. I had no
> choice but to get into it. But in reality I was a lot less of a bully,
> at least I like to think I was a lot less of a bully than.... [trails
> off] I mean I befriended two guys from north London, both
> white, who I became very good friends with. In the end they
> both got shipped out because of the bullying. One of them was
> beaten senseless. The other one [long pause]... I managed to be
> able to establish a strong enough relationship with him to keep
> everybody off his back as long as I could. I mean I would speak
> to people and say, 'No, he's all right, he's safe.' But once [starts
> to laugh], once Mad H from Peckham Rye comes in, mate, it's
> all over, do you know what I mean?

'Pals from road were there'

As the participants spent longer in prison, and their awareness and
knowledge of it increased, they began to respond in different ways
to the conditions of their confinement. They developed various understandings of what prison is for; the nature of its design, organisation
and management; how to avoid trouble; what to do to pass the time;
and so on. An important feature of this adaption process was how
to relate to other prisoners. Criminal network analysis has found

that, owing to the possibility of betrayal and deception, offenders generally are extremely wary of entering into relationships with people whose reputations they are unsure of (Chattoe and Hamill 2005). As a result, most crews or criminal gangs are comprised of small groups of individuals who know each other well. As described in the previous chapter, such alliances were formed by many of the participants at an early age from groups of people they had grown up with in the same residential area. Common sense suggests that when offenders from the same local neighbourhoods are incarcerated together, these criminal alliances or networks are likely to carry over into prison.

Most of the participants explained that in order to cope in prison they relied on the support of a small circle of friends with whom they had associated previously with on the outside. Because 'all prisoner relations are built around where you come from, and everyone sticks to the people they know', the best way of 'doing time' is 'to stay in your own group ... and keep yourself to yourself.' As we have seen already, in respect to theories of personal and place identity, the notion is sometimes expressed that 'you are where you live', there is an intertwining of personal identity and place attachment (Kintrea *et al.* 2008). It has been suggested that this is weakest in socially deprived areas, especially those which suffer high levels of crime (Livingston *et al.* 2008 in Kintrea *et al.* 2008). However, perhaps owing to the insularity of the social worlds inhabited by persistent criminals (Coles 2001), area-based identification and territorial allegiance appeared to be a significant factor in the early lives of most of the participants; some disregarded this on the outside, but now it was utilised as an important source of protection and security within the uncertain environment of prison. Indeed, mirroring recent research, 'postcode pride', used 'as a way of anchoring belonging to somewhere external to the prison ... often usurped or overlaid identities organized through "race" or ethnicity' (Phillips and Earle n.d.: 4; see also Phillips 2007). Associating with people they knew from home engendered a sense of embeddedness and safety, company and support. Sean explained why being associated with a particular place of residence was so important to him:

> There's all little groups in here. Everyone's got their little groups. There's a group from Stratford, there's a group from Dagenham, and a group from all different places. And we all know each other and we're just all friends and we try not to go out of our little circle. At least you know you can trust each other.

And Jimmy stressed how every time being admitted to prison, in order to obtain certain everyday necessities, most importantly drugs, it was essential first of all to seek out 'people from the road'.

> Pals were there and people you knew from road and they make it easier for you. You know, you get a puff, you get a puff in the daytime and keep it until you're banged up, and you've got something to get your head down with.

Because most of the participants were being held in prisons local to where they lived, it was highly probable, of course, that they would know at least a few prisoners from 'road' in and around their home neighbourhoods. To gauge the extent to which residential location is a shared characteristic of the London prison population, the participants were asked to estimate how many prisoners they were currently incarcerated with they had known previously outside, either as a friend, associate, or acquaintance, or by reputation. All of them knew some prisoners. Most knew between 30 and 70, while a few claimed to know 'literally hundreds' or 'millions of them'. Mika, for example, claimed to know 'about 60 per cent of this prison from outside'. However, as was shown in Chapter 2, because mobility in and around London is relatively easy, geographic offence patterns and criminal alliances tend to be more spread out than in other parts of the country. The extent to which prisoners in London are also part of a wider criminal network which is equally insular but nevertheless extends beyond the boundaries of immediate places of residence was revealed by the participants generally but especially those who had spent time in YOI Feltham. Currently, the only YOI in Greater London, 69 per cent of YOI Feltham's juvenile, and 70 per cent of its young adult, population are drawn from a 50-mile catchment area (HM Chief Inspector of Prisons 2005). Despite this, 'in Feltham everyone knows everyone else.' Theo explained that his perceived status in Feltham was the outcome of having a reputation that preceded him in the prison:

> Most of them knew me, yeh. I wasn't really good with names, but faces I could remember. Everyone knew me or heard of me, yeh. And, I don't know, like a boost thing… people used to like boost each other's names and that would create, I don't know, bad behaviour or rep. Do you know what I mean?

Similarly, Mika explained:

Feltham had already been paved for me coming from Brixton. I had a reputation before I ever stepped in there. So a lot of the time they'd say, 'Who are you?' I'd say, 'I'm Mika.' 'What? Mika from Brixton?' 'Yeh, right' and, 'Oh, I've heard of you.' So very much I was all right. 'Cause a lot of people I know they've already been in there. My name's come up in conversations or arguments or gossip, whatever. It was just for me to prove that I was this way and, you know what I mean, I wasn't a coward.

Gangs and landings

Although the above suggests that identity and status are features of criminal networks, and that feelings of security and mutual support often stem from area-based solidarities, it is not certain what impact this has on prisoner adaptation generally. As referred to in Chapter 2, in the United States violent confrontation organised around the territorial cohesiveness of street gangs is now an endemic feature of everyday prison culture. Indeed, according to Wacquant (2001: 111), gang activity based on ethnicity, religious affiliation, and area of residence has become so prevalent in some prisons that social relations between prisoners have shifted from a form of adaptation based previously on '"doing your own time" to one now based on "doing gang time"'. Overall, the participants did not think that a similar situation obtains in the UK. Although they were aware that gang rivalry, which is imported from outside, 'doesn't change in the system', gang violence had not reached a level of organisation or sophistication that it affected life on a daily basis. Jimmy passed it off as the product of a mutual obligation to help settle petty disputes. It was 'mostly small-scale stuff. Your friends might have a grievance with some other guys, nothing to do with you, but you're brought into it because it's your pals.' As shown in Chapter 4, interpersonal violence is a routine, everyday occurrence in prisons. But the extent to which gang violence contributes to this is unproven. To date, the major explanations of collective violent confrontation – collective discontent at the paucity of prison conditions, and an imbalance between 'security, control and justice' (Woolf and Tumim 1991) – have not identified local gang rivalry as a significant causal factor. Nevertheless, as Matthews (2009: 72) has argued, 'explanations of riots ... need to begin from a recognition of the social, structural and institutional contexts in which they take place, the causal mechanisms which underpin them, and the "triggers" which set these mechanisms off.' According to the testimonies of the participants, the social, structural and institutional context of London prisons is changing. Gang activity is increasing, especially among younger prisoners, and in local establishments. Therefore, responding to the threat of violent confrontation between prisoners from rival neighbourhoods, as well as different parts of the city, is key to maintaining security and control. Hari described how, on being admitted to YOI Feltham for the first time, he had been recruited into a gang:

> Feltham is like what I used to get outside. Gangs, this area, that area, and everyone wants to prove something, you know, fighting. It's like when you go in, as you go in, you just get picked and taken, you know what I mean? And before you know it, you're already in it. It's like areas now, like east, west, north, south and that.

Liam tells a similar story about Feltham:

> How most of the trouble used to start was via the Hackney and Tottenham thing back in my time in Feltham. Once I got to the B side of Feltham, the Hackney and Tottenham thing had started so anyone from Hackney would stick together and anyone from Tottenham would stick together. That's when it was all kicking off. Do you get what I'm saying, once that fight kicks off, either one of you is getting moved off that wing and then you could get moved to a wing where there's another one and then it kicks off again.

It is incumbent on prison staff to be constantly aware of the potential for violence and disorder this can cause. According to both official and unofficial information, the interior space of all prisons is closely organised and regulated to reduce the threat of bullying and violence. In all closed establishments, known vulnerable prisoners are accommodated on separate wings and violent prisoners in designated segregation blocks. And at local institutional levels, prison officers are also free to 'manipulate the system to achieve more individual objectives' (McDermott and King 1988: 369). According to some of the participants, fully aware of the potential for violence between rival groups of prisoners, prison staff routinely allocate prisoners to specific accommodation blocks in order to keep different factions apart, a practice particularly evident in local establishments in London, where rival gangs from neighbouring areas are more likely to come into contact with each other. Depending on the location of their arrest and the court in which they are tried, prisoners in London are liable to serve time in any one of a number of local prisons. As a consequence, the participants had to be constantly aware of how accommodation blocks, wings and landings were organised, and where different groups of prisoners were located. Joshua described the problems that can arise when prisoners are first admitted to a local prison.

> If you don't know about the wings, you will go on there blinded, not knowing who anybody is. You might see a couple of guys from your area, and they will, you know, give you the information really and truly this is an east London wing. So know just how you step, you understand? You can ask to move, but you have to give a good enough reason. If they want to put you on a wing where there's loads of east London and you're from north, you're going on that wing whether you like it or not. They can do that, they have the power to do it. If they don't like you, like the look of you, you ain't getting nothing. You're on your own.

To a large extent, the danger presented to individual prisoners in these circumstances stems from traditional enmities engendered by territorial conflicts or 'postcode wars'. As described in Chapter 5, this is a feature of life in cities generally, a characteristic of young men displaying hyper-aggressive domination and control over urban space. Although the classic teenage gang based on the American model is not as manifest in the UK, an increase in gun crime in recent years has focused attention on criminal gangs and 'gang culture' (Pitts 2008), and new forms of professional crime and violent 'street culture', particularly in 'London, the West Midlands, Manchester and Merseyside, where a disproportionate amount of gun crime occurs' (Hallsworth and Silverstone 2009: 374). It follows that local prisons in metropolitan areas such as London are likely to be prone to the threat of violent disturbance and reprisal attacks imported by prisoners from the streets outside. Rivalries between different areas in London have increased in recent years, in some cases involving the territorial control of illegal drug markets enforced with the use of guns (e.g. Hales *et al*. 2006). For some of the participants, this had immediate consequences for their personal safety and security in prison. For example, Jimmy, from East London, refused to attend education classes on another wing because he claimed it was 'like the fucking Bronx, South London versus East London, a fucking war down there':

> There's all these young guys, yeh, just coming up through the ranks... people walk around with guns, knives, won't think twice about shooting yer or stabbing yer. Now you got one side of the wing is South London and the other side of the wing is East London. Now, if I go over there, all my pals are over there on East. So where will I have to go? I will have to go on the East side, and it's a situation where I'm 33 years old, I got three kids. I ain't got no time to be getting in no war in prison and then when I go on road, the war carries on because at the moment there's a big war going on with Tottenham and Dalston.

Liam was prepared to divulge only so much about his previous gang activities. Following some off-hand comments, he tells me, 'You're going too close and I won't tell you that.' However, he does tell me that

> being in prison and being from Hackney, I couldn't be put on specific wings. I couldn't go to specific gaols because knowing certain people in them gaols, I know I would be putting my life in jeopardy, or putting their life in jeopardy. I'm on D wing right now but I was on B and G wing. I've only been on D wing for three weeks now 'cause D wing is a convicted wing. When they told me I was moving to D wing, I actually turned around and said to them, 'Look, I'm from Hackney.' I told them about the Hackney Tottenham thing even though most of them are aware of it because a lot of the fights that do happen in prison is from, is from coming from the streets. It's what's happening on the outside, if you're with me, like the crews and the gangs. It's everywhere. It's Brixton and Peckham, Birmingham, Manchester the same thing, it's everywhere.

Places of 'de-communication'

Any standard history of imprisonment will relate that during the first half of the nineteenth century prisons were founded on a strict penitentiary regime of solitary confinement, separation, and silence. But later, towards the end of the century, owing to concerns about rising levels of prisoner insanity, and the growing realisation that imprisonment was engendering high levels of prisoner insanity, the Gladstone Committee of 1895 heralded the phasing out of systems of enforced silence and the beginning of a new penal welfare approach founded on principles of reform and rehabilitation. Today, however, despite more than a century of experimentation with various means of rehabilitation, including controlled association, a lack of meaningful human contact remains a key deprivation characteristic of everyday prison life. According to Toch (1992), it is a fundamental characteristic of imprisonment that the severing of contact with the outside world creates 'a psychological vacuum' which can lead to distress, anxiety, and an overall failure to cope. As a consequence, prisoners often escape into an interior fantasy life. Owing to the way prison environments are strictly controlled and isolated from the outside world, 'prisoners turn to "inner time" and become more involved with their own experiences' (Matthews 2009: 39).

The remoteness of imprisonment impacts significantly on everyday social relationships and interaction patterns. Although the participants agreed that most prisoners grow up in unstable and disrupted family circumstances and suffer from a lack of education and a drug habit, they did not think this shared background cohered into a common outlook on life, or a unified behavioural response to imprisonment. Instead, prisoners are contradictory, unpredictable and capricious. Living in overcrowded, cramped conditions and having no privacy caused them to behave in ways that often are difficult to read. As a consequence, prisoners felt that it was necessary to avoid becoming too closely involved with other prisoners unknown to them. It was important 'to judge people's character and you learn to do that quickly' because 'what you see in people's attitudes is often not what's going on in their heads – you have to keep alert.' Moreover, you have to constantly 'watch what you talk around with people, because it can get very nasty, and then lights out and you don't wake up in the morning.' Harvey explained what to him was the main difference between life inside and that outside prison:

> Being in here you get up and make sure no one's in your cell. Being on the outside you know you ain't going to lose nothing if you don't get up. In here there's a lot of chance someone will walk in and steal something. Outside no problem. So you get up to protect yourself. Protect what you got.

A mantra often recited was that to survive in prison it is necessary 'to keep yourself to yourself'. On being asked how this is possible in an overcrowded prison where everybody lives on top of everybody else, Peter snapped, 'I put myself in the cell and fucking never come out unless I need to, because I don't want to fucking talk to no one.' Others thought that it meant withdrawing from everyday prison life emotionally, 'to not get too involved', 'keep your head down and just get on with it'. To do this, it was necessary to 're-programme yourself in prison', 'hide your true personality', and become 'different to the person you are outside'. It has been suggested that enforced apathy, and a loss of interest in anything but surviving prison condition many prisoners to behave as if they are ill. Deprived of autonomy and security (Sykes 1958), they suffer a loss of personal agency, 'institutional neurosis' (Barton 1966), and 'behavioural deep freeze' (Zamble and Porporino 1988). Theo revealed:

> On the out, I'm really sociable; do you know what I mean? Yeh, I like getting to know new people all the time. But in here, I don't know, I feel like I don't really want to get involved with so much people. You can be frustrated because like your true inner self's like, I don't know, yearning to come out of you, do you know what I mean? But you don't want people getting too comfortable with you.

Fitzgerald and Sim (1982: 58) have written that 'overall, the most striking feature of daily life in prison is the routinized boredom of people passing rather than spending time.' The rules and regulations which restrict any opportunity to make decisions or exert choice mean that 'the lives of most prisoners follow repetitive and restricted courses that dull their senses and corrode their abilities' (Irwin and Owen 2005: 99). 'Doing time' involves suspending human agency and avoiding trouble until 'normal life' can be resumed on the outside (Irwin 1970). For many of the participants, the overriding consequence of this was that prison is 'boring', 'monotonous' and 'uneventful'. Most of the time is spent 'sleeping, getting my head down', 'doing nothing at all', 'banging my door shut', 'smoking joints', 'just sitting back and getting on with it', 'watching soaps' 'sitting in my cell doing nothing', 'chilling', and 'sleeping'. Everyday life is like the film *Groundhog Day*, a repetitive cycle of mindless, routine activity which recurs because 'there's nothing else to do'.

Although they described prison as a small world, a place in which 'everyone knows everybody else', 'full of the same faces, over and over again', 'like a big family', most of the participants made it clear that there is a distinct lack of camaraderie or intimacy in prison.

In fact, other prisoners were described mostly in derogatory terms, as 'stupid, all they know is how to act on their emotions' or 'like leeches, people that are going to latch onto you'. For this reason prisons have been labelled places of 'de-communication' (Gallo and Ruggiero 1991), where, given the opportunity, prisoners spend the majority of time 'banged up' sleeping, or seeking 'escape into the fantasy life of television' (Johnson 2005: 256). Most importantly, prisoners avoid talking about themselves, their problems, children and families, or their hopes and plans for the future. Showing a personal or vulnerable side is risky, because other prisoners will 'think you're moaning and you can't do your bird', or 'start thinking they can come and disrespect you'. Adusa explained:

> If you find someone you can relate to, someone you can talk to, and someone who will become your friend, not for what you've got, it's a good thing to have. Someone you can express your problems to. But it's impossible in these sorts of places.

Of course, an everyday relationship prisoners are unable to avoid, is that with prison officers, the largest group of employees in any prison establishment. Although it is a condition of their employment that prison officers contribute to rehabilitative programmes and services, their main priority is to ensure that security is maintained, and prisoners abide by the rules and routines of the prison regime (Liebling and Price 2001). Unsurprisingly, this fundamentally affects how they relate to prisoners. Given the impersonal and authoritative atmosphere of prison (Scraton *et al.* 1991), as well as the way 'the imprisoned criminal [is] incessantly examined, observed and judged' (Duguid 2000: 57), staff–prisoner relationships for the most part are impersonal, cold and mechanical. Some prison officers are guided by a sense of vocation and grow frustrated at the inability to develop the role, and respond genuinely and creatively to prisoners, owing to pressures of overcrowding and staff shortages. However, in much the same way that prisoners are affected by imprisonment, prison officers also internalise the norms of the closed environment they spend time in every day. As a consequence, many become inured to the job, pragmatic, disciplinarian, cold and emotionless (Arnold 2005).

A few of the participants considered it to be in their best interests to maintain civil relationships with staff. Indeed, Nige conceded that he had grown to like some of the officers: 'I've never had a problem with any of them. They respect me, I'll respect them. I make jokes with them and they have a little joke with me.' However, the opinions expressed by most were perfunctory at best, downright hostile at worst. Prison officers were reified as screws who 'just want an easy life', or 'they're just in the job to annoy people'. Tim thought that prison officers abuse their position by 'getting in my face and doing certain things to me. Whereas outside they might check their actions, in here they haven't got that fear.' And Tanveer expressed frustration at the way he was regularly spoken to by staff:

> They have a nasty, general attitude towards inmates, just horrible. Being spoken to rudely, arrogantly, abusive, being shouted at for no reason, being ordered for no reason. And then you see they actually like being that way. Obviously there are a few officers who are just genuine, normal, straight-going people who are there doing their job and fair enough. But the majority of officers, I don't know, are on some power trip or whatever, you know giving commands. They actually enjoy it.

However, despite the resentment they felt, whereas once they might have responded to staff with violence and anger, the longer the participants spent in prison, the more they had come to realise it was futile to resist its authority and regimentation. As Jimmy explained, 'The system always wins no matter what you do, shit your cell up, or go against the screws; you will not win, so you go with the flow.' To cope, it is best to 'clam up', accept that 'you no longer have any control', and 'abide by the rules'. And although this is 'not an easy thing to do', it is necessary because 'sometimes you got to look at the bigger picture'. Mika explained that he had survived each of his previous 25 prison sentences by assuming the role of a subordinate:

> For me, personally, I adopt very much an army private role. To me this is just... we're just on a battlefield here, so I feel like I'm in the army, you know what I mean, I got to follow me orders.

To an extent, this suggests a tactical response (de Certeau 1984) to imprisonment, a deliberate manoeuvre 'born of inertia', which instead of being simply oppositional, 'is both a preservative and a creation of something new: rather than presenting the inverse of power, it offers a different and pluralized account of powers' (Highmore 2002: 152–3). Barry contrasted the way he tended to conform as a prisoner to the freedom of being able to do just as he pleased outside:

I don't toe the line out there. Society cannot tell me what to do. In here there's rules and regulations, and I don't like them taking days off me, so I become a model prisoner. I don't get nicked or nothing. But out there, there's no chains, there's nothing to hold me back. So I tend to push them boundaries. I tend to push 'em, doing what I want, when I want, how I want.

For some, the deliberate withdrawal to an interior state of being applied as much to family and friends outside prison as it did to prisoners and staff inside. Surviving intact involved severing all links with the external world, and leading a new life based solely on the immediate day-to-day circumstances (Irwin 1970). It is sometimes asserted that the 'depth of imprisonment' (Downes 1988) renders prisoners uncertain and powerless to such an extent they often lose interest in previous or future lives. However, rather than a conditioned or thoughtless response, the participants who expressed an unwillingness to engage with families and friends outside insisted this was a conscious, premeditated decision they could justify and were prepared to explain. It is often asserted that strong family relationships encourage prisoners to desist, because of the practical support they provide (Ditchfield 1994); for instance, temporary or permanent accommodation immediately after release and help in finding employment (Woolf and Tumim 1991). However, as we have seen, family life does not have a single, fixed meaning which is necessarily positive or supportive. Because the family backgrounds of offenders are often disrupted, unstable and abusive (Walmsley *et al.* 1992), it is necessary 'to take account of the nature of power and its distribution in these micro situations' (Sim 1994: 109), and 'identify which family relationships are likely to be (if possible mutually) supportive and beneficial' (Smith 1995: 65).

As revealed in the previous chapter, many of the participants had experienced the family home as a constraining and abusive place they had to escape from. Family relationships had broken down a long time ago and were now irreparable. Others, who had been brought up in families they described as supportive and caring, had become separated from parents, wives, partners and children as a consequence of increasingly lengthy spells in prison. Accepting this as an inevitable consequence of his criminal behaviour, Sammy described how, on finding out he had been imprisoned for the first time, his parents:

were disgusted, disowned me, yeh, really. I was away six months and they didn't come and visit me at all to punish me. I mean my mum and dad have always been workers. I don't think my dad's ever been arrested, and I don't think my mum has ever been arrested, and for me to do something like that, it put the cat among the pigeons, and they didn't like it.

And Peter explained that his father

always said to me if you go to prison, I'll never visit you, which I don't blame him really. If you've spent your whole life being a straight guy, you know what I mean, it's to keep away from places like this. And it's different if I was in here for something I didn't do and he felt sorry for me, you know, but he doesn't feel sorry. He feels sorry for me to the extent where, you know, maybe drugs have influenced me and that, but it's all my own doing at the end of the day.

For others, the idea of maintaining contact with family members was anathema. Having chosen to embrace criminality as a way of life, they felt that it was important to take the consequences. Indeed, it was a sign of weakness 'to think that I come to gaol crying mummy and daddy'. For Joshua, coping with imprisonment without the support of family and friends had become a matter of principle:

My last three-year sentence I done it without contacting a single person, without even getting a single penny sent into me, do you understand? I did that all by myself, working in the prison, doing all the stuff that I had to do. So, it was like I done it on my own back. And I know I can do it again here. I will just lock off all outside contact with my family, parents and all that stuff, not contact a single person and just get on with it. That's what I'm here to do. I put myself here. My mum and dad never put me here, my friends never put me here, I put myself here, you get me?

Although family ties are commonly recognised as a crucial factor in promoting prisoner resettlement (SEU 2002; Niven and Stewart 2005), the complexity of the relationships involved is often discounted or ignored by policymakers and practitioners on the assumption that 'we know what we mean by family ties in this context' (Smith 1995:

64). The complexities of feeling some of the participants expressed towards their birth families, as well as their own families, suggests that this is misguided. Some had no intention of maintaining contact with their children through a basic lack of care and responsibility. Others claimed to have been prevented from seeing their children by former wives, girlfriends, and 'baby mothers'. Reflecting previous research which has found that many offenders marry, or form relationships with, women who are also offenders (West 1982), a few explained that their former wives or girlfriends were in prison and criminals themselves, or had serious drug problems and so were likely to encourage them to reoffend after release. Rick was of the opinion that 'girls are like that, they don't want you in prison, but when the money's there they like it.' Others maintained contact with their partners and children but strictly on their own terms. While they wrote and received letters and made telephone calls, they were reluctant to accept visits. There were a number of reasons for this. Eric explained that he would see his family only when he had gained the strength to give up drugs, and was 'confident that I will do it this time before I contact them because I've fucked up so many times in the past'. Whereas Maurice was mindful that prison visits were stressful for his parents, explaining that 'my mum's ill and my dad's diabetic, and I don't want to put them through all this in their old age'. Others were embarrassed their children would see them 'poorly dressed', 'looking unhealthy', 'looking all rough', 'depressed and subdued', or 'with bruises from fighting'. Billy would not talk to his children because 'they're obviously going to ask where am I, and all that rubbish.' John was worried his younger brother might 'see prison life as a good life, and follow in my footsteps'. And Barry had severed all contact with his children and baby mothers. He explained why:

> Relationships with my children, that will come later in my life, when I've got myself sorted, when they know that I'm stable and not going to go back into gaol, or relapse back into drugs. It's not fair on them. At the moment they've got a good life and I don't want to rock it, and I don't think they need that unstableness in their life. Kids are very impressionable, aren't they? and it can fuck 'em up psychologically, and I'm not the person to do that.

Drugs and crime

On the question of what prisoners talk about, the two topics of conversation mentioned most frequently were the lowest common denominator ones: drugs and crime. For many, crime is the great leveller, the reason they are in prison. Every day, drugs, alcohol and cigarettes, are in constant demand. Tanveer, who was being held on a 'drug-free wing', and claimed not to take drugs, complained:

> There's probably more drugs on this wing than any other wing [laughs loudly]… so obviously I keep away from the majority of people. It's disgusting to have, every second, someone ask you, 'Have you got any burn, or got any Rizla?' It's just, 'Keep away from me, I don't want anything to do with you.'

All of the participants explained that drugs were freely available in every prison they had been to (Ruggiero 1995). As tranquillisers and anaesthetics (Matthews 2009: 39), taken to relieve the stress and boredom of everyday life (Turnbull *et al.* 1994), drugs helped to 'keep me calm and pass the time', and 'block out the outside world and help me to sleep'. Having experimented with 'recreational drugs' in the past, a few described how the exposure to all kinds of drugs in prison influenced them eventually to become injecting drug users (Gore *et al.* 1995). Much of this was to do with the pervasive drug culture in prisons. For example, Stuart, had learnt how 'to wash up cocaine and turn it into crack, how to chase the dragon, what speedballs are. All the jargon that goes along with drug taking became a part of my vocabulary.' Barry, on the other hand, blamed the way drugs were policed in prison for the escalation in his drug use, in particular the introduction of mandatory drug testing:

> You can always get your hands on drugs. All forms of it. The screws they used to turn a blind eye to drinking and puffing, and as soon as they brought out that piss test, people then turned round to heroin because it's only in your system for three days, whereas puff is 28 days. The first time I started taking heroin was when I was about 25, pretty late in life, and that was down to these piss tests. You know I got a positive for puff, so I'm thinking, fuck this I'll have a bit of this, and since then I have been off the scales.

The idea that imprisonment functions as a 'school for criminal learning', or 'university of crime', has been cited as its major failure since the early seventeenth century (Sharpe 1990). It remains an enduring assumption that through a process of collective interaction, socialisation and peer group influence, prisoners mutually reinforce criminal behaviour, resulting in 'the maintenance of delinquency, the encouragement of recidivism, the transformation of the occasional offender into a habitual delinquent, the organisation of a closed milieu of delinquency' (Foucault 1977: 272). Given the lack of other things to do, Maurice explained that talking to your cellmate was unavoidable, and crime an inevitable topic of conversation:

> You sit in a cell for 23 hours every day yeh, banged up every day with a geezer. What are you going to be talking about? He's going to tell you about his ideas of how he does things, and I'm going to tell him my ideas.

Most of the participants admitted that they had become more able and skilled criminals as a consequence of going to prison. They had learnt 'how to do burglaries, how to deal with the alarms, whereas before I was just booting the door down'; how 'not to leave prints, the less you move around, the less you leave as evidence'; and how to 'jimmy locks open, and then I was in my element, you know'. Prison also provided contacts and associates 'ready to aid and abet any future criminal act' (Foucault 1977: 267); for example, drug-dealing networks (Ruggiero and South 1995), and gangs and crews to engage in street and armed robbery (Little 1990). Theo recounted how he regularly committed street crime with friends and associates from 'Feltham, yeh, 'cause we used to keep contact with each other, and they started to visit me in the hostel, and we used to go out at night and take cars and do robberies, whatever.' Robert, who described himself as a 'big guy', claimed to be in constant demand:

> I am a bouncer, they use me for my size I suppose to, urm… hurt people and commit robberies and stuff like that. Associating with a lot of criminals in prison, you tend to get offers. If you want to get involved and make money, the kind of money they're making, which they say you can basically, they'll call me and contact me when you get out, whatever. And you're very tempted.

Prison as home

All of this indicates that the daily rhythm and intensity of social relations in prison is highly criminogenic. A main effect of imprisonment is to teach and reinforce antisocial norms and behaviour patterns, which lead to reoffending because they revolve around drugs and the sharing of criminal knowledge and expertise. However, while this suggests that prisons function primarily as 'schools of crime' (Maruna and Toch 2005: 152), there is also evidence they function as homes, with similar consequences. In Chapter 5, the importance of the home was highlighted as a place in which people experience a sense of rootedness and connection – a familiar place where 'one is attached by myriad habits of thought and behavior – culturally acquired, of course, yet in time they become so intimately woven into everyday existence that they seem primordial and the essence of one's being' (Tuan 1998: 7). This is not necessarily a conscious experience, a product of 'discursive consciousness' (Giddens 1984); it is also that 'home place and quotidian life *feel* real' (Tuan 1977: 145; my emphasis). In a study of social order in prison, Sparks *et al.* (1996) have suggested that prison can engender a sense of lived, unobtrusive 'ontological security', in that the routine nature of everyday life serves to instil 'trust in the reliability and durability of the life-world' (*ibid.*: 75). They go on to argue that:

> All this is of course most likely to happen (1) when the 'locale' in question is fairly small, and bounded, and (2) when many of those spending time in the locale have been there (or been back and forth from there) for an extended period, so that they know intimately aspects of the history, traditions, and culture of the place, and significant events which, in the past, have helped to shape the way that social life is now lived there. (*ibid.*: 77)

The view that imprisonment acts as a 'cognitive and emotive anchor' (Giddens 1991: 36) to ground feelings of ontological security was substantiated by some of the participants, who admitted they had come to treat prison as a place of refuge, where they could withdraw, recharge and take stock of things. Compared to the chaos, randomness and poverty of their lives outside, prison provided respite, routine, regularity, 'a lighter load'. Jimmy described the lack of pressure he felt in prison:

You just wake up in the morning. The only thing I have to do to make sure I'm all right is I've got a smoke and what's that? I ain't got no bills, no responsibilities, no worries for paying rent, buying food, supporting the kids. Out there you got to make sure you got money for petrol for your car. You got to make sure you got electric, gas, all them things.

However, although Jimmy was content to come to prison, and 'get my nut down, get away from my girl, get away from the kids [laughs], get my bearings, and do my bird, as they say', he was also bored and frustrated: 'That's the only thing about prison, boring. Wouldn't be so bad if there was work, or there was things on offer all the time.' While this suggests a degree of critical scrutiny and appraisal of the prison experience, Declan, on the other hand, admitted that he had come to accept, even relish, the inactivity and routine. Considering his cell to be 'just like home... my own little bedsit', he described a typical day in his life:

> I get up at half eight; I have a wash; I go to education from nine o'clock; ten o'clock I have a cigarette break; I'm back here on the wing at eleven; have my food at half past eleven; get banged up until two, so I have a little nap until two; back in education at two o'clock; cigarette break at three outside; finished at four; come back, have a shower; then I have my dinner; close my door; and then I chill out for the night; I watch *The Weakest Link*, I watch *The Simpsons*, and I watch the programmes as the nights go on and the weeks fly by [laughs]. So I'm afraid I'm beginning to like it.

This was not a view shared by all of the participants, however. Acutely aware of the ameliorating effect of imprisonment – its power to control and reprogram prisoners and render them helpless (Clemmer 1940) – some scoffed at those, like Declan, who treated prison as somewhere 'they get their meal, somewhere to sleep, you know warmth basically, three meals a day'. Prison was 'nothing', 'easy' and 'relaxed', but it was also 'mind numbing', 'like a trap getting into the system'. They missed their freedom, girlfriends, children, someone to talk to. Prisoners who had become complacent and comfortable, particularly those who appeared to actively enjoy coming back to prison, 'to see old friends', were dismissed as 'pathetic', 'depressing', 'upsetting', and having 'nothing in their lives'. Tim explained:

I'll tell you a lot of prisoners when they come back... I've seen people since I've been on this sentence go and come back, and they come back happy. When they see you, it's, 'Ah, how you doing?' and all that, like they're meeting old friends. I call them returnees. I don't talk to them, it upsets me.

Not that this caused Tim to consider the consequences of continuing to engage in crime and the likelihood of coming back to prison. Prison was boring, uneventful, and frustrating, but the prospect of returning did not act as a significant restraint on his behaviour after release. He went on to explain the reason for its lack of deterrent effect:

Like in certain situations that might stop me acting on impulse. You think, 'Ah, I could go to prison', but when you've been to prison you're like... I don't know, you don't want to come back, but there's no apprehension about coming back. Obviously, you'll be annoyed and you'll miss everything, but it's like nothing really.

Peter was more disparaging:

I can think of various people, particularly now, that seem to not give a shit. They literally do not give a fuck. They run around this place like it's a fucking holiday camp, like Butlins, yeh. Doing this and doing that, and it's fucking like they think it's great or something. It makes me laugh.

It is of note that some of the participants were critical of improvements made to prison conditions and regimes in recent years, which they thought had made prison 'too easy', 'no big deal', 'not like prison at all'. Indeed, Keifer claimed that compared to the domestic pressures they faced outside, prison had become so comfortable for some offenders that they now sometimes committed crimes with the specific intention of being rearrested and re-imprisoned:

You haven't got the pressures that you've got on the outside in prison. You haven't got to worry about where you're going to live, what you're going to eat, what time you're going to get up, how you're going to get through the day. I think gaol's easy. It is now, it's easy. I mean I know certain people that like coming to gaol. They like it 'cause they've got no responsibilities whatsoever in gaol. You got no worries, you're in gaol, 'don't stress me, I'm in gaol, leave me alone'. I've seen people go out deliberately to do crime to get caught. They've been on the out and it's coming close to Christmas. I know it's mad, but I've seen it.

Nige described the contents of a typical prison cell:

You can probably get drugs on this wing more easy and quicker than you can outside. It's not like prison. Prison should be restrictive, but it's like people make drink in here. People make hooch, and then they're sitting there with a spliff. You've got a stereo, a radio, a TV, DVDs, your kettle, tea bags, sugar, your toaster, blankets for your bed, curtains and stuff like that... with a fucking glass of hooch, TV, radio on. You're just sitting in your bedroom really, ain't you?

Joshua described what he thought were the wider social implications of holding prisoners in conditions of relative comfort:

Kids of 11 and 12 are saying they want to go to gaol. I know, I've had kids come and tell me that for a fact. It's easier, they do what they want. You know it's better than living at home with their mums, so they say. Where they get that idea from I do not know, but obviously it's someone who has gone into prison and given them that info. The more easy you make it for people to commit crime by making the prisons more relaxed and, you know, more futuristic, if that's the word, the more people are going to come in.

For some readers, this will no doubt call into question whether recent improvements to prison standards and conditions, and also the adherence to a rights-based culture in prisons, contravene the principle of less eligibility, whereby, in order to exert a deterrent effect on individual and public behaviour, conditions in prison must be worse than those experienced by the poorest law-abiding person outside. Yet, just how bad do prison conditions have to become to achieve this? And is it necessary to measure one person's poverty, misery and degradation against another's to find out? Are the opinions expressed above a critical reflection on the state of prisons, or on the conditions some sections of society must endure outside? These are important questions, because they impact not only on the utilitarian function of imprisonment to deter offenders, but also its function to reform them. Prisoner rehabilitation is discussed below in the concluding section to this chapter.

'A law-abiding and useful life'

How does this square with the statement of purpose of HM Prison Service, 'to [keep] in custody those committed by the courts ... and to help prisoners lead law-abiding and useful lives in custody and after release'? Neither the propensity of some prisoners to remain pragmatically compliant while resisting adjustment and retaining self-belief, nor the inclination of others to savour passively the respite prison affords from the harsh realities of life outside is likely to disturb the well-documented inevitability that many offenders reoffend after release. It is increasingly accepted that imprisonment is not experienced in the same way, but because strategies of coping and adaptation remain understated and largely unchallenged, they remain little understood. Imprisonment is an *in camera* experience. Some prisoners find it unnatural and frustrating, others comforting and secure; but the resigned attitude most present to their captors is not predictive of behaviour that will be carried over into the world outside after release (Matthews 2009). It is an appearance, an act and therefore a temporary thing. Irrespective of whether the effects of imprisonment are negligible (Zamble and Porporino 1988), or inculcate a sense of dependency (Irwin and Owen 2005), they tend to perpetuate criminal behaviour.

A major reason for this is that the particularity of prison militates against the possibility that prisoners will personally re-evaluate social values, and appraise future prospects (Duguid 2000). According to some academic criminologists (see Feeley and Simon 1992; Garland 2001), the impersonality of prison life has become more deeply embedded in recent years owing to the introduction of control measures which are less to do with 'normalising' than 'warehousing' prisoners. For instance, Jewkes (2002) has argued that the disconnection with 'real life' outside prison has become more distinct since the introduction of in-cell television. With little or no encouragement to reflect on past, present or future life, the 'dead time' of television provides prisoners with a distorted view of the real world, which they consume in 'a mildly comatose state' (Johnson 2005: 265). As Lefebvre (2008 [1961]: 76) has observed generally, television introduces 'non-participation and receptive passivity'; it rolls over the viewer 'like a succession of waves, churned out and repeated and already indistinguishable by the simple fact that they are pure spectacle: they are overpowering, they are hypnotic.' Thus, everyday life becomes 'the non-place ... of desire, the place where desire dies of satisfaction' (Lefebvre 1984 [1968]: 118). Keifer explained the deleterious effect of television in prison. Whereas previously he had been inclined to read, 'nowadays I think I've been to the library twice. I just watch a load of crap on TV.' Television has been introduced to manage and regulate movement in prison. Moreover, as with other ameliorative perks, it is granted or denied depending on standards of conduct and behaviour. However, while it provides a ready-made and powerful control mechanism, the widespread acceptance of television as a benign influence on prisoner conduct has diminished the importance of more constructive activities such as offender-based programmes or group activities. For example, earlier lock-up times have been introduced, and association and educational opportunities curtailed (Jewkes 2002).

Nevertheless, while penal strategies of social integration and inclusion may have 'become increasingly irrelevant to policy makers', and as a consequence prison conditions and regimes have prioritised regulatory systems of supervision and control, remedial work in prison 'has not disappeared or been scientifically discredited' (Garland 2001: 137). Prisons continue to provide resources and services which aim to rehabilitate prisoners and prepare them for release. They provide work, education and training; through case management, they address individual factors linked to criminal behaviour, such as thinking skills and anger management; they encourage the maintenance of family relationships; and they help prisoners to overcome various health, drug and alcohol, finance, benefit and debt problems. A few of the participants were willing to receive such help. They expressed misgivings about continuing to commit crime (Cusson and Pinsonneault 1986), which they had experienced before only to see them evaporate soon after release. Prison afforded time to think about time wasted, family and friends. For some, it was an opportunity to attend drug rehabilitation and get healthy. However, the usual, everyday priorities soon regained precedence once they had returned home. To put an end to this cycle of behaviour, Peter stressed the importance of receiving 'professional help because I can't do it on my own. That's very apparent to me now, you know.' Keifer also had come to realise that 'I'm a bit arrogant. I thought I could do it on my own, and I can't.'

Institutionally, prisons face considerable barriers to providing rehabilitation and reintegration services on a consistent and regular basis. A lack of constructive regime activity is a feature of all prisons but is most commonly associated with local establishments. Owing to the high turnover of prisoners on remand and awaiting trial or transfer, local prisons lack both space and the resources to provide constructive and purposeful activities for prisoners to engage in (Cavadino and Dignan 1997). In comparison, training prisons tend to be protected from overcrowding. They are also better resourced to provide regime activities customised to meet the specific needs of the category of prisoners in their charge (*ibid.*). However, for the most part, this distinction was lost on many of the participants. They readily listed the names of different prisons they had been held in and also noted obvious distinguishing features about them such as the security category, age and architecture. Furthermore, they noted that, whereas local London prisons were 'full of familiar faces', training prisons in rural areas of England and Wales were anonymous places, 'out in the country somewhere', 'full of people from Norwich and Newcastle and Manchester and all those far-out areas', 'with strange accents I couldn't understand'. But in terms of how they spent their time on a day-to-day basis, most agreed that 'prison is prison'; 'they're all the same – you do your bird and you get on with it.'

In important respects, the willingness of prisoners to use time productively is dependent on sentence length. Most of the participants serving long sentences explained why and how they intended to use their time in prison as productively as they could, in some cases to effect fundamental change in their lives. Dalmar, a lifer, had applied for a course in plumbing:

> I want to take it to the highest level. I've made up my mind that I can't be the same person when I come out of here, so it's a personal aim that I need to achieve myself, because I've promised my family that I will do something. I'm going to have to do something because I'm sitting in gaol for 14 years.

Stuart described how during a previous five-year sentence he had 'started to get my education':

> I was able to work on myself and work on the areas of my own personal development I felt were important to me. Whereas in all the previous sentences while I was doing this stuff, while I wanted to do this stuff on myself, either the facilities weren't available or security categorisations wasn't open to me, or you just didn't have the people with the openness of mind and the

power to pursue any sort of rehabilitative programmes, so it was always stuck within the prison walls.

In contrast, the participants serving short sentences were generally dismissive of rehabilitative activities and programmes. While some attended education and vocational training courses that they hoped would help them find work after release, others did so simply to fill in time. Education provided 'something to do', an opportunity 'to learn new things about how the world works'. Jimmy attended classes to 'get in the screws' good books, make it a little bit easier for me, make it not so behind the door all the time, get out so you can make a phone call'. Others still had decided that attending education and training was not worth the effort. Harvey had gained qualifications in catering, mechanics, painting and decorating, but these were irrelevant to his future plans and expectations. The money these jobs paid 'was not enough, so that's why I went back to what I was doing'. Robert expressed similar sentiments:

> I need to live, I need to be doing something, I've got a lot of ambition and I've got a lot of responsibilities. A nine to five, I don't know, I don't think it's going to get me where I want to be in life.

To some extent, the inappropriateness of much prison work and training for employment outside in new service, financial and knowledge-based markets has been recognised officially. For instance, a review of 'what works' in correctional services recently concluded that 'the emerging evidence of basic skills training in prison suggests that these courses can improve prisoners' skills but the extent to which these can be improved sufficiently to have a positive impact on employment prospects by prison training alone is still in doubt' (Harper and Chitty 2005: 78). Aware of the lack of good-quality and relevant training opportunities in prison, some of the participants had been persuaded that, if they were to support themselves and their families legitimately after release, it would be as a result of their own efforts. Paul explained:

> Prison can't rehabilitate you; you have to rehabilitate yourself because there's not enough courses that can help you. And the courses they do do are short-time, and they only do them sometimes to make their books look good. So I do things in prison to benefit myself, to make me feel good in myself.

And according to Liam:

> Coming to prison and coming out on the streets is hard. Trying
> to get a job today is hard, let alone knowing you got a criminal
> record. I'm talking from experience here. I have actually realised
> there is no one and no kind of establishment that is actually
> helping people like me. In this establishment, in Feltham, and
> in every other gaol there ain't no help for us. You got probation,
> but probation is there to monitor, maybe refer you here, refer you
> there. So right now I'm trying to use prison to my advantage.
> I'm using my time, I'm reflecting on life, I'm defining all my
> problems, I'm brainstorming, I'm evaluating the consequences.

As we saw in Chapter 1, research carried out by Maruna (2001: 147)
has suggested that criminal desistance stems in large part from the
internalisation by offenders of complete responsibility for overcoming
personal and social problems in their lives: 'whereas active offenders
… seemed to have little vision of what the future might hold,
desisting interviewees had a plan and were optimistic that they
could make it work.' Although none of the participants in this survey
could be classified as successful desisters, while some held negative,
pessimistic expectations of staying away from crime, others thought
the problems they faced were within their control and surmountable.
For example, Theo explained that staying away from crime 'is hard,
if I make it hard. You can get anything you want if you put your
mind to it. It will only be hard if I'm slack about it.' Harvey agreed:
'You have to see what happens, you don't know until you try. If you
have a go in life you'll succeed'. And according to Stuart, 'You might
need the breaks but you have to work for those breaks. You've got to
be in it to win it.' Paul was first convicted at the age of 15 and has
been to prison three times. Now at the age of 29 he wants to give up
crime. He explains:

> I want to be a person that's making a difference, putting
> something back. Everything I have done I have took away
> from. I've stolen from people, I've threatened people. I've been
> a victim myself, but other people have been a victim because
> of my crimes and stupidity, and I want to just gain something
> out of life and put something back on the table and say, 'Look,
> although I've always taken away, if I can do it, you can do it.'
> I'm 100 per cent positive about life now and I know in my heart
> that once I get out I won't be coming back to prison.

As Maruna (2001) has argued, such sentiments may indeed be crucial indications of the self-motivation necessary to act upon and maintain criminal desistance (see also Zamble and Quinsey 1997; Farrall and Calverley 2006). However, owing to a lack of meaningful engagement with prisoners on a personal level – for instance, as citizens who after release must attempt to re-engage and resettle in society (Farrant and Levenson 2002) – no attempt is made to determine how prepared they are to confront the problems they face and achieve legitimate and lasting reintegration.

There is little in the way of prison rehabilitative services which support narratives of change, enable prisoners to develop pro-social thinking and attitudes, build on opportunity, prepare for release, and plan for the future. It is not surprising, therefore, that, although some of the participants expressed confidence and a commitment to stay away from crime, on a practical level they were ill prepared to make the transition from criminal to law-abiding citizen. Indeed, some of them entertained wholly unrealistic expectations of what potentially they could achieve in the outside world through legitimate and legal means (Uggen et al. 2004). Previous experiences of release are recounted in the next chapter.

Chapter 7

'On the out': after-prison experiences

Introduction

This chapter assesses the experiences of persistent offenders in relation to how the meaning of previous place of residence changes, as they make the often repeated transition back and forth between prison and home, and the effect this has on reoffending and criminal desistance. As noted in Chapter 1, a key focus of attention in recent policy approaches to reduce reoffending has been the personal and social circumstances of former prisoners, and practical measures taken to address these (SEU 2002; Petersilia 2003). Guided by this, the chapter begins by assessing the meanings, motivations and desires of first-time and short-term prisoners with respect to the places they return to, as compared to prisoners who have served repeat and longer prison sentences. It then considers the extent to which the personal and social needs of ex-prisoners are place specific. This leads to a brief discussion of resettlement policy and practice, which is explored in much greater detail in the Chapter 8.

Returning home

It is commonly assumed that in the days leading up to release many prisoners become anxious about how they are going to survive in the outside world. According to Goffman (1961: 71), they are daunted by the prospect of having to move 'from the top of a small world to the bottom of a large one'. However, this is a transitory feeling; the impact of imprisonment on them is not long-lasting. The behavioural adaptations they have made in prison tend to dissipate on release, 'partly because of the availability of secondary adjustments, the presence of counter-mores, and the tendency for inmates to combine all strategies and play it cool' (*ibid.*: 69–70). This observation requires some qualification. As we have seen throughout this book, people identify most intimately and unself-consciously with places they are exposed to for a significant period of time (Relph 1976). It follows that prisoners who serve long sentences or have been to prison repeatedly are likely to experience its effects more profoundly than short-term or first-time prisoners. For instance, they may suffer 'more subtle, hidden kinds of psychological and emotional disability' (Jamieson and Grounds 2005: 55), depression, anxiety, fear, and rejection (Liebling 1999), as well as various forms of diagnosable post-traumatic stress disorder (Liebling and Maruna 2005). More generally, they may also have a tendency to become passive and reliant on staff for the distribution of various benefits and privileges, or grow accustomed to confrontation and violence. As a consequence, 'the destructive manifestations are not left behind the walls when the prisoner is released but often become part of his "taken for granted" world on the outside' (Sim 1994: 103).

In contrast, most short-term prisoners, because they 'float through their sentences with little damage to their persons or impact on prison society' (Irwin and Owen 2005: 115), are released from prison relatively unscathed. Having been imprisoned for the first time at a relatively early age, most of the participants returned home after serving a short, first prison sentence bitter and resentful towards conventional society (Irwin 1970). Angry at being caught and unwilling to acknowledge the legitimacy of the punishment they had received (Scheff and Retzinger 1991), they soon returned to crime. Rather than suffer shame (Braithwaite 1989) at what they had done, they emerged defiant and proud to have survived prison intact. Indeed, some of them felt 'big headed', 'like my virginity had been broken', and with 'no care for people that was not in my circle'. Rick described how on release he immediately re-established contact with former friends and resumed the criminal activities he had engaged in previously:

You're running before you hit the pavement. When you come out you're supposed to sit back for a few months, get your head together, get a plan, what you're going to do, this, that and the other. But I didn't have that plan, I just came out. Where's my friends? Where's the girls? And you know, that was it. I was just all over the place and back into crime.

It has been suggested that in some high-crime communities going to prison has become accepted by many young people today as unproblematic, a fact of life, even a 'rite of passage' (Houchin 2005: 25). Moreover, having gone to prison and demonstrated they are 'willing and even inclined to live life in a challenge' (Goffman 1967: 182), young offenders are often welcomed home and treated with respect by friends and associates. Maurice remembered being released from Feltham after his first prison sentence:

> It was an experience because you know it was like a bit of a street thing. I'm not even lying because everyone that'd been to Feltham was like 'Right, he's been to Feltham' at the time. Now it's uncool to go to prison, a waste of time. But at that time, it kind of gave you a bit of street cred. This is the truth. It made me feel good. In Tottenham, if you'd been to prison before, like even just for a week, you got a bit of respect.

And Mika explained how going to prison enhanced his reputation within the local neighbourhood:

> Prison is a place where people feel sorry for you. They know the pain you're going to go through. But if you go in and come out and can still hold your head high and walk straight with a spring in your step, they will think you had to be a hard man to survive it. So your hard man reputation, if you haven't got one already, it's enhanced. And women tend to throw themselves at men that's been in prison. They do, women have shown a lot more interest in me.

Unsurprisingly, this further embedded the participants within close-knit social networks comprised of other criminal peers and ex-prisoners (Moore 1996). As a consequence, their criminal activity escalated. Experiencing prison for the first time made some of them feel 'like I'd been down the stream', 'more advanced in what I was doing', 'a criminal properly now'. They 'got deeper into crime', 'started doing bigger and better things', 'really robbing hard'. Going to prison reinforced the impression that 'crime is good, and if you do it properly, you can earn your money'. Joshua had 'started doing all kinds of things, anything and everything. If it was a good enough plan, and I thought we'd get away with it, I'd go and do it'.

Ultimately, of course, for some the tendency to escalate criminal activity inevitably results in rearrest, reconviction and re-imprisonment. As they grew older and the number and length of the prison sentences they received increased, wearing previous experiences of imprisonment as something to be proud of, a 'badge of honour', lost its appeal. Most began to view time spent in prison in a far more negative light than they had done previously as young offenders. Indeed, the idea that going to prison is somehow creditable they now considered puerile and childish. Barry admitted:

> I was shy and I was silly. I was young and I was very silly. And I used to think I was bad and it made you feel good, and people would see you and they would have a bit of respect for you. He's done a bit of bird and that. It had an impact on a time in my life when I was very impressionable.

In this respect, the narrative accounts of the participants provide evidence of the role of ageing (Gottfredson and Hirschi 1990) combined with rational choice (Clarke and Cornish 1985) in the criminal desistance process. As they grew older, nearly all of them admitted to questioning the appeal of crime and pondering the trouble and upset it had caused. Even those who fully intended to return to crime cited reasons for wanting to give up. For instance, they needed to support their families, see girls and get off drugs. They were also tired of being harassed by the police, bored with prison and fearful that sentences would get longer. Others had come to accept that the lifestyle they had constructed for themselves was a sham, short-lived and situational. For example, Mika realised his dream of becoming a successful gangster was exactly that, 'a dream which only happens in cartoons and films':

> In my original gangster plan I'd have already retired a couple of years ago. In my original plan I was already a 25-year-old millionaire on a yacht in the middle of the West Indies, surrounded by women. Mr T was jealous. You know what I'm saying, it hasn't worked.

Such sentiments are not uncommon; many offenders profess a desire to abandon crime while in prison (Burnett 1992). This leads to the question, why is the path to eventual desistance so often marked by false starts and unfulfilled intentions? In response, Maruna (2001: 23) has observed simply that, 'deciding to desist and actually desisting are two very different things.' The participants offered a variety of explanations for lapsing back into crime. Some admitted the decision to give up crime was lightly made. For the same reasons they had started to offend, they shrugged off the propensity to reoffend as an inevitable consequence of enjoying the party lifestyle (Shover 1996) and, having 'champagne tastes'. For others, returning to crime was a pragmatic decision, a means to an end, 'the only way I know how to get money', 'the only thing I can do'. In comparison to the thrill seeking they had engaged in when younger, crime was now an instrumental solution to having no money, a simple matter of survival. Joshua described how, after prison, he lived

> with my baby mother and two daughters in bed-and-breakfast hotels. Whenever I was strapped for money, I would commit burglary. There was no rush and it was not enjoyable. It was strictly a money thing. You know, it was not fun knowing that you have to go into someone's house and take their goods to make money for yourself.

As noted in Chapter 1, Maruna (2001: 121) has argued that in order to successfully desist, ex-prisoners must learn new motivations and patterns of behaviour that provide 'the same sense of empowerment and potency they were seeking (unsuccessfully) through criminal behavior'. Ex-prisoners turn away from crime for good only when they establish a permanent non-criminal identity able to control a range of personal and social problems that await them after release. Therefore, offender reintegration should concentrate on supporting ex-prisoners to construct new life histories for themselves which engender a sense of personal agency and self-worth through legitimate rather than criminal means. Despite the shared expressions of regret, most of the participants appeared not to have made any progress towards changing in this way. A tendency to justify lapsing back into crime given the complexity of the problems they faced was evident in most of the testimonies. They gave no indication that it would be possible to alter and overcome various structural, social and personal problems they felt constrained them after release. These included 'drug addiction', 'being broke', 'the responsibility of looking after my children', 'worries about where I'm going to live', 'trying to get a job', 'lack of education', 'no training', 'the stigma of a prison record', 'getting dragged back into the areas where I've been getting into trouble', 'hanging around with the same old people', and being 'a known geezer'. Feeling that the problems he faced back home were unsolvable and therefore 'condemned' him to lead a life of crime, Sean explained:

> I always go back home because that's where my people are. That's where everyone loves me. That's where I'll probably always go back to. It will always claw me back somehow. That's what I always say. It will always claw me back, and it will always be my downfall.

The sense of resignation, hopelessness and insecurity expressed in this case returns us to the dichotomy of structure and agency outlined in Chapter 1. As future offending is influenced by offenders' thinking and attitudes, as much as by social circumstance (Zamble and Quinsey 1997), criminal desistance is a process that involves offenders actively developing the human capital necessary to overcome structural and social difficulties they face (Maruna 2001). However, while it may be true that, in comparison to habitual criminals, offenders who successfully give up crime are often disdainful of the notion that behavioural change is not possible in certain environmental situations (*ibid.*: 153), this cannot be taken to be a refutation of the fact that human agency is socially structured. Individuals are never wholly determined to act according to external constraints, but the capacity to decide consciously and intentionally upon new courses of action is always shaped by the social worlds they inhabit. As argued in Chapter 4, the work of Giddens, Bourdieu, de Certeau and Lefebvre offers useful theoretical insights into the ways this dialectical relationship plays out. Given that the career paths of many persistent offenders tend to be structured around prison and certain socially deprived urban neighbourhoods, to a significant extent their life-course experiences, and the attitudes, beliefs and actions they engender, are situationally specific. As MacLeod (1995: 255) has observed in relation to street gangs that operate in certain low-income neighbourhoods in the United States, in everyday circumstances of social and spatial inequality, 'social structures reach into the minds and even the hearts of individuals to shape their attitudes, motivations, and worldviews.'

So, while a pessimistic frame of mind may be commonly associated with habitual offending, the practical problems ex-prisoners face on returning home act as significant barriers to successful re-entry into society (Petersilia 2003). A crucial time, of course, is the period immediately after release, when all ex-prisoners must make arrangements for their well-being and security. With insufficient money to survive more than a few days, many have no financial support for the sometimes lengthy periods of time it can take to arrange benefits and secure housing (SEU 2002). Those that on returning home find family life has deteriorated, often because of a failure on their part to contribute financially to the upbringing of their children (Rose and Clear 1998), are likely to be reliant on social services for support with housing and employment. As agencies which address structural and social impediments to offender reintegration are in short supply in many deprived urban communities (Petersilia 2003), ex-prisoners frequently have no option but to live in whatever temporary accommodation they can find to avoid becoming homeless. Then, if they are to desist successfully from crime over the long term, they must develop personal resources and the social capital necessary to achieve full civic participation as law-abiding citizens (Uggen *et al.* 2004). This includes avoiding previous criminogenic influences such as delinquent peer networks and finding a permanent job (Caspi and Moffitt 1995).

Given the structural uncertainties the participants faced after release, the personal and social circumstances of their lives were characterised on the whole by cheap and poor-quality housing, as well as social networks structured around informal, entrepreneurial activities – legitimate, borderline and illegitimate – which persist in some parts of London despite significant economic and social change within the capital as a whole (see Hobbs 1985 on East London, and Foster 1990 on South London). As we saw in Chapter 2, as a consequence of conflicting entanglements between financial and production sectors, private enterprise and public services, and the rapid hikes in property prices which have stemmed from these, London has become the most unequal region in the UK (Massey 2007). As a global city, London's identity is heterogeneous, but for Londoners without the means to actively participate in the negotiation of the places they live, poverty and insecurity remain contextual factors which significantly locate identity, choice, and action. This does not mean the urban poor are distinctive, set apart from broader society. As we saw in Chapter 3, identity is never homogeneous, predetermined by structural, spatial and social constraints. The residents of socially deprived communities 'demonstrate quite clearly ... the open-ended manner in which individuals and groups respond to structures of domination' (MacLeod 1995: 136). What it does mean, however, is that attention must be paid to the different responses of individuals and groups, and the physical and social contexts in which these are made. Foster (1997: 121) has written that

> popular perceptions of council housing – and the very poorest and most difficult-to-let estates in particular – as alienating environments in which there is little tenant interaction and support, are too simplistic. Instead of condemning such places as 'dreadful enclosures' we should look more closely at patterns of interaction between tenants in these contexts. We need to understand more about how they are characterised, in what ways they influence tenants' perceptions of the estates on which they live, and how different individuals and groups, who have had little or no choice in their housing allocation, manage to co-exist.

In assessing how the participants reacted to returning home after release from previous prison sentences, the following sections consider the extent to which the development of conscious choice and deliberate decision making leading to new pro-social identities and a permanently crime-free lifestyle is hindered by structural, spatial and social constraints, and the identities, choices and actions engendered by them.

Somewhere to live

Of the 30 participants included in the sample, five said they always returned to the parental home after prison, while another four lived with siblings, friends or girlfriends nearby, or some distance away from the areas they had grown up. Of the remainder, 13 said that they were of no fixed abode prior to coming to prison this time, three were sleeping rough, two lived in squats, two lived in a hotel, and one lived in bed-and-breakfast accommodation. All of them lived in various parts of London to which they mostly felt little affinity or sense of belonging. It is common to assert that securing adequate housing is one of the most important problems ex-prisoners must address on returning to the community. In the UK, around a third of prisoners lose their housing on being imprisoned and a further third have nowhere to live on release (SEU 2002). Although just over 70 per cent of prisoners attempt to arrange accommodation prior to release (Niven and Stewart 2005), many return to areas where social housing and support for the homeless is unreliable and in short supply. This is particularly the case in London where house prices and rents are the highest in the country, and half of the private accommodation available is in insecure, assured short-hold tenancies (GLA 2002). Unsurprisingly, because it exacerbates other barriers to integration such as accessing education and training or finding a job, insecure housing is often linked to reoffending and reconviction. It has been estimated that around two-thirds of ex-prisoners who live in unstable accommodation reoffend within 12 months of release (Joseph Rowntree Foundation 1996).

The participants described a variety of unstable and temporary housing outcomes experienced after prison. Barry 'found somewhere to sleep by living everywhere, friend's places, floors, settees', while Theo stayed with 'girls that keep me on a level when I ain't got nowhere to go'. Although most had children, only a small number returned to live with wives or partners owing to relationships having broken down irretrievably. Moreover, for the small number that did resume former relationships and return to the family home, incompatible lifestyles, mostly caused by a failure to assume responsibility for the problems they faced, meant that living arrangements could be precarious and suddenly terminated. Jimmy described how his behaviour had led to arguments with his wife and eventually to his becoming homeless:

> There's a situation when I go home. She wants me out the house. She sees it like I'm taking the piss. I was really 'cause I weren't giving her no money. I was spunking the money, going out raving, whatever. So I'll be indoors and, I don't know, something might go pear-shaped and she'll say, 'Get out of my house' and I'll just get up and go.

A hedonistic lifestyle, mostly involving high levels of drug taking, was often a decisive factor in whether the participants were able to maintain permanent, stable, living arrangements. For example, Barry explained he had been unable to return to the family home because of his heroin addiction:

> I wanted to go home, or as far as I was concerned I wanted to see my brother. I just needed a cuddle. You know, I'd been in gaol. I'd had no letters, no phone calls, no visits from anyone in my family because I chose not to have it. So then when I went back to my area, I phoned my brother and he turns round to me and he says, 'You what, I don't need that shit around me.' He's

talking about the heroin. And he says, 'Look, I'm not blowing you out, but I don't want that shit around me. I've got children, blah, blah, blah.' Well, I'm not hearing that, I'm hearing just rejection, 'fuck off', you know what I mean, and I just went bollocks and ended up a user. I relapsed, proper relapse.

Keifer had a different story to tell but with a similar outcome. Before coming to prison this time around, although remaining in close contact with his wife and six children, he had been living in a hostel a short distance from the family home. He explains why:

I was doing too much drugs and the place I was living with my kids I didn't want them to see me doing the amount of drugs I was doing so I made myself homeless so I could get somewhere else. I went to the homeless unit. They had to come and see you sleeping on the street at least twice, so I was actually sleeping on the street for about three months and then they got me a hostel.

On the corner

An argument commonly made by desistance authors is that, whereas habitual criminals often maintain intimate contact with delinquent peer groups, offenders who give up crime succeed primarily because they are able to relinquish them (Knight and West 1975; Caspi and Moffitt 1995; Graham and Bowling 1995; Warr 1998; Rex 1999). The reason for this, the pervasive influence of 'street corner society', is also well documented (Whyte 1943). In closely defined 'criminal areas', constant contact with antisocial networks is often unavoidable (Meisenhelder 1977). Unless ex-prisoners physically remove themselves by moving away from high-crime neighbourhoods, it is therefore often a requisite of criminal desistance to adopt 'social avoidance strategies' (Graham and Bowling 1995). For example, in order to maintain a pro-social and law abiding identity in the face of negative, criminogenic influences, it is necessary to 'negotiate "the system", to play by the code of the street with the street element and by the code of decency with others' (Anderson 2001: 150). Just as they have resorted in the past to creative criminal means to achieve respect and distinction in close-knit criminal communities, offenders must draw on these selfsame qualities to avoid crime in the future (*ibid*. 1998: 68). In this way, desisters negotiate the loss of 'credibility, props (deference), and, ultimately, protection' (*ibid.* 2001: 144) afforded by previous association with delinquent peers and establish a new life for themselves at variance with that of career offenders who live in close proximity to them. Substantiating the proposition that successful desistance is not dependent on moving out of local criminogenic neighbourhoods (Maruna 2001), Nige explained that since he had had a child his former friends and criminal associates had fundamentally changed how they reacted towards him:

> People got to know that I'm completely different now. So people respect that, even people that I've beat up in a school. They'll walk past me and speak to me, say, 'How's it going, is this your little boy?' I'll say, 'Yeh, "say Hello, Phillip"', and he says 'Hello', and people can respect that I've changed.

However, in contrast to this, it was common for most of the participants to explain why they thought the social context within the local neighbourhoods they returned to after release caused them to retreat further into close-knit criminal circles and ultimately return to crime. Several mentioned the need to disassociate themselves from delinquent peers and develop new contacts with people who were not crime-oriented. To effect this change, Kev considered it necessary to avoid the pull of certain locations and the negative influence of the former friends and associates who frequented them:

> You know, it would be a risk for me to put myself back in where I knew if I went into such and such a pub that half the people in there that I knew were dealing or involved in some form of criminality. I mean after a few drinks I'd be like susceptible to any kind of suggestion if I didn't have a buck in my pocket and stuff like that. Now I need to surround myself with people who are working, family-orientated and, you know, law-abiding, basically to give myself any type of chance of surviving.

As discussed in Chapter 4, research has shown that ex-prisoners are more likely to reoffend if they return to communities which lack social capital, or at least have the wrong kind of social capital (Clear *et al.* 2003; Farrall 2004). Having relied on close-knit relationships and group membership as children and adolescents for 'mutual acquaintance and recognition' (Bourdieu 1986b: 248), several of the participants revealed how social relations and interaction patterns in the places they returned to after prison obstructed their efforts to avoid reoffending, and that, through constant exposure to crime as a visible everyday occurrence, they assimilated seamlessly back into criminal networks. Building on Goffman's (1967) observation that individuals perform roles and stage-manage impressions within specific contextual situations, Meisenhelder (1977, 1982) has shown how changes in social setting can reinforce new pro-social roles and personal identities. More recently, Barry (2006: 161), too, has investigated the extent to which changes in social position enable offenders to both accrue and spend social capital, and this, in turn, allows them to 'experiment and interact with different people at different phases, and to achieve eventual recognition within the wider society'. Rick explained why he thought moving to an environment in which most people were employed would change the nature of his social relationships and make it less conducive for him to have an active criminal lifestyle.

> If you live in an area where everybody is actively working, you're not going to stand up on the corner all day because you're going to feel like a punk. But if everybody's standing up on the corner, you know what I'm saying, it ain't nothing to stand up on the corner. So, obviously, where they put you determines kind of how you're going to be or what opportunities you get.

For the participants who had difficulty living independently owing to being homeless or having drug or mental health problems, 'where they put you' was mostly in various forms of supported accommodation, including specialist hostels run specifically to house ex-prisoners. Although this is a viable, albeit temporary, alternative to night shelters or living on the streets, and, for some, provides a period of respite in which to make future arrangements, it can also present a precarious, potentially dangerous situation for ex-prisoners. As noted by Maguire and Nolan (2007: 154), 'individuals with histories of long-term offending and substance abuse are housed together, and despite the best efforts of staff, this can easily produce an environment which is not conducive to desistance or resettlement.' Moreover, bail and other government-funded hostels are often poorly managed and violent places where young offenders are liable to make new criminal contacts, and gang rivalries are intensified (Rock 2005). Placed in a hostel after serving his last prison sentence, Theo recalled how he regularly used to sneak out at night with other residents to steal cars and commit violent street robberies:

They never used to keep tabs on us. They were young people and they weren't really, I don't know, tight with surveillance. So they were a bit laid back. We used to climb through the bedroom window, down the pole and whatnot. They had rules and regulations that you had to abide by, but I didn't keep up with them, yeh. No one stopped me, yeh. And I had a couple of fights in there, and you weren't allowed to have girls in there, and they used to find girls in my bedroom. All those things went against me in the end so I left.

A further problem is that supported accommodation is often not situated in locations near to employment opportunities, or away from people likely to exert a negative influence on ex-prisoners (Mackie 2008). As discussed in Chapter 3, people with housing needs generally, and minority groups in particular (Beider 2009), often have little or no choice but to live in areas of economic and social decline characterised by low levels of social capital (Cheshire 2007). For many ex-prisoners, living in areas where conventional opportunities are constrained and criminal opportunities readily available can all too easily lead them back into crime. Paul explained he is unable to stay at his mother's home after release any more because 'it's not room enough for me. My brother's got my old room now.' Moreover, 'my step-dad's still around and he's a crack addict and he tends to be very violent.' Therefore, after prison he either 'lives with girls or in a hostel'. We met Paul in the previous chapter. He says he wants to give up crime. In pursuit of this, before coming to prison this time, he says, 'I was on my own a lot and I felt better within myself because I knew that if anyone was to try and take me down the wrong road, I would know that it wasn't what I wanted, you know.' He goes on to explain the reasons for his subsequent relapse:

I was living in a hostel, and basically the hostel was in a place known for selling crack cocaine, cannabis and whatnot, all sorts of different things. And they put me in the heart of it again. The problem is that if I tend to be around people that are addicts and things like that, I just can't live in that environment.

Rick had also been placed in a hostel in an area where large numbers of people were buying, selling and using drugs. Having previously exploited similar street environments with a high degree of entrepreneurial skill and success (Hobbs 1995), he explained that this presented him with numerous opportunities to make quick and easy money. Initially inclined to resist the temptation, he described how the business man in him eventually won out and led him back to crime:

> They can't put me in a hostel when I come out of here in the middle of crack city and don't expect me to make a bit of money. That defeats the object; you know what I'm saying? That's what they done last time. They put me out in the middle of crack city. Every time I come out of my house, I got rushed by about 10 junkies. Have I got this? Have I got that? 'No, No, No.' Come back in the evening, there's about 20 of them there. Have I got this? Have I got that? 'No, No, No.' Until I decided, do you know what, I could make a bit of money here.

Friends (dis)reunited

As the participants received longer sentences, they found the places they returned to after release had changed. Material circumstances had changed, as had the social, economic, cultural and political contexts which shape social relations and interaction patterns. This is not an experience unique to ex-prisoners, of course. Massey (2005: 124; emphasis in the original) has emphasised that, owing to constant and rapid transformations in the economic and social infrastructure, 'the truth is that you can never simply "go back", to home or to anywhere else. When you get "there", the place will have moved on just as you yourself will have changed.' As discussed in Chapter 1, as well as earlier in this chapter, changes in social relations play an important role in criminal desistance. Residential changes in the housing infrastructure, for example, affect community structures, routine activities, social interaction patterns, and the composition of peer groups in ways that may help or hinder the efforts of ex-prisoners to give up crime (Meisenhelder 1977, 1982).

Of immediate concern to most of the participants was that, in their absence, former friends and acquaintances had developed new interests and priorities in life. In some instances, these centred on a steep escalation in new forms of criminal activity. Mika explained that 'when I first came out of prison all of them had changed; they were doing professional jobs for like £50,000 a time.' In contrast, however, most found the people they had associated with previously on the outside had ceased to commit crime at the same level of intensity, or had stopped completely. Given that most young offenders are criminally active for only a short period of their lives (Smith 2002), they no longer sought thrills and excitement as they had done when they were younger. Instead, they had developed responsibilities, started families, secured mortgages and acquired steady jobs. As we have seen, contexts such as marriage, employment and education, which affirm the value of pro-social structured activities and result in new, law-abiding peer relationships, can inhibit deviant behaviour (Sampson and Laub 1993). Since some of his former friends had drifted away from crime, Paul had begun to question the life decisions he had made so far:

> There's a feller now who's been going to work since we was all out there and he's been our friend. And there's a few of them that work and they've all got houses now and mortgages, and half of us is stuck in prison. But it tells you something, I suppose. We are the stupid ones, the lot of us. We've had a good time but so have they. They've had a good time as well.

A negative outcome of such relationship changes, however, is that friendship groups that once provided social capital, support and camaraderie may no longer be available to the recently released prisoner. Stuart explained how on leaving prison he felt a strong sense of dislocation from the social networks to which he had previously belonged and the problems this caused him:

> If you go away for a month or so you can basically pick up from where you left off, but after a long prison sentence people just don't know you any more. People have moved on, they have matured in different ways, and the things that you used to do with them, and the way that you used to relate to each other, you can no longer relate to them on that level. So you find yourself becoming distanced, and it can be a very lonely, isolating situation. For example, you go into prison and before you go into prison a friend of yours was on the dole and, I don't know, living in a hostel, and when you come out after two years he's got his own cleaning company and he's married. Do you know what I mean? You're talking to a totally different person.

Several of the participants said that they, too, had begun to change. For instance, they had come to realise that former friends had been a bad influence on them. They were 'negative people', 'drug takers'; people that, as Keifer admitted, 'ain't really friends at all, they're associates who just want to sell drugs and sell me drugs.' Nevertheless, most agreed that continued attachment to former friends and associates after prison stemmed largely from a need for company and support. Not having developed the life skills necessary to participate fully within legitimate society, they were drawn to associate with people of a similar criminal disposition. Inevitably, these included other ex-prisoners. While a few claimed to have friends who were not criminally motivated and 'flitted from one group to another', the majority found it difficult to maintain friendships with people who 'do not live the same way as we do'. As we have seen before, this encouraged the resumption of everyday social activities associated with crime (Moore 1996). In important respects, the everyday habits and routine activities of ex-prisoners differ both temporally and spatially from those of law-abiding people. For instance, because many ex-prisoners are unemployed, they are not constrained to travel to and from the same place of work every day, or do daily chores such as shop for food at particular times. With large amounts of unstructured time on their hands, some of the participants described how loose and shifting social networks often formed as a consequence of chance meetings on the street, not from engaging in fixed routines, purposefully going from place to place, but while they were idly walking around in search of something to do (de Certeau 1984). This parallel trajectory through the city, characterised as it is by the everyday unconscious desire to resist anonymity, boredom and inertia, seamlessly spilled over into crime. Stuart explained:

> You come out of prison and, all right, you can't go round to what's his name's house today because he's working. And when he gets home from work he's tired and he's got to be up in the morning. And if you're not working yourself and you've just come out of prison and you want company, you're going to go to people who are around. And you're walking down the street one day and you see somebody you know vaguely, and it's like, 'I'm just going down the pub' and 'Are you coming?' And then a couple of others, strays, come in, and you're all sitting there drinking and, 'You know what, there's some money to be had around here' and it's like 'How much?' and it's off.

'Placelessness'

Illustrative of geographical life-course perspectives which suggest the way people relate to place is age graded (Laws 1997), most of the participants no longer looked upon their 'homes', the streets and open spaces they had played in as children, as arenas of excitement. Nor did they consider home in a nostalgic light, an intimate place that retained significant collective and community values. For some, this was an outcome of having to live down a criminal reputation, of being 'a known geezer', and treated with fear by local people and suspicion by the police. Community-based stigma is commonly linked to reoffending (Braithwaite 1989), although the extent to which it also impedes the intentions of ex-prisoners to give up crime has not been well documented. In addition to ex-prisoners having to contend with discriminatory housing (Shelter 2007) and employer recruitment practices (Fletcher *et al.* 1998), as we saw in Chapter 3, the tendency to treat them as deviants first and human beings second (Goffman 1963) within 'punishing communities' (Worrall and Hoy 2005) can obstruct their chances of reintegrating fully and productively into community life (Uggen *et al.* 2004). Rick explained:

> Everybody's going to know I'm fresh from gaol, especially in my area, whether it be shopkeepers or whatever because everybody's used to seeing me. So when you've gone away for such a long time people talk and automatically people come to a conclusion, 'Yeh, he must be away.' It will be hard for me. Like I ain't going to get no work unless it's people that I know.

A few of the participants had more pressing reasons for feeling insecure in their home areas after release, which they claimed related to the circumstances of their specific offences. For example, Harvey had been convicted of attempted murder. Because his girlfriend had subsequently received death threats from the family and friends of the victim, he explained:

> I'm moving up north when I get out. I'm moving away. I've said to my girl already, we'll move away and she said, yeh. A fresh start basically. I get out, all it takes is for one person to say I said something to them, to ring up police and say, 'He threatened me' and they're going to come and hit me and haul my arse back in here. Don't want that.

More generally, experiencing a growing sense of 'placelessness' (Relph 1976), many of the participants described the home neighbourhoods they returned to as filthy, dangerous and hostile, where young people act like 'complete head cases', 'completely out of control', 'far more violent than we had ever been'. Pitts (2003: 101) has noted how, during the 1980s, 'people most vulnerable to criminal victimisation and those most likely to victimise them were progressively thrown together on the poorest housing estates.' As a consequence, 'old social ties, constructed of kinship, friendship or familiarity, withered away to be replaced by transience, isolation and mutual suspicion.' Of course, as children and adolescents, mistrust and hostility would not have bothered the participants unduly. As we have seen, it was mutually accepted as an ingrained cultural characteristic, a habitus of the environment in which they had grown up. Now they were older, however, some had become acutely aware of the dislocated and corrosive nature of local community life. Farrall and Calverley (2006: 167) have observed how, owing to a lack of choice over where to live, irrespective of whether they give up crime or not, many ex-prisoners become '"socially caged" in poorer housing estates where crime is prevalent and embedded [and therefore] in this respect, persisters and desisters experience the same levels of victimization as one another because both live in areas in which crime is common.' Kev described the changes he thought had occurred in his home area:

> In the 1980s and 1990s, Brixton transferred from the softer drugs to the harder drugs. Everybody was looking and the stakes were raised. But people weren't really understanding what was happening on that level with the unemployed, the homeless and all these types of issues and drugs. In those days people turned a blind eye to it. Growing up in Brixton from my early childhood, the earliest memories I have of Brixton are quite happy because my front door never had to be locked and if my grandmother came out onto the step and said 'Kev?', then a neighbour would say, 'Oh, he's here.' People didn't fear about letting their children out of their house. If you look at the whole picture, it's gone from that to now you've got to have a steel door.

Nige explained why he thought the neighbourhood where he had grown up was no longer a suitable place to bring up his son:

There's 15-year-olds running around where I used to live with guns now. It's just ridiculous, 15-year-olds selling crack with guns. And my son's 5 now. By the time he gets to 10, 13, what's it going to be like for him? It's going to be in the schools, and I don't want him brought up around that.

Unsurprisingly, some of the participants thought their motivation to abandon crime would be aided significantly if they moved out of these criminogenic environments, 'away from everyone that's around me whose life is just crime oriented'. For those who intended to resume crime after release, returning home was an instrumental decision, necessary to continue the life of a professional criminal (Hobbs 1985). So, having grown up surrounded by people who condoned and encouraged crime, Barry saw home as 'where I've got family, friends or thieving people, people who will buy stuff when I go out, stolen gear'. In contrast, most of the participants described their home neighbourhoods as places they 'always got into trouble', went 'from bad to worse', involving them in 'a lot of rubbish', 'a no-win situation', 'drugs and crime again'. This was often expressed simply as a need to 'just go somewhere else', 'somewhere nobody knows me', 'anywhere at all, I don't care'. The few who had effected this change in their lives, made the break, and moved away, described the impact this had had on their criminal lifestyles. Liam explained why he had moved out of Hackney:

I cut them all off. Not one person in Hackney, not one of my friends actually come to visit me, actually knew I lived in West London. They might have heard from the bird but no one would ever know where to find me. No one ever knew where I lay my head down or where my front door is. I was a new person. It was a fresh start. I put my whole heart into this fresh start. I really wanted it and I stopped doing what I was doing. I got a permanent place, a nice little one-bedroom flat, and started going to university, believe it or not.

And John explained why he had moved out of Dagenham:

If I go back to Dagenham I'll end up slipping back into my old ways because all the police know me. They'll keep getting on my nerves, pulling me over, trying to get me for this and that. And I'll end up getting so fed up with it I'll end up retaliating and throwing everything back at them ... I moved away and got my life sorted out. I got off the drink, I got off the drugs. I got away from my friends. I just pushed them to one side and moved on. I got my own place in Southall with my Mrs and I'm happy. I haven't been in trouble once up there with the Old Bill, not once. Not been stopped by police or anything.

Reflecting research which has found that drug users are more likely to desist when they associate with non-drug-using friends and associates (Sampson and Laub 1993), and that recovering addicts who return to places associated with previous addictions are prone to relapse (Rawson 1999), the participants who were serious drug users were particularly insistent on the importance of moving to a new area where the temptation to resume drug taking would be easier to resist. For example, Adusa explained:

It would help if I went to an area where I didn't know where the drugs was, somewhere I don't know nobody. Because the line of thinking I'm on now is I want to stay clean, you know. If I go back I'm going to relapse, because I know where I can get it. Being around the people that do it, you know.

Although, for some, prison offered a time-limited respite from habitual drug taking, on release they always relapsed. Hari used prison to 'get away from drugs. I don't want to take drugs in prison, I want to go gym, I want to do this, I want to do that. But it's when I go out there, that's the thing.' Adusa also refrained from drugs in prison. Moreover, he had 'read loads of books on the effects of drugs and how to avoid relapse, [but] every time I get out all my good intentions go out the window, and I find I just can't say no.' Therefore, it was generally accepted by the participants who were habitual users that staying clean on a permanent basis could only be achieved with professional help. Eric explained why:

When you're locked up, yeh, it's not like being out. There's so many temptations out there. There's not much here, you know. A lot of people here, you know, go on rehab and say I'm never smoking drugs again and as soon as they reach the gate that's the first thing they do. Even to myself, you know, I promised myself I'm never going down that road again, I love the way I look, I like feeling, you know, like a human being. And then as soon as I come out, and the pressure is too hard, I turn to drugs. And basically I am going to need support, you know, I don't think I'm strong enough.

This chapter concludes by assessing the responses of the participants to the professional help and support made available to ex-prisoners in the community, in particular that provided by social services and employment agencies.

'Social services'

It has been suggested that many of the problems ex-prisoners must solve after release are no different from those of people generally who rely on social services and community support. Yet, faced with problems and situations they feel ill equipped to resolve, there is a tendency for offenders to choose 'a maladaptive, often criminal, response as a misguided coping effort' (Zamble and Quinsey 1997: 10). Research has found that:

> In the case of offenders there was no evidence that the problems encountered outside of prison were distinctive in kind or severity from the ordinary challenges that most people encounter. However, their ways of dealing with these situations were at best ineffective and often exacerbated the original problems. (*ibid.*)

It follows that, as well as the social circumstances in which offenders make decisions and act upon them, rehabilitative interventions need to address individual factors such as impulsivity, confidence and motivation (Rex 2001). Certainly, many of the participants expressed a strong sense of impatience, frustration and anger at having to deal with public bodies such as benefit and housing departments, job agencies, and the probation service. Owing to the unique structural and social impediments of imprisonment (Richards and Jones 2004), many long-term prisoners after release do not possess the skills to communicate on a level considered acceptable within wider society. Stuart thought a major reason for this was the competitive and often callous masculine culture which tends to predominate in prisons (Sykes 1958):

> Inside, you have to have an exterior that you're tough. You have to because if you don't, you will get fucked. It's as simple

as that. You have to speak the speak, and people have to know that you're not somebody that can have the piss taken out of. And we all do that, we do it in different ways, but in prison it is on a very physical level, a very showy level, and it's all very verbal. But when you're on the outside it doesn't work, it doesn't wash, and it's a different context. If you've spent a long time in prison, those patterns of behaviour you try to transfer them when you come out of prison. For example, if you're going into a situation where you're trying to claim a civil right and the person standing on the other side of the counter is working for a public body, and you're all [grunts like an ape], they're not going to buy it. Your attempts to gain your entitlements will be thwarted because you're unable to communicate in the sort of way you need to communicate to get those things.

Failing to secure the help and support they thought was deserved and appropriate in their situation and believing the problems they faced required urgent attention, some of the participants had decided it was futile to engage with public bodies and had given up claiming housing or employment benefits. Barry described dealing with his local housing department:

Housing, they always fob me off, fanny me off, and I don't know why. I'm sick of it, to tell you the truth. I think, what the fuck, oh shag it, forget it. I won't beg for something, you know what I mean.

Unsurprisingly, the decision to reject the support of social services and spurn benefit entitlements led some of the participants further into crime. Prior to coming to prison, Billy had been cohabiting illegally in council-owned property with a friend. As a consequence, he had been unable to claim unemployment benefit or disclose his home address to official organisations such as banks, housing associations and prospective employers. This had resulted in his becoming 'stuck in a place I did not want to live but which I could not leave':

I wasn't signing on so housing benefit wasn't paying my rent. So, you know, things went downhill. Like I said to you, I didn't want to be living there but I have tried to go for jobs but my friend wouldn't let me use his address as a place of residence for them to send me bank statements; you know, things like that. So I'd say I committed crime to survive really.

On leaving his wife and children and becoming homeless, Jimmy recounted his failure to persuade the probation service to provide him with alternative accommodation:

> So I leave home, I go to probation. I said, 'haven't got nowhere to live'. 'There's nothing I can do for you.' 'What do you mean, there's nothing you can do for me?' I said, 'I'm still on licence, I just finished four years'. She says – now listen to this – I'm only vulnerable for the first six to eight weeks of coming out. Now don't you think that's bollocks? I've just come out of doing four years, I've done two years eight months, and she's telling me I'm only vulnerable for the first six to eight weeks. I ended up living in my car. That's when it all went pear-shaped.

In some cases, the failure to comply with rules and regulations required by the social services extended to supervision arrangements imposed by the probation service. As it is common for offenders to delegitimise conditions of licence intended to regulate movement and activity, many fail to comply with the mandatory requirements placed upon them (Winstone and Dixon 2000 in Ellis and Winstone 2002). As a consequence, there has been an increase in the number of offenders who have breached conditions of release and been returned to prison (Prison Reform Trust 2005). Prior to coming to prison, John had been subject to a judicially ordered supervision order, which he considered inappropriate and unfair:

> The probation service keep trying to drag me back into the areas where I've been getting into trouble, and I keep saying I don't want to go back to those areas. And they breached me for not going to probation in that area and living in that area. I don't like it down there no more. I've just had enough. The people I used to know, I just don't want to know those people any more. But they don't want to help. So I just get fed up and think, sod it, I'm not going to bother going back to probation, so that's why I'm in here now.

While these testimonies appear to support the view that offenders respond to everyday social situations and common problems ineffectively, the assertion that the difficulties they face are the same as those of vulnerable people generally fails to acknowledge the specifics of the social situation many of them return to after prison. Ex-prisoners are entitled to a range of benefits including income support, housing benefit, jobseeker's allowance and community care grants. However, it is commonly the case that the loss of formal identification, as well as delays in processing urgent claims for food and clothing, means that many must survive the first few weeks after release without any financial support (SEU 2002). For those who manage to secure benefit entitlements and somewhere to live, the next step to successful social integration is finding a job, and this raises a further problem unique to ex-prisoners: the requirement to disclose criminal records to potential employers.

Finding a job

Employment is commonly linked to housing as a significant factor which supports prisoner reintegration because it is thought that 'the possession of a job will enable suitable accommodation to be secured and any problems within the family will be solved by [the ex-prisoner's] assuming his traditional role of breadwinner' (Soothill 1974: 23). Therefore, securing and retaining a job is 'significantly related to changes in adult crime' (Laub and Sampson 2001: 20). As noted in Chapter 1, as well as providing an income and self-esteem, employment promotes pro-social relationships, reduces unstructured time and helps offenders construct a new 'legitimate' identity for themselves (Farrall 2004: 64). Criminality subsides when through employment offenders develop conventional adult social bonds which reinforce legitimate forms of behaviour (Warr 1998). Depending on the quality of work available and the commitment to hold down a permanent job (Sampson and Laub 1993), employment provides structure to daily life, develops independence and self-worth, and aids the maturation process (Farrall 1995). Some of the participants appeared to be aware that a job would lock them into the rules and conventions of legitimate, everyday social life (Giddens 1984). For example, Billy thought that a job would establish patterns of behaviour at variance with his normal criminal routines:

Through those doors, you know, I might just say fuck it and jog it on for a couple of days and then it's a couple of weeks, a couple of months. But I hope on the day of coming out I want to be through those doors and straight into work because I believe that if I work for at least one week, two weeks or maybe one month it will be imbedded in me, you know, that lifestyle. But usually I smoke weed in the day, and I get up

> when I want, play computer, go out when I want, come back when I want, don't have to go to bed at a certain time. I don't want it to be like that, I want it to be organised.

Although a few of the participants had never worked and insisted they had no intention of ever doing so, most had been employed for short periods of time in a variety of manual or service sector occupations. Reflecting research which suggests that offenders commit twice as much crime when unemployed (Farrington *et al.* 1986), many had reduced or suspended criminal activities during periods they had been in work. Ian explained that although he did not relinquish contacts with his former friends during periods of employment:

> I'd link up with them, we'd go raving and stuff like that, but I had steady money, that was the thing. I had a wage every week and sometimes they didn't, even though they probably made a lot more money that I did. And they used to say, you need to come back in and you need to do this and you need to do that, and I'd say, 'No, I'm all right'. Until my mum died and then, I think, for about six months I just done nothing, just sat around smoking weed, can't even remember where to be honest – everywhere I suppose.

This would suggest that the relationship between employment and giving up crime is far from certain. Crucially, its role in supporting desistance is mediated by other factors. Soothill (1974: 7) has observed that 'offering employment in isolation is unlikely to have significant effects in lowering the recidivism rates for the general run of the prison population.' Although they professed to like the security of a weekly wage, there were a variety of reasons, all equally subjective, that the participants gave for giving up work and returning to crime. Given that only repetitive and poorly paid jobs were available, crime provided far more money than could realistically be achieved in legitimate forms of employment, which, anyway, they viewed as boring and monotonous. Dalmar explained:

> Even when I was doing a job, I was going every day and all that, right, doing it because of my mum and that. I wanted to give it a go and see what it was like. But I was never happy, get me. Even when my mum said I was going to be much, much happier, I was never happy, because the money that I was getting paid was not sufficient enough. Because I could

make like exactly the same thing in an hour or something on the streets.

For others, a predilection for 'raving' meant they were often unable to conform to employer expectations that they be punctual and conform to reliable and consistent standards of performance. Ian gave up his job because 'I couldn't get to work on time, I was a proper crackhead, going out raving all the time.' On being asked why he had returned to crime after working for an estate agent for over a year, Tim replied:

Urm... partly money, and partly just to survive and just live life. The money I was getting wasn't enough to live out in the community. Like I was a young person, I wanted clothes. I wanted to eat good, I wanted to drink, I wanted to smoke weed, I really wanted to impress girls, I wanted a car. There were loads of things I wanted.
NF: Did you get all those things?
Yes, I did [laughs].

Despite these caveats, employment causes offenders to scale down criminal activity, and a large number of studies have found that ex-prisoners are more likely to permanently desist from crime if they are employed (e.g. Sampson and Laub 1993; Farrall 1995; Graham and Bowling 1995; Lipsey 1995; May 1999; Raphael and Winter-Ebmer 1999). It is surprising, therefore, given this substantial body of work, that 'very little systematic and intensive work-related support is currently available to ex-prisoners after release' (SEU 2002: 58). Perhaps a reason for this is that, owing to the difficulty of securing work in highly skilled labour markets, coupled to the reluctance of many employers to recruit known offenders, especially during a period of labour surplus, the few programmes which are available have been unsuccessful (Fletcher et al. 1998). As we have seen, this difficulty is magnified because many ex-prisoners return to deprived areas which suffer high rates of unemployment. Given that early criminal convictions and imprisonment often preclude entry into training and employment, most of the jobs open to ex-prisoners are low skill and low wage; involve long, unsocial hours; and have few or no prospects of promotion (Nagin and Waldfogel 1995). Acutely aware that only poorly paid and oppressive jobs are available to the working poor (Young 1999), and convinced that the requirement to disclose criminal records to potential employers disqualified them from finding gainful employment anyway, most of the participants had been dissuaded from applying for jobs through professional agencies (Niven and Stewart 2005). Jimmy explained:

> I ain't got no qualifications. I can read and I can write, but when you go for a job now who's going to employ me? I've got 33 convictions, and the first thing you see on a piece of paper is, have you got a criminal record? And if I lie they can find out and then they wipe their hands of you.

Consequently, those that attempted to find work relied on informal networks of family and friends. Of course, this is a pragmatic solution to the barriers to employment they faced. However, as noted in Chapter 4, it is a form of social capital which has the potential to embed offenders further into intimate criminal networks. Uggen *et al.* (2004: 269) have observed that, in failing to 'expand their limited social circle to access jobs of higher quality', ex-prisoners often fail to develop the social and cultural capital necessary to establish a new permanent non-criminal identity based on independence and self-worth. Ericson (1975: 210), too, has articulated why it is that many ex-prisoners who maintain social networks which revolve around former friends and acquaintances become excluded from mainstream employment opportunities and prone to reoffend:

> the ex-inmate tends to experience gross exclusion from distant others and gross inclusion from intimate others. He therefore begins to establish the meaningful aspects of his existence among his close associates rather than through wider community associations or the employment sphere. It is in this connection that a form of crime can re-enter the person's life.

Reflecting the tendency of ex-prisoners to rely on their own kind, Adusa explained that the only way he had been able to find work in the past was through contacts he had developed with ex-prisoners:

> If it's a small place and the employer is someone who's an ex-offender, he might give you a chance. But most places, if you tell them you've been in prison, they just throw you through the door. They just say, 'Go away', you know. But I know where to go. I know the people to go to for my jobs. That is why all my friends are ex-prisoners.

Aside from a few participants who had previous experience of manual occupations and were considering returning to work as bricklayers, painters and decorators, or roofers, most considered there were two main routes to employment open to them. They could become counsellors and work with young criminals, drug users, and ex-prisoners, or become self-employed and work for themselves. Again, given their situation, these are not unrealistic career options. However, as most had not sought or been offered guidance and advice to develop skills and secure the work experience necessary to realise these ambitions, the plans they outlined came across as naive and self-defeating. Barry claimed:

> I'll make a damn good counsellor 'cause I've been taking drugs since the age of 9, and I've got a degree in it, so who better to help another drug user than a drug user? You know, they can't sit there and say, 'You don't know how I feel.' Well, you know what, 'I do know how you feel 'cause I've been there and I've done it.'

The desire to help others has been taken to be a precursor of criminal desistance, a sign that ex-offenders are prepared to make amends and repair the harm they have caused (Burnett and Maruna 2006). However, while such 'generative activities' may provide opportunities for offenders to 'demonstrate their value and potential and make positive contributions to their communities' (*ibid*.: 86–7), none of the participants appeared to be aware of even the most obvious occupational restrictions they faced, given their offending background, in attempting to secure work of this kind. A similar lack of understanding and planning was evident among those who had considered the self-employment option. For example, Sammy could not drive but wanted to be a long-distance lorry driver. Robert could neither read nor write but wanted 'to work for a big IT company, a well-paid job working with computers'. Jimmy was going to rely on his innate talent to 'sell sand to Arabs' and be 'a successful entrepreneur'. And Maurice intended setting up a car-clamping business:

> I think if I had my own business, like waking up in the morning at 9 o'clock, having to go and do this and do that, it's something that's going to occupy my mind and my time. So that's what it basically boils down to, yeh. I've looked into car clamping. I've

already found out about it from my cousin. He looked it up on the Internet. It's not hard or nothing like that, do you know what I'm saying? It's just getting it up and running, getting on the outside, getting up on the road and getting it up and running.

Acknowledging the difficulties offenders face in finding work, Farrall (2004) has suggested, albeit tentatively, that probation services should attempt to create jobs in the form of sheltered employment. Once again, this is a pragmatic policy proposal given the circumstances faced by most ex-prisoners in today's highly competitive employment market. It is based on the understanding that ex-prisoners have access to few viable employment opportunities in the places they return to after prison, and are hampered by a lack of work experience, as well as naive and unrealistic expectations about what it is possible to achieve. Social capital is increased when offenders are able to demonstrate 'a record of employability in the form of people who can be approached to provide references and, as such, may well provide the basis of further jobs in other occupations' (*ibid*.: 73). In this way, offenders are empowered to develop knowledge and capabilities, secure better employment options, and choose a life they value. The next and final chapter discusses offender reintegration policy in more detail.

Chapter 8

Implications

Introduction

It has been a recurring theme of this book that narratives of self and space are intricately bound up together. As we have seen throughout, the intrinsic difficulty of representing the truth of the relations between people and place has resulted in divergent and contradictory approaches being taken. As Holloway and Hubbard (2001: 234) observe, owing to the fluid and contested nature of the concepts involved, nothing can be taken for granted 'in the face of vigorous debates about the type of relationships that exist between society and space, social structure and human agency or nature and culture'. An obvious outcome of this is that consensual social policy is hard to arrive at. And yet, given the pressing need to solve practical problems of access to resources, services and welfare (Titmuss 1976), there has been no shortage of policy prescriptions developed to address spatial and social differences in poverty, health, education, employment, social welfare, racism, social justice, citizenship and so on. Throughout its history, criminology in particular, including spatial analysis, has rarely been detached from social policy. Garland (2002: 8) attributes this to the convergence of two separate traditions – 'the Lombrosian project', which employs scientific method to discover the causes of crime, and 'the governmental project', which administers justice and empirically analyses the work of the criminal justice system. However, although these traditions come together in the sense that academic theories lead to governmental ideologies which seek to resolve social problems caused by crime, in reality the process by which criminological theoretical positions are translated into action is beset by pressure and conflict.

As we saw in Chapter 3, a fundamental tension between psychology and sociology has tended to privilege personality and trait theories of criminal behaviour, on the one hand, and structural and social context on the other hand. While some argue that 'a general personality and social psychological approach to understanding criminality is a very promising route to risk management and risk reduction' (Andrews 1995), others contend that the traditional focus on individual levels of analysis has marginalised community psychologies of therapy and counseling (Nelson and Prilleltensky 2004), and more generally has obscured the need for economic and social change (Albee 1990). A methodological concern underlying this dispute is the uncertainty of applying abstract concepts such as 'reflexive practice', 'habitus', 'social practice', 'social capital' and 'the dialectics of everyday life' to an area of social policy concerned for the most part with the instrumental matter of assessing risk and reducing crime. The sub-discipline of environmental criminology in particular has remained suspicious of theories that focus on subjective factors associated with criminality, and has concentrated instead on the manipulation of behavioural triggers and criminal opportunities within specific locations. According to Young (1999: 33), the rational choice perspective which guides much environmental criminology, although highly context-sensitive (Tilley 1993), assumes that crime is simply a product of 'basic human frailty'. Therefore, the notion that crime may be prevented by applying actuarial solutions – that is, by calculating the probability of negative events occurring by statistical methods derived from the insurance industry – reduces understandings of the social world to 'a relatively simple structure' (Young 1999: 130).

This chapter discusses the implications of the theoretical ideas on people–place relationships presented throughout the book for prisoner reintegration policy. After discussing recent policy developments and interventions, it develops an argument that a conceptual approach, broad and nuanced enough to assess 'criminal behaviour in context', should take into account individual criminal histories – past experiences, present situations and future prospects, including the personal motivations, attitudes and understandings that stem from these (Visher and Travis 2003), as well as the unique structural and social challenges faced by offenders in the places they are drawn from and return to after prison (Sampson and Laub 2005; Farrall and Calverley 2006; Ward and Maruna 2007). The book concludes with some contextual observations on human capabilities and constraints associated with this life-course perspective.

Prisoner reintegration: recent policy and practice

As noted in the introduction, the rise in the prison population in both the United States and the UK over the past 15 years or so, and the consequent increase in the numbers of prisoners re-entering the community, have placed prisoner reintegration firmly back towards the top of the penal policy agenda. This has led to heightened interest in the crime profile and social status of prisoners, as well as the communities to which they return (Clear *et al.* 2005). In the United States, public and professional disquiet over the 600,000 or so prisoners released back into certain communities every year has led to a reappraisal of the prisoner re-entry system. Prisoner rehabilitation and treatment programmes, legal and practical barriers to reintegration and aftercare support services have all been the subject of review (Petersilia 2003). Informed by a new 'community justice ideal' – the five core elements of which focus explicitly on neighbourhoods, problem solving, decentralisation of authority and accountability, community quality of life, and citizen participation (Karp and Clear 2000) – various policy interventions have been introduced or revised. For example, the Office of Justice Programs of the US Federal Department of Justice has introduced 'Reentry Courts', in which judges oversee the reintegration of ex-prisoners back into the community, as well as 'Reentry Partnerships' between criminal justice, social service and local community groups.

As detailed in Chapter 2, the impact of large numbers of prisoners returning to certain disadvantaged communities has not been identified as a problem on the same scale in the UK. Nevertheless, owing to increasing rates of imprisonment, reoffending and re-imprisonment, the need to improve offender rehabilitation and reintegration has generally been recognised. Reviews of prisoner resettlement (Home Office 2001b), the sentencing framework (Halliday 2001), and criminal courts (Home Office 2002a) have led to the implementation of the Criminal Justice Act 2003, which, *inter alia*, identified rehabilitation as a primary purpose of sentencing. In tandem with a review of correctional services (Carter 2003), these have informed a 'Reducing Reoffending National Action Plan' (Home Office 2004b), the major component of which is a new, single National Offender Management Service (NOMS), charged to reduce reoffending through 'seamless sentences' delivered by the prison and probation services in partnership. In addition, new risk needs assessment instruments have been introduced, including the Offender Assessment System (OASys) for adult offenders and 'Asset' for young offenders, to assess harm and the likelihood of reoffending in relation to a set of 'criminogenic' needs such as accommodation, employment, relationships, drug misuse, and thinking and behaviour.

Although these are not inconsiderable developments, they need to be put into context. In the United States, prisoner reintegration programmes remain additional to parole services, which continue to prioritise control-oriented activities designed to manage the risk of reoffending. More fundamentally than this, however, they have been implemented in response to policies which continue to drive up the number of offenders incarcerated each year. As Petersilia (2003: 246) has pointed out, it is a peculiar characteristic of the political climate in the United States that calls for additional offender programmes are 'quickly dismissed as being liberal on crime and are likely to be disregarded as irrelevant to the current public mood and national policy trends'. The social problems caused by high rates of reoffending committed by former prisoners are real enough but 'in matters of prison policy, liberals who want more programs are pitted against conservatives who want more cells' (ibid.).

It is early days, but the overall policy approach to the reintegration of prisoners in the UK has also attracted criticism. Again first and foremost, although academics and policy advisers continue to question the efficacy of imprisonment to rehabilitate offenders (Maruna and Toch 2005), and recommend that 'custody should be recognised as the ultimate sanction and as such be reserved for the most serious, dangerous and highly persistent offenders' (Carter 2003: 30), imprisonment rates continue to rise. In large part, of course, rehabilitation in prison is affected by the physical environment and living conditions, the differential distribution of material goods and facilities, overcrowding, and high staff turnover (Lewis et al. 2003). It follows that, depending on whether there are procedures in place to 'identify those at risk, provide advice at the point of sentence, and follow through with effective and sustained support ... a prison sentence can be an opportunity to improve or can actually worsen those factors that are either known to cause or are heavily associated with the likelihood of re-offending' (SEU 2002: 38). Some of these problems are managerial; more fundamentally, however they are contextual. As far as it is possible to do so, account therefore needs to be taken of 'social and institutional factors [which] enable prisoners to use the treatment programmes successfully' (Clarke *et al.* 2004: 40). Given that evaluations of prison-based treatment programmes to date have produced only mixed results (*ibid.*), it would appear that there are fundamental and systematic obstacles to overcome if effective rehabilitation services are to be delivered in prison establishments.

On a wider community level, Maguire and Raynor (2006) have argued that offender rehabilitation remains beset by unresolved tensions between the need to supervise offenders, increasingly through the use of 'technocorrectional innovation' such as electronic monitoring (Nellis 2006) and, the need to deliver interventions which are less impersonal and more 'people focused' (Liebling 2004), and which encourage offenders to make the internal behavioural changes necessary to desist from crime. In line with the overriding priority to protect the public, the key guiding principle of NOMS is that resources should follow risk: the 'principle of risk and principle of need inform which interventions are to be selected for which offenders in order to try to achieve reform and rehabilitation' (Home Office 2006a: para. 6.4). Yet, although it is purported that 'reform and rehabilitation is about change' (*ibid.*: para. 6.2), offender reintegration remains compromised by 'a clash between the often short-term goals of immediate victim safety and community protection and the longer term goals of behaviour change' (Kemshall 2007: 284).

There is a historical precedent for this. Ever since the May Committee reported that 'the rhetoric of "treatment and training" has had its day' (May 1979: para. 4.27), and, in so doing, realigned the purposes of imprisonment to emphasise containment over rehabilitation, relationship work with prisoners has been marginalised. Similarly, 'aftercare' work has been downgraded. Acceptance by government of the proposition that 'social work for offenders … can only command the priority which is consistent with the main objective of implementing non-custodial measures' (Home Office 1984) has 'limited the discretion of the individual probation officer and focused on the management of supervision rather than on its content' (Worrall and Hoy 2005: 84). As a consequence, the favoured model of offender rehabilitation today is based on personality and social psychological approaches to risk management and risk reduction. Indeed, for some, any other intervention is considered to be a waste of time and resources (Andrews *et al.* 1990). Guided by rigorous managerial systems of accreditation designed to ensure that programmes address risk, target need, and respond to the specific learning style of offenders, the current paradigm of offender rehabilitation privileges cognitive behavioural techniques. A side effect of this is that one-to-one work with offenders based on empathy, mutual understanding and respect has been neglected (Burnett 2004b). The potential of relationships between offenders and practitioners to support processes of rehabilitation and desistance is assessed below.

Relationships

As identified in Chapter 6, it has been found that during periods of imprisonment many offenders profess a desire to give up crime (Cusson and Pinsonneault 1986). While for most this is nothing more that a whim which dissolves as soon as new criminal opportunities arise, those that do make a concerted attempt to change either develop the strength of will to sustain non-criminal behaviour, or are hindered from doing so by a failure to address negative structural and social influences on them (Maruna 2001). Therefore, in order to support narratives of change, it is necessary to understand how offenders develop the confidence and motivation necessary to overcome the obstacles they face, and how concepts of self, personal maturity, and attitudes and feelings towards desistance from crime impact on the decisions they make.

In order to build on the doubts offenders express about continuing to lead a life of crime – for example, to positively confront fatigue with 'street life' (Shover 1996), frustration at receiving repeated and longer prison sentences (Clarke and Cornish 1985), and disillusionment at not having achieved a career or started a family (Uggen et al. 2004) – Burnett (2004a: 170), for example, has advocated one-to-one counselling conducted in such a way that 'the relationship between the worker and the individual becomes the safe "place" where personal history can be revealed and where conflicting feelings and dark thoughts can be brought into focus and explored.' In this way, offenders may be encouraged to reflect critically on personal factors which obstruct desistance such as lifestyle, consumer choice, everyday activities, and relationships with family and friends. Most effective when offenders feel valued and engaged in the supervision process (Trotter 1999), relationship work with offenders is intended to confront ambivalent attitudes and reinforce positive action (Miller and Rollnick 1991). It also encourages offenders to solve their own problems by providing advice and guidance and jointly exploring normative processes which facilitate behavioural change (Rex 1999) – normative processes which focus, for example, 'on some of the mundane events in offenders' lives especially the problems they encounter, how they manage these problems, and their moods and emotional reactions' (Zamble and Quinsey 1997: 149).

Person-centred methods which support biographical development in this way include 'pro-social modelling' and 'motivational interviewing' (Raynor and Maguire 2006). By no means new to probation practice, these techniques have garnered considerable attention and support. McNeill, for example, has recently developed a 'desistance paradigm for offender management' based on the establishment of trust and mutual collaboration, which, in assessing the complex interfaces between technical and moral questions in rehabilitation practice, 'forefronts processes of change rather than modes of intervention' (2006: 56). In the context of imprisonment, too, there is a growing acceptance, academically at least, that relationships, for instance, 'how material goods are *delivered*, how staff *approach* prisoners, how managers treat *staff*, and how life is *lived* through talk, encounter or transaction, constitute (above a minimum threshold) key dimensions of prison life' (Liebling 2004: 50; emphasis in the original). As we saw in Chapter 6, an overall lack of communication in prisons means that, for the most part, the perceptions, attitudes and emotions of prisoners remain a closed book. Consequently, it is difficult to gauge which prisoners are likely to reoffend as a result of either conscious choice or individual deficiency (Sampson and Laub 2005), or, alternatively, identify the readiness of other prisoners to give up crime. Therefore, to support processes of desistance, prisons should develop 'moral performance' criteria based on qualities of justice, fairness, humanity, relationships, trust, respect, and safety, as well as opportunities for personal development (Liebling 2004).

At present, rather than constitute a guiding framework for work with offenders, such approaches remain supplementary to the predominant model of offender rehabilitation based on addressing risk and the treatment of perceived deficits or needs. In contrast to the narrowness of the basic assumptions which inform the 'risk-needs-responsivity' approach, Ward and Maruna (2007: 112) have advocated a 'strength-based' or 'good lives' model of rehabilitation, which assumes that, 'because of their status as human beings, offenders share the same inclinations and basic needs as other people.' It is suggested that, by focusing on the goals or 'primary human goods' they seek through criminal means, offenders 'do not need to abandon those things that are important to them – only to learn to acquire them differently' (*ibid*.: 108). It is only by addressing 'the role of identity and agency in offending' (*ibid*.: 105), and taking into account 'the match between the *characteristics* of the individual and the likely *environment* he or she will be released into' (*ibid*.: 118; emphasis in the original), that it is possible 'to understand the internal and external conditions that are associated with, or in fact constitute, the offender's criminogenic needs, and to build interventions around the amelioration of these problematic conditions' (*ibid*.: 106). As we have looked at the internal processes of behavioural change, the following section assesses the external conditions associated with the agency characteristics of criminal desistance – the goals and goods that offenders value and desire in everyday life and have reason to pursue. Inevitably, this involves discussing the personal and social contexts in which offenders live, and the area-based and community approaches to them.

Area-based initiatives and social exclusion

Policy initiatives implemented to tackle the problems of cities and pockets of deprivation within them often highlight the issue of urban crime, the governance of crime and local community safety. In the UK, originating with the 'Five Towns Initiative' and the 'Safer Cities Programme' in the 1980s, urban regeneration policy over recent decades has prioritised crime reduction directly, or encompassed it as a feature of wider government initiatives such as the Urban Programme, Single Regeneration Budget, and Urban Renaissance and Sustainable Communities Programme. Through implementing principles of architectural design and mobilising local community support, many of these have attempted to synchronise urban-regeneration and crime-reduction measures in order to create 'defended spaces' (Cochrane 2007) and develop 'sustainable' and 'entrepreneurial' communities. Today, it is a key aim of the government's 'National Strategy for Neighbourhood Renewal' to reduce the gap between the 4,000 most socially excluded neighbourhoods and the rest of the country by tackling health, unemployment, housing and crime together (SEU 1998). To do this, central government departments with responsibility for tackling various structural and social components of poverty, unemployment, education, health, urban regeneration, housing, equal opportunity, and social justice have been harnessed to work alongside agencies within the criminal justice system. Based on Local Area Agreements (LAAs), local community programmes, such as Employment, Health and Education Action Zones, New Deal for Communities, SureStart, the Safer and Stronger Communities Fund, the Neighbourhood Renewal Fund, the Working Neighbourhoods Fund, and the Community Empowerment Fund, have been rolled out to encourage urban renewal, promote community development, and fight crime through strategies of integrated local action (Newman 2001). In addition, the 'Cleaner, Safer, Greener' agenda has been implemented to improve play spaces, parks and leisure facilities; in sum, what is referred to as the 'liveability' of local urban environments. And in terms of crime and community safety specifically, multi-agency Crime and Disorder Reduction Partnerships (CDRPs) have been established to reduce crime in local areas, including the incidence of low-level disorder, incivility and antisocial behaviour.

As we saw in Chapter 3, although together these programmes constitute a significant outlay in public spending, a major criticism of this overall approach is that it is contradictory. On the one hand, it promotes social inclusion and local community development, but, on the other hand, through the 'criminalisation of social policy', it attempts to purify urban space. As Hughes (2007: 168) has observed, city regeneration projects are driven by 'a neo-liberal economic agenda of global competitiveness and footloose entrepreneurism and a moral communitarian social agenda aimed at remoralizing communities as object, site and agent of governance'. According to Cochrane (2007: 84) 'in this context, the pursuit of urban policy through forms of policing supported by the planning system can effectively operate to imprison some people in the dangerous places in which they live, while apparently "protecting" others.' Mixed up and implicated in all of this is the much vaunted policy concept of social exclusion, a broad discourse which suggests that certain groups of people who would like to participate in society are unable to do so for a range of reasons beyond their control (Burchardt *et al.* 1999). As such, it encompasses a range of non-spatial factors such as gender and class, as well as factors such as housing, schooling, employment, crime and community breakdown, which, *inter alia*, are affected by physical location (Buck 2001). However, despite the specificity of its overall agenda, captured in policy statements to the effect that within 10–20 years no one shall be seriously disadvantaged by where they live (SEU 2001: 44), social exclusion is a contested idea defined, interpreted and understood in wholly contradictory ways (Young 2002).

Levitas (2005) identifies three separate discourses: a redistributivist discourse (RED), framed in reference to entrenched social divisions of income and relative deprivation; a social integrationist discourse (SID), more narrowly defined in terms of marginalisation from the labour market; and a moral underclass discourse (MUD), based on the view that inequality is a product of the moral and cultural failings of the socially excluded themselves. Each has been drawn upon to investigate the reasons that increasing numbers of marginalised people are unable to participate in society, and the extent to which social exclusion is geographically bounded (Lister 2004). The discourse favoured most in policy circles, however, constructs the problem 'in terms of social and cultural processes (schooling, ill health, lack of access to training opportunities, possible racism) rather than in terms of lack of material resources' (Newman 2001: 29); that is, through SID and MUD rather than RED interventions. As such, the social exclusion agenda stops short of 'proposing routes to a more spatially integrated urban society as opposed to the thinning out of poverty or its superficial amelioration in targeted areas' (Atkinson *et al.* 2005: 171). Although it is emphasised that area and crime-based urban regeneration initiatives should be informed by the concerns of local people, and that nothing is ruled out and nothing ruled in, in practice policies on crime reduction and community safety have been driven by the government's Anti-social Behaviour Respect Action Plan (Home Office 2006b). As Gilling (2007: 220) has pointed out, based on strategies of 'duty' and 'responsibilisation', 'the lion's share of the armoury is devoted to enforcement measures, and even when support measures are "offered", they are offered with the threat of enforcement for non-compliance.' The overall outcome has been to redefine the urban neighbourhood as a moral space which engenders a decrease in tolerance of individuals and groups who, it is assumed, lack social and cultural responsibility (Callinicos 2001). Moreover, the repositioning of antisocial behaviour and crime as a problem caused predominately by young people (Hughes 2007) has privileged the spatial management of crime over its social, economic and political antecedents. As such, it serves to rehabilitate space rather than people (Coleman 2003).

It is within this overall policy context that current offender reintegration initiatives have been developed and implemented. As we saw in Chapter 2, the Reducing Reoffending National Action Plan (Home Office 2004b) has been informed by studies of social exclusion in particular (SEU 2002). In England and Wales, high rates of reoffending have been linked to a 'sharp rise in social exclusion, in areas such as child poverty, drug use, school exclusion, and inequality' (*ibid.*: 5). Similarly, in Scotland, it has been found that 'the relationship between social exclusion and imprisonment is systemic. Risk of imprisonment is as much a correlate of social deprivation as are poverty, chronic unemployment or poor life expectancy' (Houchin 2005: 77). However, although measures to address social exclusion are generally accepted as a precondition of crime reduction and community safety, and the connection between social exclusion and imprisonment has been clearly made, reflecting the contradictory discourses and approaches taken with respect to social exclusion generally, there is little consensus on the policy prescriptions needed to address increasingly high rates of reoffending and re-imprisonment specifically. A key point of departure is the importance attached to place. For example, in drawing a direct line between place of residence, social deprivation and imprisonment, the report on social exclusion in Scotland recommends a RED and SID policy approach based on a strategy of regeneration within the relatively few communities from which the evidence shows that the majority of Scottish prisoners are drawn. Suggesting that offending is 'normal role behaviour, normatively governed and approved within its social context' (*ibid*: 80), it notes that:

> The number of communities in which such profound development is needed in order to have a significant impact on the numbers of young men requiring punishment is relatively small and highly concentrated, particularly in Glasgow and to a lesser extent in three other of our cities and a small number of Unitary Authority areas in the West of Scotland. The concentration of the problem in the City of Glasgow marks it out as standing alone in its need for social regeneration. (*ibid.*: 86)

In contrast, the report on social exclusion in England and Wales pays scant regard to the geographical location of offenders, or the extent to which it correlates to spatial patterns of social deprivation. Observing in the most general terms that prisoners are drawn from socially deprived metropolitan areas, it recommends equally generic policy interventions based on SID and MUD approaches; for instance, a national strategy of rehabilitation programmes to address individual risk factors such as attitudes, thinking and behaviour, as well as measures to improve social opportunity outcomes on accommodation; education, training and employment; mental and physical health; drugs and alcohol; finance, benefit and debt; and children and families (SEU 2002).

Partnership working and information sharing

This does not mean, of course, that rehabilitation and reintegration work is not undertaken in England and Wales. Indeed, a key driver of the new approach has been 'that the national strategy should make strong links with effective regional and local partnerships, including Crime and Disorder Partnerships' (SEU 2002: 135). Accepting that the police, courts, prisons and probation service have only a limited capacity to tackle crime and community safety, non-criminal justice agencies are encouraged to play a more proactive role in community-based offender reintegration. This requires a multi-agency, local partnership approach. For 'end-to-end offender management' and 'seamless sentences' to work effectively, there needs to be close coordination and 'continuity of service' (Clancy et al. 2006) between prisons, probation services, other criminal justice agencies, and mainstream community services (Home Office 2001b; SEU 2002; Carter 2003). As such, the government's 'Five-Year Strategy for Protecting the Public and Reducing Re-offending' (Home Office 2006a: 30) includes 'facilities for less serious offenders, and for those getting close to release, which are local, which link to the local community, and to local services'. In particular, there is 'a critical role for local government to play, working in partnership with NOMS, local probation boards, and youth offending teams, in reducing re-offending and protecting the public' (Department for Communities and Local Government 2006).

However, while it is generally acknowledged that complex, 'wicked' problems such as crime require a response which no single agency can provide, partnership, like social exclusion, is beset by conflicting policy objectives and contentious and politically infused relationships at local, regional and national levels of government (Hughes and Rowe 2007). Policies for the urban and civil renewal of local communities have been developed between national and local government (Newman 2001); and as enshrined in the Crime and Disorder Act 1998, in partnership with the police, local authorities now have a statutory responsibility for community safety and crime prevention. However, as many critics have pointed out, power differentials between national and local government influence the strategic direction taken (ibid.). Most crucially, in relation to the reasons and circumstances, expenditure is allocated to locally based, bottom-up policies. For example, Simmie et al. (2006) have commented that funding made available by national government is often too short-term to impact on the success or failure of local urban economies. Moreover, it is allocated without the benefit of local knowledge. As detailed in Chapter 2, this is a significant failing. Global and national forces have resulted in significant differences in the economic and social trajectories of urban environments throughout the UK, a clear indication that 'difference and diversity can no longer be reconciled through universalist projects' (Amin and Thrift 2002: 139). In order to tailor policies appropriately, local information and expertise must be brought to bear on the problems at hand, a level of analysis often far too detailed for central government to contemplate. As a result:

> English city regions have very weak powers over their local economies. Central government macro-economic and fiscal policy combined with mainstream as opposed to spatially targeted funding programmes make and pay for most of the key decisions concerning urban economies. Local authorities have very limited powers and resources when it comes to strategic decisions concerning their economies. (Simmie *et al.* 2006: 12)

Such inherent tensions in 'joined-up government, public participation and public–private partnerships have hampered the crime-reduction agenda ever since the Morgan Report (1991) first recommended a multi-agency approach to community safety. As Crawford (1998: 171) has observed, 'deep structural conflicts exist between the parties that sit down together in partnerships. Criminal justice agencies have very different priorities and interests, as do other public sector organisations, voluntary bodies, the commercial sector and local community groups.' As we have seen in Chapter 1, such conflict is very much at the heart of current debates over whether offenders grow out of crime without the assistance of formal correctional treatment (Farrall 2002; Maruna *et al.* 2004). For instance, Maguire and Raynor (2006: 32) have pointed out that the process issues involved in the unification of traditional 'what works' cognitive-behavioural approaches and broader criminal-desistance perspectives are likely to 'depend on interagency collaboration of a kind that will not be easy to reproduce'. It is predictable, therefore, that progress in relation to offender reintegration has been both slow and piecemeal.

To date, various voluntary and community sector organisations have been engaged; in particular, those with remits already closely linked to crime and penal policy, such as the crime-reduction charity Nacro, the Rehabilitation for Addicted Prisoners Trust, and Partners in Reducing Reoffending. However, so far, there has been little evidence of a meaningful contribution from organisations that operate outside the criminal justice system such as local government and local business. Indeed, according to the Local Government Association (LGA 2005), civic leadership has been marginalised, local knowledge and expertise ignored, and local problem-solving capabilities undermined. In the light of the evidence that prisoners 'tend to come from particular neighbourhoods; those neighbourhoods which are well known because of their social problems and deprivation' (ibid.: 2), it follows that services should be targeted at and local expertise harnessed within the same communities to which they return. Because:

> localities differ markedly from one local authority to another and within their boundaries from one neighbourhood to another, NOMS should engage with local government at the local level to understand the complexities, concerns and creativity of communities, as well as the services available in a local area where an offender will be a member of the community. (ibid.: 19)

This chimes with arguments outlined in Chapter 1, for instance, the finding that although processes of criminal desistance play out within the community, 'many have neglected to include the role of "the community" in their investigations of probation supervision' (Farrall 2004: 62). According to Raine (2006: 8), the main reason for the neglect of local communities and local people is systemic; in particular, the management arrangements adopted within NOMS for the devolution of power and responsibility for offender reintegration. The specific mechanism for this is 'contestability', an arrangement whereby Regional Offender Managers (ROMs) commission services from local organisations. However, in seeking to ensure that accountability is tightly controlled and monitored from the centre, NOMS has relied too much on the application of New Public Management techniques, and too little on the 'process issues that will determine just how effective the new framework can be in meeting the twin targets of crime reduction and enhanced confidence expected of it' (ibid.). As a consequence, its overall administrative and management structure remains 'some distance removed from the task of constructing local situations, schemes or relationships that would benefit individual offenders, victims or communities and achieve some reconciliation between them' (Faulkner 2006: 86).

It is against this background that new proposals for the devolution of funding and criminal justice reinvestment in local communities have recently been assessed. Based on a geographical approach to prisoner reintegration piloted in the United States, the 'Justice Reinvestment' project seeks to divert funds away from custody budgets in order to pump-prime non-criminal justice employment, health, education and housing services in the local communities where they are likely to have the greatest impact. By using GIS to identify the neighbourhoods which receive the most released prisoners, 'million dollar blocks' have been identified that contain concentrations of offenders removed to prison at a cost exceeding a million dollars. As there is no logic 'to spending a million dollars a year to incarcerate people from one block in Brooklyn ... and return them, on average, in less than three years stigmatized, unskilled, and untrained to the same unchanged block' (Tucker and Cadora 2003: 2), it follows that significant savings can be made by diverting certain sections of the prison population to less expensive community sanctions. For instance, by reducing the sentences of short-term prisoners or those returned to prison for technical violations of parole, state legislatures are able to redirect spending from correctional budgets in order to invest in at-risk local communities.

Applying these ideas to the UK, the International Centre for Prison Studies has piloted a similar project in the local authority area of Gateshead in north-east England (Allen and Stern 2007). By diverting short-term prisoners away from custody, it is suggested that money would be made available to the local authority and probation service to coordinate multi-agency resettlement partnerships and establish neighbourhood-based justice centres in the areas where most ex-prisoners live. To a limited extent, the government, too, has responded to the idea. The Ministry of Justice has introduced 'diamond districts', an initiative intended to coordinate resettlement services in three local authority areas and that is targeted at neighbourhoods where the largest numbers of ex-prisoners reside, although no commitment has been made to divert offenders from custody or invest in non-criminal justice services in order to finance this (Commission on English Prisons Today 2008). Moreover, the House of Commons Justice Committee (Ministry of Justice 2009c: 2.38) has reported that 'England and Wales could benefit from this kind of focus on the local community'. However, the committee goes on to comment that much needs to be done to achieve this. Reflecting concerns articulated throughout this book, it finds that 'the emphasis of strategic planning here has not usually addressed information about where offenders live or how best to reduce the local deprivation which may give rise to their offending' (*ibid.*).

The problem is twofold: it involves both information recording and information sharing, a source of seemingly permanent tension within partnership working arrangements, particularly those between national and local government to address crime reduction and community safety (Gilling 2007). The first issue to note is that, although data are kept by the police, the courts, Crime Disorder Reduction Partnerships (CDRPs), the probation service and the prison service, the data are partial and not usually kept in an accessible form. For instance, the Police National Computer contains postcode information on crime location, but does not contain address information that may be extracted in usable form. This is also true of the Offenders Index, which contains court disposals relating to standard list offences, but not geographical information about where offences were committed or who committed them (Home Office 2002b). Moreover, as explained in the Appendix, prisoner addresses are neither systematically nor accurately recorded. An obvious source of information is that collected by NOMS for risk assessment and prediction purposes. Both of the risk assessment tools, OASys and Asset, contain information on offences, thinking and behaviour, and attitudes, as well as various social issues such as relationships, lifestyle and associates; education; employment; and, crucially, the quality, suitability and location of accommodation (Howard et al. 2006). Together, these instruments consistently collect a comprehensive source of data. Yet, as Webster et al. (2006: 19) have observed, there is little sense in which such information is used 'in any meaningful way' to assess the local neighbourhood context; for instance, to coordinate services, identify gaps in provision, and improve applications for housing. In assessing the reasons for the lack of quality of offender address data, the House of Commons Justice Committee (Ministry of Justice 2009c: 2.71) concludes that

> Priority-setting to concentrate effort on existing offenders in particular areas is hampered by both the poor quality of data available locally and lack of accessibility to data that is available. We find it remarkable there are still problems with information sharing when it is over 10 years since the Crime and Disorder Act make it quite clear that information can be shared for the purposes of preventing offending.

The Justice Reinvestment initiative has garnered considerable support, not least because it provides a local strategic planning approach to socially deprived and high-crime urban communities. Nevertheless, translating the approach from the state legislature context of the United States to much smaller governmental administrations within the UK poses significant managerial problems. It also raises the crucial question of how savings are to be used and, closely associated with this, by whom and for what purpose. As the Justice Committee

(Ministry of Justice 2009c: 2.33) points out, 'the dividends from reducing spending on custody would not be received automatically by those agencies responsible for the spending to reduce, or enable the reduction of, its use.' The key issue here is that, although defining social issues locally targets provision on communities most in need of support, such initiatives are likely to prove ineffective if policy decisions made nationally – such as, in this instance, those which affect sentencing and the prison population, but also prison conditions, and the work of the probation service – take no account of local interests and concerns. Equally, as we have seen, it is a feature of area-based approaches generally to deprioritise larger national and global forces, and the economic and social policies emanating from them that give rise to local problems (Cochrane 2007). Below, two broad social issues commonly associated with crime and reoffending, employment and housing, both affected significantly at the local level by national and wider economic and social policies, are briefly reassessed before the book concludes with some final thoughts on agency and structure.

Constraints and capabilities

It is often argued that employment is the primary route out of social exclusion and crime. As evidenced by the priority accorded to such programmes as the New Deal for the unemployed and the Connexions youth support programme, providing skills training and improving equal opportunities in local job markets has been a central component of recent government policy on social exclusion and crime reduction (Gilling 2007). Yet, according to some commentators, the approach is fundamentally flawed. Given that jobs simply are not available in socially deprived neighbourhoods (Young 1999; Byrne 2005; Levitas 2005), Wilkinson (2005: 284) has argued that employment opportunity policies rest on the erroneous assumption that

> you can reduce the unpleasantness of unemployment while leaving the real rate of unemployment unchanged simply by helping some people to get jobs in place of others.... The substitution of equality of opportunity for equality of outcome as a political aim reflects a monumental failure even to begin thinking seriously about the causes of our society's problems.

As discussed in Chapter 1, it is not work itself that encourages offenders to give up crime; rather it is the meaning and value attached to work that instigate behavioural change. In order to instil 'self-efficacy' (Bandura 1982) – the belief that individuals can influence events and attain a desired goal – lifelong learning is necessary to facilitate a move out of poverty and benefit dependence, update knowledge and skills, and support offenders to navigate the demise of traditional forms of employment. Unless policies are put in place, both locally and nationally, to redistribute socio-economic resources and create entry-level jobs of sufficient quality, those who receive basic forms of training are unlikely to move out of 'in-work poverty', a condition which in some communities is now as much a characteristic of social deprivation as unemployment (Dorling *et al*. 2007).

As with unemployment, there is a good deal of evidence to suggest that homelessness and unstable housing are linked to reoffending (SEU 2002), and that helping ex-prisoners find appropriate accommodation supports criminal desistance (Joseph Rowntree Foundation 1996). However, housing is not predictive of a non-criminal lifestyle. Like employment, housing type determines whether it is valued or not by ex-prisoners. Those not returning to prior accommodation, living in temporary accommodation with family or friends, or eligible for sheltered accommodation, have three options. As they are considered to have a 'priority need', in that they are 'vulnerable as a result of having been remanded or having served time in custody', they are eligible to apply for social housing. Alternatively, they may attempt to secure a privately rented tenancy, or seek shelter in bed-and-breakfast accommodation, or in a hostel.

For a variety of reasons, ex-prisoners face considerable difficulty in negotiating any of these options. First, less than a fifth receive help to find accommodation after release (Niven and Olagundaye 2002). Second, there is a systemic lack of affordable housing available to them. Finally, they are often subject to inequitable and unfair housing-allocation policies. As Maguire and Nolan (2007) point out, local authorities and housing associations do not always fulfil their obligations to those who have served time in custody. For instance, they may be denied accommodation by housing officers who subjectively evaluate worth based on perceptions of dependability and honesty – for example, whether they are likely to pay rent or are legitimately homeless. Moreover, since antisocial behaviour has become a housing issue, social landlords often routinely reject applications from individuals that they consider will disrupt the social balance of the area (Flint 2006). Even those who secure housing often find themselves in precarious situations. For example, as Houchin (2005) has shown in the context of Glasgow, prisoners who return to prior accommodation mostly come from 'ACORN Type H' housing, the poorest type of council estate. Such areas, in which much social housing is situated, are often characterised by criminogenic 'neighbourhood effects' linked to poverty, unemployment and high population turnover (e.g. Weatherburn *et al*. 1999; Newman and Harkness 2002; Reid-Howie Associates 2004), which serve to sustain long-term criminal careers (Hagan 1993).

Finally, let us revisit and conclude the guiding themes of this book. The failure to secure adequate employment and housing is an indication that processes of criminal desistance and offender reintegration are shaped by where offenders live. Moreover, where they live is determined by an overall system of capitalist reproduction which is highly unstable and generally locates groups of people differentially according to the availability of resources: education, training, employment, housing and civil entitlements (Castells 1977). Uneven geographic development is an systemic outcome of social relations and socio-economic processes within modern capitalism (Harvey 1973; Lefebvre 1991 [1974]). It follows that relying on government to facilitate effective economic and social interventions for ex-prisoners relegated to urban neighbourhoods characterised by high levels of structural unemployment and homelessness is unrealistic. Therefore, social policy must concentrate on developing what Sen (1999) has termed 'competencies', 'skills', 'capabilities' and 'functionings'. While the capability of individuals to make use of resources and opportunities is repressed by the denial of access to adequately resourced and managed space, it is enabled and supported by social networks (Sen 1985, 1992, 1999). As argued throughout this book, the motivation and confidence to overcome structural and social challenges and achieve behavioural change both recreate and are created by the physical and social environment. Policy responses to economic and social problems do not emerge unbidden; they are precipitated by complaint and resistance, through which 'social actors, on the basis of whatever cultural materials are available to them, build a new identity that redefines their position in society' (Castells 2004: 8). However, while some develop the 'agency aspect' to accumulate social capital on their own and so impose themselves on their environment, given the diversity of preferences and predicaments of different individuals in society, others require institutional support (Sen 1992). Freeing individuals of the constraints which confine them to communal modes of thought and behaviour is a fundamental characteristic of a just, well-ordered and healthy society. It is also suggestive of a policy to rehabilitate and reintegrate offenders.

Appendix

A note on the methodology

This book is based on both quantitative and qualitative research. Quantitative research methodologies are associated with a 'positive' scientific tradition which explains the social world according to laws and rational logics. Qualitative methodologies, on the other hand, are associated with an 'interpretive' tradition based on the understanding that social reality cannot be studied independently of human experience. Miles and Huberman (1994: 1) suggest that the distinction between the two is characterised by the use of numbers rather than words; and Hammersley (1992: 163) suggests that it is by precise and imprecise data. However, most social researchers would agree that, when appropriately applied, 'both of these paradigms complement each other, rather than compete' (Black 1993: 3). In fact, combining quantitative and qualitative research methodologies to explore the link between crime and place dates back to Victorian times when social reformers such as William Mayhew used quantitative data to map urban poverty and crime in London and qualitative research to describe their everyday social consequences. Throughout the early part of the last century, the Chicago sociologists also employed multiple research methodologies, including statistical spatial analysis, in-depth interviewing and ethnography, to explain urban concentrations of crime and criminality. More recently, human geographers have employed quantitative and qualitative methodologies to investigate historical, social, economic, political, and cultural dimensions of urban life; and personalise abstract statistical detail (Ley 1985).

Although the quantitative and qualitative elements of this project were not intended to be interactive, separately they each serve a specific purpose. The quantitative account of prisoners' residential distribution is intended to increase the 'generalisability' of the research design as a whole (Maxwell 1996). Most importantly, it confirms that the meanings and interpretations expressed by the prisoners who were interviewed are related to the experience of living in particular areas, whereas the qualitative account is better suited to the study of 'social interaction processes, definitions of situations, decision-making processes, and contingencies and turning points in the life course, and the ways in which larger scale contextual factors such as social structures are dealt with by social actors' (Ulmer and Spencer 1999: 106). Combining quantitative and qualitative research methodologies in this way ensures that 'the process which is claimed to be typical is shown to be adequately grasped on the level of meaning and at the same time the interpretation is to some degree causally adequate' (Weber 1978: 10).

Address data for the quantitative component of the research were collected from an 'Inmate Information System' database of prisoner records. Information was gathered on both remand and sentenced prisoners with a home address in Greater London. It needs to be pointed out that procedures adopted to record prisoner address information raise important issues of validity and reliability. Normally, address information is recorded during the first few days of a prisoner's sentence. It comprises a 'home address', 'reception address', 'discharge address', 'next-of-kin address', 'curfew address', and 'another address'. Details are relayed verbally by prisoners and recorded by hand by prison officers. Prisoners are under no compulsion to provide an address and often they do not. Moreover, because prisoners who are registered as homeless are eligible for a higher discharge grant, the number of 'no fixed abode' prisoners is likely to be overestimated (SEU 2002). The reliability of the data is further compromised by the ad hoc way information is recorded. Most of the address fields are left empty and the addresses that are recorded are often incomplete or misspelled. As a consequence, although inaccurate and incomplete addresses were investigated, using the Royal Mail's address-finder database, the number of postcodes used to plot the geographical distribution of prisoner addresses within Greater London was significantly reduced in size. The final sample comprised 5,139 postcodes, 35 per cent of the total population of 14,614 prisoners who were recorded as having an address in Greater London from the period October 1993 to May 2005.

This data set is visually represented in Chapter 2, using a geographical information system (GIS). GIS relates data to places.

It differs from iconic representations – scaled down models of the real thing – in that it 'preserves the unique attributes of places and particular time periods, while retaining the power to generalize about events that occur in different places and times' (Longley 2004: 109). In this case, prisoner postcode information was correlated with 2001 Census Area Statistics in order to show whether areas of prisoner residence conform to areas of social deprivation, including socio-economic classification, occupation, health, educational qualifications and housing tenure.

GIS is widely used. As a means of presenting data graphically, it guides the operations of government departments and agencies including the police, local authorities and other practitioners involved in crime control. It is also used by private businesses to link personal data to demographic information and thereby target new customers and potential markets (Clarke 1999). A primary attribute of GIS is that it provides a simplified version of the world. This is both a strength and a weakness. GIS provides quick answers to problems of a spatial and temporal nature in an easily recognisable map form, but it is unable to reveal information of substance relating to more complex areas of social life. In terms of crime, for instance, GIS is used mainly to analyse patterns and, to a much lesser extent, to explain the causes of a crime problem or evaluate the impact of an intervention (Weir and Bangs 2007). Moreover, because there are many ways in which the data tools contained within GIS can be utilised, individuals and organisations are able to mould the system to particular needs in a way that forces complex issues into overly simplistic categories and boundaries (Clarke 1999). Human choice concerning what to put in and what to leave out, and how the resultant data set is manipulated, can therefore lead to meanings and explanations that satisfy an innate preference for 'a world of black and white, of good guys and bad guys, to the real world of shades of grey' (Longley *et al.* 2001).

In the light of this, the use of GIS to correlate the spatial distribution of offenders with indices of social deprivation also raises important issues of validity and reliability. First, because maps produced by GIS cannot be more accurate or contain more detail than the source data that produced them (Martin 1996), it is necessary to include information on how the data were gathered, manipulated and presented; and also to identify gaps, errors and omissions contained within the data (Laurini and Thompson 1992). As explained above, there were important inaccuracies and inconsistencies contained within the postcode data used to map the spatial distribution of prisoners within Greater London. Second, for reasons of data protection, most

GIS applications are constrained by the need to aggregate data and preserve confidentiality (Longley 2004). Nevertheless, visual representations produced by GIS are frequently considered accurate enough to warrant drawing conclusions and taking effective action – 'a form of instrumentalism that is proliferating in many spheres of GIS use whether the object is a parcel of land, terrain for military action, or a neighbourhood of like consumers' (Pickles 2002: 240). Therefore, it should be emphasised that there is no simple, cause-and-effect relationship between the physical and social characteristics of an area and the characteristics of the individuals or groups who live there. Individuals do not experience or relate to the places they inhabit in the same way. Furthermore, postcode areas, boroughs and wards are not natural areas; they are arbitrarily imposed. They are also large and often diverse enough to include neighbourhoods which are different in character. As discussed throughout this book, neighbourhoods are composed of interconnections that operate at different spatial scales from the local to the global. They are 'not a closed system of social relations but a particular articulation of contacts and influences drawn from a variety of places scattered, according to power relations, fashion, and habit across many different parts of the globe' (Massey 1998: 124). Therefore, it is important to avoid drawing erroneous conclusions about the nature and behaviour of people in particular areas that can arise from aggregation-based systems and socio-economic data (Martin 1996).

The central concern of the qualitative component of the research was to uncover social and environmental processes linked to criminal desistance and the degree to which these are related to the places inhabited by persistent offenders over the life course. This necessitated a narrative phenomenological approach, one guided by the working assumption that people do not exist apart from the real world; the two are indivisible and people are intimately and intentionally immersed within it (Moran 2000). Biographical, narrative or storytelling research is a method of excavating the ways individuals develop a sense of self, and how they see and experience the world around them. Rather than collect facts, it gathers personal experiences and descriptions of social background and specific situations and places (von Eckartsberg 1998). A strength of this approach is that it focuses on 'naturally occurring, ordinary events in natural settings' (Miles and Huberman 1994: 10). Therefore, it is suited to 'locating the meanings people place on the events, processes, and structures of their lives: their perceptions, assumptions, prejudgements, presuppositions and for connecting these meanings to the social world around them' (ibid.). However, a common criticism of phenomenological and qualitative research in general is that it lacks a guiding hypothesis. Social processes are considered 'too complex, too relative, too elusive, or too exotic to be approached with explicit conceptual frames or standard instruments' (*ibid.*: 17). The social world is real only because individuals experience it as real. It follows that 'there is no unambiguous social reality out there to be accounted for, so there is little need to evolve methodological canons to help explicate its laws (*ibid.*: 2).

Research of this kind with offenders is rare. However, two previous studies – Cohen and Taylor (1972) on the effects of long-term imprisonment, and Maruna (2001) on criminal desistance – guided the design of the research in order to address the inherent messiness of qualitative methodologies. To a degree, the semi-structured approach to life-history interviewing adopted for the study was also influenced by the work of Parker (1966), particularly with regard to establishing a relationship of trust with the participants, although, given the time available for each interview, the opportunity to explore specific aspects of the stories they told was limited. Bar one interview conducted with a participant outside prison, the interviews were conducted throughout 2006 with 29 serving male prisoners (both sentenced and unsentenced) in three local prisons in London, each situated within an area where the quantitative analysis showed there to be a particular concentration of prisoner addresses: Pentonville in the north of the inner city; and Wandsworth and Brixton in the south. The mean age of the sample was 29, and the mean length of offending career, dated from age at first conviction to age at the time of the interview, was 14 years.

Owing to the small sample size, it was decided to restrict the study to male prisoners. Including women would have raised contrasting gender issues relating to criminal desistance and place. Women generally commit less serious crime far less persistently than men (Graham and Bowling 1995). Because there are relatively few female compared to male prisoners, they also tend to be held long distances from their homes, often in remote parts of the country (Cavadino and Dignan 1997). Furthermore, the only female prison in London, Holloway, draws its population from the whole of the south of England and so does not function in the same way as local male prisons, each of which serves a specific local catchment area. Therefore, a separate study is warranted to assess the relationship between the imprisonment of women and place of residence.

The sample was selected according to whether participants lived within the area of Greater London and the number of prison sentences served. Statistics show that first-time prisoners are 23 per cent less likely to be reconvicted and 13 per cent less likely to be re-imprisoned than prisoners with one or two previous convictions (Home Office 2003). Therefore, in order to ensure that a recurring cycle of offending and re-imprisonment had been established, the sample was restricted to prisoners who had served at least two previous prison sentences. As it turned out, over two-thirds of the participants had been convicted five times or more. Most had committed a large number of different offences before they reached the age of 21. The most common crimes were theft, taking and driving away, domestic and commercial burglary, assault and street robbery, drug dealing, fraud and armed robbery. One participant had been convicted of manslaughter, another of rape, and two were serving life sentences for murder.

All interviewees were self-selecting, having learned about the research from leaflets and posters, or they had been referred by prison staff. It has been noted that prisoners rarely refuse requests to be interviewed because 'taking time out' with researchers offers a diversion from everyday prison routine (Burnett 2004a: 156). Normally, the participants expressed an opinion as to why they had consented to the interview. For some it was an opportunity to do something different, get 'off the landings' for a while. Others claimed to be interested in the topic and wanted to talk about where they grew up and what they were going to do and where they were going to live after release. This is possibly indicative of selection bias. Interestingly, however, many of the participants explained that previously they would never have disclosed information about themselves as young offenders.

Interviews were scheduled to last two hours and structured to allow participants the opportunity to tell their own stories in their own way and bring in tangential matters which, for them, were meaningful and had a bearing on the main subject (Hakim 2000). Of course, in asking participants to divulge personal details, it is entirely possible the accounts received would be fictionalised, idealised and also heavily censored. Moreover, given the well-known propensity of offenders to 'rationalize their behaviour with a whole gamut of techniques of neutralization' (Gadd and Farrall 2004: 148), it is unrealistic to expect 'that authentic accounts of what "things are really like" will be given in moments of emotional intimacy where souls are bared and pretence is stripped away' (Seale 1998: 209). The only real certainty is that the participants told their life stories in their own words, unaware of the contextual analysis that informs studies of space and place, the dichotomy of structure and agency, the impact of space/time compression, the 'spaces of postmodernity' and so forth. Because 'truth is also always personal and subjective' (Denzin 1997: 265–6), in following the narrative development of their lives in relation to this contextual analysis, it is up to the reader to make a judgement on the validity and reliability of the conclusions about space and time that are drawn from it.

Bibliography

Adorno, T. (1991) *The Culture Industry*. London: Routledge.

Akers, R.L. (1990) 'Rational Choice, Deterrence and Social Learning in Criminology: The Path Not Taken', *Journal of Criminal Law and Criminology*, 81: 653–76.

Albee, G.W. (1990) 'The Futility of Psychotherapy', *Journal of Mind and Behavior*, 11: 369–84.

Allen, C. (2007) *Crime, Drugs and Social Theory: A Phenomenological Approach*. Aldershot: Ashgate.

Allen, R., Jallab, K. and Snaith, E. (2007) 'Justice Reinvestment in Gateshead: The Story so Far', in R. Allen and V. Stern (eds), *Justice Reinvestment: A New Approach to Crime and Justice*. London: International Centre for Prison Studies.

Allen, R. and Stern, V. (eds) (2007) *Justice Reinvestment: A New Approach to Crime and Justice*. London: International Centre for Prison Studies.

Amin, A. and Thrift, N. (2002) *Cities: Reimagining the Urban*. Cambridge: Polity.

Anderson, E. (1998) 'The Social Ecology of Youth Violence', in M. Tonry and M.H. Moore (eds), *Youth Violence*, vol. 24. Chicago: University of Chicago Press.

Anderson, E. (1999) *Code of the Street: Decency, Violence, and the Moral Life of the Inner City*. New York: W.W. Norton.

Anderson, E. (2001) 'Going Straight: The Story of a Young Inner-City Ex-convict', *Punishment and Society*, 3 (1): 135–52.

Andrews, D. (1995) 'The Psychology of Criminal Conduct and Effective Treatment' in J. McGuire (ed.), *What Works: Reducing Reoffending – Guidelines from Research and Practice*. Chichester: John Wiley and Sons.

Andrews, D.A., Bonta, J. and Hoge, R.D. (1990) 'Classification for Effective Rehabilitation: Rediscovering Psychology', *Criminal Justice and Behaviour* 17: 19–52.

Arnold, H. (2005) 'The Effects of Prison Work', in A. Liebling and S. Maruna (eds), *The Effects of Imprisonment*. Cullompton: Willan Publishing.

Atkinson, R., Buck, N. and Kintrea, K. (2005) 'Neighbourhoods and Poverty: Linking Place and Social Exclusion', in N. Buck, I. Gordon, A. Harding and I. Turok (eds), *Changing Cities: Rethinking Urban Competitiveness, Cohesion and Governance*. Basingstoke: Palgrave Macmillan.

Atkinson, R. and Kintrea, K. (2001) 'Disentangling Area Effects: Evidence from Deprived and Non-deprived Neighbourhoods', *Urban Studies*, 38 (12): 2277–98.

Atkinson, R. and Moon, G. (1994) *Urban Policy in Britain: The City, the State and the Market*. Basingstoke: Macmillan.

Augé, M. (1995) *Non-places: Introduction to an Anthropology of Supermodernity*. London: Verso.

Baldwin, J. and Bottoms, A.E. (1976) *The Urban Criminal: A Study in Sheffield*. London: Tavistock.

Ball., S.J., Maguire, M. and Macrae, S. (2000) *Choice, Pathways and Transition Post-16: New Youth, New Economies in the Global City*. London: Routledge.

Bandura, A. (1973) *Aggression: A Social Learning Analysis*. Englewood Cliffs, NJ: Prentice-Hall.

Bandura, A. (1977) *Social Learning Theory*. Englewood Cliffs, NJ: Prentice-Hall.

Bandura, A. (1982) 'Self-Efficacy Mechanism in Human Agency', *American Psychologist*, 37: 122–47.

Banfield, E. (1974) *The Unheavenly City Revisited*. Boston: Little Brown and Co.

Barry, M. (2006) *Youth Offending in Transition: The Search for Social Recognition*. London: Routledge.

Barton, R. (1966) *Institutional Neurosis*, 2nd edn. Bristol: Wright Publishing.

Baskin, D.R. and Sommers, I.B. (1998) *Casualties of Community Disorder: Women's Careers in Violent Crime*. Boulder, CO: Westview Press.

Baum, A. and Paulus, P.B. (1987) 'Crowding', in E. Stockols and I. Altman (eds), *Handbook of Environmental Psychology*, vol. I. New York: Wiley-Interscience.

Bauman, Z. (1989) 'Hermeneutics and Modern Social Theory' in D. Held and J. Thompson (eds), *Social Theory of Modern Societies: Anthony Giddens and His Critics*. Cambridge: Cambridge University Press.

Bauman, Z. (1998) *Work, Consumerism and the New Poor*. Buckingham: Open University Press.

Bauman, Z. (2001) *The Individualized Society*. Cambridge: Polity Press.

Bauman, Z. (2004) *Identity*. Cambridge: Polity Press.

Baumgartner, M.P. (1988) *The Moral Order of a Suburb*. New York: Oxford University Press.

Beccaria, C [1767] (1995) *On Crimes and Punishments and Other Writings*, ed. R. Bellemy. Cambridge: Cambridge University Press.

Beck, U. (1992) *Risk Society: Towards a New Modernity*. London: Sage.

Becker, H. (1963) *Outsiders: Studies in the Sociology of Deviance*. New York: The Free Press.

Behan, B. (1958) *Borstal Boy*. London: Hutchinson.

Beider, H. (2009) 'Guest Introduction: Rethinking Race and Housing', *Housing Studies*, 24 (4): 405–15.

Bennett, T. and Holloway, K. (2004) 'Gang Membership, Drugs and Crime in the UK', *British Journal of Criminology*, 44 (3): 305–23.

Bentham, J. [1789] (1996) *An Introduction to the Principles of Morals and Legislation: Works of Jeremy Bentham*. Oxford: Oxford University Press.

Bentham, J. (1791) *Panopticon*. London.

Berger, P. and Luckman, T. (1966) *The Social Construction of Reality: A Treatise in the Sociology of Knowledge*. New York: Doubleday.

Berman, M. (1983) *All That Is Solid Melts into Air: The Experience of Modernity*. London: Verso.

Black, T.R. (1993) *Evaluating Social Science Research: An Introduction*. London: Sage.

Blumer, H. (1969) *Symbolic Interactionism: Perspective and Method*. Englewood Cliffs, NJ: Prentice-Hall.

Blumstein, A. and Cohen, J. (1987) 'Characterizing Criminal Careers', *Science*, 237: 985–91

Boeck, T., Fleming, J. and Kemshall, H. (2006) 'The Context of Risk Decisions: Does Social Capital Make a Difference?', *Forum Qualitative Sozialforschung/ Forum: Qualitative Social Research*, 7 (1), Art. 17.

Bosworth, M. (1999) *Engendering Resistance: Agency and Power in Women's Prisons*. Aldershot: Dartmouth.

Bottoms, A. (2006) 'Desistance, Social Bonds, and Human Agency: A Theoretical Exploration', in P.-O. Wikström and R.J. Sampson (eds), *The Explanation of Crime: Context, Mechanisms and Development*. Cambridge: Cambridge University Press.

Bottoms, A.E., Claytor, A. and Wiles, P. (1992) 'Housing Markets and Residential Community Crime Careers: A Case Study from Sheffield', in D.J. Evans, D.T. Herbert and N.R. Fyfe (eds), *Crime, Policing and Place: Essays in Environmental Criminology*. London: Routledge.

Bottoms, A.E. and Wiles, P. (1992) 'Explanations of Crime and Place', in D.J. Evans, N.R. Fyfe and D.T. Herbert (eds), *Crime, Policing and Place: Essays in Environmental Criminology*. London: Routledge.

Bottoms, A.E. and Wiles, P. (1997) 'Environmental Criminology', in M. Maguire, R. Morgan and R. Reiner (eds), *The Oxford Handbook of Criminology*, 2nd edn. Oxford: Clarendon Press.

Bottoms, A.E. and Wiles, P. (2002) 'Environmental Criminology', in M. Maguire, R. Morgan and R. Reiner (eds), *The Oxford Handbook of Criminology*, 3rd edn. Oxford: Oxford University Press.

Bourdieu, P. (1977) *Outline of a Theory of Practice*. Cambridge: Cambridge University Press.

Bourdieu, P. (1986a) *Distinction: A Social Critique of the Judgement of Taste*. London: Routledge.

Bourdieu, P. (1986b) 'The Forms of Capital', in J.G. Richardson (ed.), *Handbook of Theory and Research for the Sociology of Education*. Westport, CT: Greenwood Press.

Bourdieu, P. (1988) *Language and Symbolic Power*. Cambridge: Polity Press.

Bourdieu, P. (1990a) *The Logic of Practice*. Cambridge: Polity Press.

Bourdieu, P. (1990b) *In Other Words: Essays Towards a Reflexive Sociology*. Cambridge: Polity.

Bourdieu, P. and Passeron, J.-C. (1977) *Reproduction in Education, Society and Culture*. London: Sage.

Bourdieu, P. and Wacquant, L. (1992) *An Invitation to Reflexive Sociology*. Cambridge: Polity Press.

Box, S. (1987) *Recession, Crime and Punishment*. London: Macmillan Education Ltd.

Boyle, J. (1977) *A Sense of Freedom*. London: Pan Books.

Braithwaite, J. (1989) *Crime, Shame and Reintegration*. Cambridge: Cambridge University Press.

Brantingham, P.J. and Brantingham, P.L. (1981) *Environmental Criminology*. Beverly Hills, CA: Sage.

Brantingham, P.J. and Brantingham, P.L. (1984) *Patterns in Crime*. New York: Macmillan.

Brantingham, P.J. and Brantingham, P.L. (1991) 'Notes on the Geometry of Crime', in P.J. Brantingham and P.L. Brantingham (eds), *Environmental Criminology*. Beverley Hills, CA: Sage.

Breckler, S.J. (1993) 'Emotion and Attitude Change', in M. Lewis and J.M. Haviland (eds), *Handbook of Emotions*. New York: Guilford Press.

Brewer, M., Goodman, A., Muriel, A. and Sibieta, L. (2007) *Poverty and Inequality in the UK: 2007*, Briefing Note No. 73. London: Institute for Fiscal Studies.

Broady, M. (1968) *Planning for People*. London: Bedford Square Press.

Brooks-Gunn, J., Duncan, G., Klebanov, P. and Sealane, N. (1993) 'Do Neighbourhoods Influence Child and Adolescent Development?', *American Journal of Sociology*, 99: 353–95.

Buck, N. (2001) 'Identifying Neighbourhood Effects on Social Exclusion', *Urban Studies*, 38 (12): 2251–75.

Buck, N., Gordon, I., Hall, P., Harloe, M. and Kleinman, M. (2002) *Working Capital: Life and Labour in Contemporary London*. London: Routledge.

Burchardt, T., LeGrand, J. and Piachaud, D. (1999) 'Social Exclusion in Britain 1991–1995', *Social Policy and Administration*, 33 (3): 224–7.

Burgess, E.W. (1925) 'The Growth of the City', in R.E. Park, E.W. Burgess and R.D. McKenzie (eds), *The City*. Chicago: University of Chicago Press.

Burnett, R. (1992) *The Dynamics of Recidivism: Summary Report*. Oxford: University of Oxford, Centre for Criminological Research.

Burnett, R. (2000) 'Understanding Criminal Careers Through a Series of In-Depth Interviews', *Offender Programs Report*, 4 (1): 1–16.

Burnett, R. (2004a) 'To Reoffend or Not to Reoffend? The Ambivalence of Convicted Property Offenders', in S. Maruna and R. Immarigeon (eds), *After Crime and Punishment: Pathways to Offender Reintegration*. Cullompton: Willan Publishing.

Burnett, R. (2004b) 'One-to-One Ways of Promoting Desistance: In Search of an Evidence Base', in R. Burnett and C. Roberts (eds), *What Works in Probation: Developing Evidence-Based Practice*. Cullompton: Willan Publishing.

Burnett, R. and Maruna, S. (2004) 'So "Prison Works", Does It? The Criminal Careers of 130 Men Released from Prison Under Home Secretary, Michael Howard', *The Howard Journal*, 43 (4): 390–404.

Burnett, R. and Maruna, S. (2006) 'The Kindness of Prisoners: Strength-Based Resettlement in Theory and in Action', *Criminology and Criminal Justice*, 6 (1): 83–106.

Bursik, R.J. (1988) 'Social Disorganization and Theories of Crime and Delinquency: Problems and Prospects', *Criminology*, 26 (4): 519–51.

Burt, C. (1925) *The Young Delinquent*. London: University of London Press.

Byrne, D. (2005) *Social Exclusion*, 2nd edn. Maidenhead: Open University Press.

Callinicos, A. (2001) *Against the Third Way*. Cambridge: Polity Press.

Campbell, B. (1993) *Goliath: Britain's Dangerous Places*. London: Methuen.

Canter, D.V. (1977) *The Psychology of Place*. London: Architectural Press.

Carlen, P. (1989) 'Crime, Inequality and Sentencing', in P. Carlen and D. Cook (eds), *Paying for Crime*. Milton Keynes: Open University Press.

Carter, P. (2003) *Managing Offenders, Reducing Crime: A New Approach*. London: Prime Minister's Strategy Unit.

Caspi, A. and Moffitt, T.E. (1995) 'The Continuity of Maladaptive Behavior: From Description to Understanding in the Study of Antisocial Behavior', in D. Cicchetti and D.J. Cohen (eds), *Developmental Psychopathology 2, Risk, Disorder and Adaption*. New York: Wiley.

Caspi, A. and Silva, P.A. (1995) 'Temperamental Qualities at Age 3 Predict Personality Traits in Young Adulthood: Longitudinal Evidence from a Birth Cohort', *Child Development*, 66: 486–98.

Castells, M. (1977) *The Urban Question*. London: Edward Arnold.

Castells, M. (1998) *End of Millennium. Volume III of the Information Age: Economy, Society and Culture*, 2nd edn. Oxford: Blackwell.

Castells, M. (2004) *The Power of Identity. Vol. II of the Information Age: Economy, Society and Culture*, 2nd edn. Oxford: Blackwell.

Castoriadis, C. (1975) *L'Institution imaginaire de la société*, 3rd edn. Paris: Editions du Seuil.

Cavadino, M. and Dignan, J. (1997) *The Penal System: An Introduction*, 2nd edn. London: Sage.

Chambliss, W.J. (1975) 'Towards a Political Economy of Crime', *Theory and Society*, 2: 149–70.

Champion, T. (2006) *State of the English Cities: The Changing Urban Scene.* London: Department for Communities and Local Government.

Chattoe, E. and Hamill, H. (2005) 'It's Not *Who* You Know – It's What You Know About People You *Don't* Know That Counts: Extending the Analysis of Crime Groups as Social Networks', *British Journal of Criminology*, 45 (6): 860–76.

Cheshire, P. (2007) *Segregated Neighbourhoods and Mixed Communities.* York: Joseph Rowntree Foundation.

Chitty, C. (2004) 'The Impact of Corrections on Re-offending: Conclusions and the Way Forward', in G. Harper and C. Chitty (eds), *The Impact of Corrections on Re-offending: A Review of 'What Works'.* Home Office Research Study 291. London: Home Office.

Church, A., Frost, M. and Sullivan, K. (2000) 'Transport and Social Exclusion in London', *Transport Policy*, 7: 195–205.

Clancy, A., Hudson, K., Maguire, M., Peake, R., Raynor, P., Vanstone, M. and Kynch, J. (2006) *Getting Out and Staying Out: Results of the Prisoner Resettlement Pathfinders.* Bristol: Policy Press.

Clarke, A., Simmonds, R. and Wydall, S. (2004) *Delivering Cognitive Skills Programmes in Prison: A Qualitative Study.* Home Office Online Report, 27. London: Home Office.

Clarke, K.C. (1999) *Getting Started with Geographical Information Systems.* Upper Slade River, NJ: Prentice-Hall.

Clarke, M. (1990) *Business Crime: Its Nature and Control.* Oxford: Polity Press.

Clarke, R.V. (ed.) (1992) *Situational Crime Prevention.* Albany, NY: Harrow and Heston.

Clarke, R.V. (1999) *Hot Products: Understanding, Anticipating and Reducing Demand for Stolen Goods.* Police Research Series Paper 112. London: Home Office.

Clarke, R.V. and Cornish, D.B. (1985) 'Modelling Offenders' Decisions: A Framework for Research and Policy', in M. Tonry and N. Morris (eds), *Crime and Justice: An Annual Review of Research*, vol. 6. Chicago: University of Chicago Press.

Clear, T.R. (1994) *Harm in American Penology: Offenders, Victims and Their Communities.* Albany, NY: State University of New York Press.

Clear, T.R., Rose, D.R., Waring, E. and Scully, K. (2003) 'Coercive Mobility and Crime: Incarceration and Social Disorganization', *Justice Quarterly*, 20: 33–64.

Clear, T.R., Waring, E. and Scully, K. (2005) 'Communities and Reentry: Concentrated Reentry Recycling', in J. Travis and C. Visher (eds), *Prisoner Reentry and Crime in America.* Cambridge: Cambridge University Press.

Clemmer, D. (1940) *The Prison Community.* New York: Holt, Rinehart and Winston.

Cloke, P., Philo, C. and Sadler, D. (1991) *Approaching Human Geography: An Introduction to Current Theoretical Debates.* London: PCP Press.

Cloward, R. and Ohlin, L. (1960) *Delinquency and Opportunity: A Theory of Delinquent Gangs*. New York: Free Press.

Cochrane, A. (1986) 'Community Politics and Democracy', in D. Held and C. Pollitt (eds), *New Forms of Democracy*. London: Sage.

Cochrane, A. (2007) *Understanding Urban Policy: A Critical Approach*. Oxford: Blackwell.

Cohen, A.K. (1966) *Deviance and Control*. Englewood Cliffs, NJ: Prentice-Hall.

Cohen, L.E. and Felson, M. (1979) 'Social Change and Crime Rate Trends: A Routine Activities Approach', *American Sociological Review*, 44: 588–608.

Cohen, S. and Taylor L. (1972) *Psychological Survival: The Experience of Long-Term Imprisonment*. Harmondsworth: Penguin.

Coleman, A. (1989) 'Disposition and Situation: Two Sides of the Same Crime', in D.J. Evans and D.T. Herbert (eds), *The Geography of Crime*. London: Routledge.

Coleman, J.S. (1988) 'Social Capital in the Creation of Human Capital', *American Journal of Sociology*, 94 Supplement: S95–120.

Coleman, R. (2003) 'Images from a Neoliberal City: The State, Surveillance and Social Control', *Critical Criminology*, 12 (1): 21–42.

Coleman, R. (2004) 'Watching the Degenerate: Street Camera Surveillance and Urban Regeneration', *Local Economy*, 19 (3): 199–211.

Coleman, R., Tombs, S. and Whyte, D. (2005) 'Capital Crime Control and Statecraft in the Entrepreneurial City', *Urban Studies*, 42 (13): 2511–30.

Coles, N. (2001) 'It's Not What You Know – It's Who You Know That Counts: Analysing Serious Crime Groups as Social Networks', *British Journal of Criminology*, 41: 580–94.

Collier, R. (1998) *Masculinities, Crime and Criminology*. London: Sage.

Combessie, P. (1998) 'The Sensitive Perimeter of the Prison: A Key to Understanding the Durability of the Penal Institution', in V. Ruggiero, N. Smith and I. Taylor (eds), *The New European Criminology: Crime and Social Order in Europe*. London: Routledge.

Commission on English Prisons Today (2008) *Localism: A Consultation Paper*. London: Howard League for Penal Reform.

Connell, R.W. (1995) *Masculinities*. Cambridge: Polity Press.

Cornish, D.B. and Clarke, R.V. (eds) (1986) *The Reasoning Criminal: Rational Choice Perspectives on Offending*. New York: Springer-Verlag.

Cornish, D.B. and Clarke, R.V. (2008) 'The Rational Choice Perspective', in R. Wortley and L. Mazerolle (eds), *Environmental Criminology and Crime Analysis*. Cullompton: Willan Publishing.

Corrigan, P. (1979) *Schooling the Smash Street Kids*. London: Macmillan.

Cox, V.C., Paulus, P.B. and McCain, G. (1984) 'Prison Crowding Research: The Relevance for Prison Crowding Standards and a General Approach Regarding Crowding Phenomena', *American Psychologist*, 39: 1148–60.

Craglia, M. and Costello, A. (2005) 'A Model of Offenders in England', in F. Toppen and M. Painho (eds), AGILE 2005 (Association of Geographic

Information Laboratories Europe), Eighth Conference on Geographic Information Science – Conference Proceedings. Lisbon: Universidade Nova de Lisboa.

Crane, J. (1991) 'The Epidemic Theory of Ghettos and Neighbourhood Effects on Dropping-out and Teenage Childbearing', *American Journal of Sociology*, 96: 1226–59.

Crawford, A. (1997) *The Local Governance of Crime: Appeals to Community and Partnerships*. Oxford: Clarendon Press.

Crawford, A. (1998) *Crime Prevention and Community Safety: Politics, Policies and Practices*. Harlow: Longman.

Crawshaw, P. (2004) 'The "Logic of Practice" in the Risk Community: The Potential of the Work of Pierre Bourdieu for Theorising Young Men's Risk Taking', in W. Mitchell, R. Bunton and E. Green (eds), *Young People, Risk and Leisure: Constructing Identities in Everyday Life*. Basingstoke: Palgrave Macmillan.

Crewe, B. (2006) 'Male Prisoners' Orientation Towards Female Officers in an English Prison', *Punishment and Society*, 11: 395–421.

Currie, E. (1985) *Confronting Crime: An American Challenge*. New York: Pantheon.

Cusson, M. and Pinsonneault, P. (1986) 'The Decision to Give up Crime', in D.B Cornish, and R.V. Clarke (eds), *The Reasoning Criminal*. New York: Springer-Verlag.

Dahrendorf, R. (1987) 'The Underclass and the Future of Britain', 10th Annual Lecture, Windsor.

Dannefer, D. (1984) 'Adult Development and Social Theory: A Paradigmatic Re-appraisal', *American Sociological Review*, 49: 100–16.

Darden, J.T. (2001) 'Race Relations in the City', in R. Paddison (ed.), *Handbook of Urban Studies*, 177–93. London: Sage.

Davies, W.K.D. and Herbert, D.T. (1993) *Communities Within Cities: An Urban Social Geography*. London: Belhaven Press.

Davis, M. (1990) *City of Quartz*. London: Verso.

Davis, M. (2006) *Planet of Slums*. London: Verso.

Davis, M.H. (1994) *Empathy: A Social Psychological Approach*. Boulder, CO: Westview Press.

de Certeau, M. (1984) *The Practice of Everyday Life*. Berkeley, CA: University of California Press.

Dear, M.J. and Flusty, S. (2002) (eds) *The Spaces of Postmodernity: Readings in Human Geography*. Oxford: Blackwell.

Dear, M.J. and Wolch, J. (1989) 'How Territory Shapes Social Life', in J. Wolch and M.J. Dear (eds), *The Power of Geography: How Territory Shapes Social Life*. Boston, MA: Unwin Hyman.

Denzin, N.K. (1997) *Interpretative Ethnography: Ethnographic Practices for the 21st century*. London: Sage.

Department for Communities and Local Government (2006) *Strong and*

Prosperous Communities: *The Local Government White Paper*. Cm. 6939-II. London: The Stationery Office.

Ditchfield, J. (1994) *Family Ties and Recidivism*. Home Office Research Bulletin 36. London: Home Office.

Dodd, T. and Hunter, P. (1992) *The National Prison Survey*. London: HMSO.

Dorling, D. (1995) *A New Social Atlas of Britain*. Chichester: Wiley.

Dorling, D. (2004) 'Prime Suspect: Murder in Britain', in P. Hillyard, C. Pantazis, S. Tombs and D. Gordon (eds), *Beyond Criminology: Taking Harm Seriously*. London: Pluto.

Dorling, D., Rigby, J., Wheeler, B., Ballas, D., Thomas, B., Fahmy, E., Gordon, D. and Lupton, R. (2007) *Poverty, Wealth and Place in Britain, 1968 to 2005*. Bristol: Policy Press.

Dorling, D. and Thomas, B. (2004) *People and Places: A 2001 Census Atlas of the UK*. Bristol: Policy Press.

Douglas, J. (1977) 'Existential Sociology', in J. Douglas and J. Johnson (eds), *Existential Sociology*. Cambridge: Cambridge University Press.

Downes, D. (1966) *The Delinquent Solution: A Study in Subcultural Theory*. London: Routledge and Kegan Paul.

Downes, D. (1988) *Contrasts in Tolerance: Post-war Penal Policy in the Netherlands and England and Wales*. Oxford: Clarendon Press.

Duguid, S. (2000) *Can Prisons Work? The Prisoner as Object and Subject in Modern Corrections*. Toronto: University of Toronto Press.

Duncan, N. (1996) 'Renegotiating Gender and Sexuality in Public and Private Spaces', in N. Duncan (ed.), *Bodyspace: Destabilizing Geographies of Gender and Sexuality*. London: Routledge.

Eaton, M. (1993) *Women After Prison*. Buckingham: Open University Press.

Eck, J.E. (2005) 'Crime Hot Spots: What Are They, Why We Have Them, and How to Map Them', in J.E. Eck, S. Chainey, J.G. Cameron, M. Leitner and R.E. Wilson (eds), *Mapping Crime: Understanding Hot Spots*. Washington, DC: US Department of Justice, National Institute of Justice.

Edgar, K., O'Donnell, I. and Martin, C. (2003) *Prison Violence: The Dynamics of Conflict, Fear and Power*. Cullompton: Willan Publishing.

Ellaway, A., Macintyre, S. and Kearns, A. (2001) 'Perceptions of Place and Health in Socially Contrasting Neighbourhoods', *Urban Studies*, 38 (12): 2299–316.

Elliot, D., Wilson, W., Huizinga, D., Sampson, R. and Rankin, B. (1996) 'The Effects of Neighbourhood Disadvantage on Adolescent Development', *Journal of Research in Crime and Delinquency*, 33: 389–426.

Elliott, A. (2001) *Concepts of the Self*. Cambridge: Polity.

Elliott-Marshall, R., Ramsay, M. and Stewart, D. (2004) 'Alternative Approaches to Integrating Offenders into the Community', in G. Harper and C. Chitty (eds), *The Impact of Corrections on Re-offending: A Review of 'What Works'*. Home Office Research Study 291. London: Home Office.

Ellis, T. and Winstone, J. (2002) 'The Policy Impact of a Survey of Programme Evaluations in England and Wales', in J. McGuire (ed.), *Offender Rehabilitation and Treatment: Effective Programmes and Policies to Reduce Re-offending.* Chichester: John Wiley and Sons.

Ericson, R.V. (1975) *Young Offenders and Their Social Work.* Farnborough, Hants: Saxon House, D.C. Health Ltd.

Esser, H. (2000) Soziologie. Spezielle Grundlagen, Band: Opportunitäten und Restriktionen. Frankfurt: Campus.

Etzioni, A. (1995) *The Spirit of Community.* London: Fontana Press.

Evans, D.J. (1980) *Geographical Perspectives on Juvenile Delinquency.* Farnborough: Gower Publishing and Retail and Planning Associates.

Eysenck, H.J. (1964) *Crime and Personality.* London: Routledge and Kegan Paul.

Ezell, M.E. and Cohen, L.E. (2005) *Desisting from Crime: Continuity and Change in Long-Term Crime Patterns of Serious Chronic Offenders.* Oxford: Oxford University Press.

Farrall, S. (1995) 'Why Do People Stop Offending?', *Scottish Journal of Criminal Justice Studies,* 1 (1): 51–9.

Farrall, S. (2002) *Rethinking What Works with Offenders: Probation, Social Context and Desistance from Crime.* Cullompton: Willan Publishing.

Farrall, S. (2004) 'Social Capital and Offender Reintegration: Making Probation Desistance Focused', in S. Maruna and R. Immarigeion (eds), *After Crime and Punishment: Pathways to Offender Reintegration.* Cullompton: Willan Publishing.

Farrall, S. (2005) 'On the Existential Aspects of Desistance from Crime', *Symbolic Interaction,* 28 (3): 367–86.

Farrall, S. and Bowling, B. (1999) 'Structuration, Human Development and Desistance from Crime', *British Journal of Criminology,* 39 (2): 253–68.

Farrall, S. and Calverley, A. (2006) *Understanding Desistance from Crime: Theoretical Directions in Resettlement and Rehabilitation.* Maidenhead: Open University Press.

Farrall, S. and Sparks, R. (2006) 'Introduction to Special Issue: What Lies Beyond?: Problems, Prospects and Possibilities for Life After Punishment', in S. Farrall and R. Sparks (eds), *Criminology and Criminal Justice,* 6 (1): 7–17.

Farrant, F. and Levenson, J. (2002) *Barred Citizens: Volunteering and Active Citizenship by Prisoners.* London: Prison Reform Trust.

Farrington, D.P. (1994) 'Human Development and Criminal Careers', in M. Maguire, R. Morgan and R. Reiner (eds), *The Oxford Handbook of Criminology.* Oxford: Clarendon Press.

Farrington, D.P. (2002) 'Developmental Criminology and Risk Focused Prevention', in M. Maguire, R. Morgan and R. Reiner (eds), *The Oxford Handbook of Criminology,* 3rd edn. Oxford: Oxford University Press.

Farrington, D.P., Gallagher, B., Morley, L., St. Ledger, R. and West, D. (1986) 'Unemployment, School Leaving and Crime', *British Journal of Criminology*, 26 (4): 335–56.

Farrington, D.P., Jolliffe, D., Loeber, R., Stouthamer-Loeber, M. and Kalb, L. (2001) 'The Concentration of Offenders in Families and Family Criminality in the Prediction of Boys' Delinquency', *Journal of Adolescence*, 24: 579–96.

Farrington, D.P. and West, D. (1993) 'Criminal, Penal and Life Histories of Chronic Offenders: Risk and Protective Factors and Early Identification', *Criminal Behaviour and Mental Health*, 3: 492–523.

Faulkner, D. (2006) 'A Modern Service Fit for Purpose?', in M. Hough, R. Allen and U. Padel (eds), *Reshaping Probation and Prisons: The New Offender Management Framework*. Bristol: Policy Press.

Feeley, M. and Simon, J. (1992) 'The New Penology: Notes on the Emerging Strategy of Corrections and Its Implications', *Criminology*, 30: 449–74.

Felson, M. (1994) *Crime and Everyday Life: Insights and Implications for Society*. Thousand Oaks, CA: Pine Forge Press.

Felson, M. (1998) *Crime and Everyday Life*, 2nd edn. Thousand Oaks, CA: Pine Forge Press.

Felson, M. (2008) 'Routine Activity Approach', in R. Wortley and L. Mazerolle (eds), *Environmental Criminology and Crime Analysis*. Cullompton: Willan Publishing.

Ferguson, H. (2009) 'Anthony Giddens', in M. Gray and S.A. Webb (eds), *Social Work: Theories and Methods*. London: Sage.

Ferrell, J. (1996) *Crimes of Style: Urban Graffiti and the Politics of Criminality*. Boston: Northeastern University Press.

Ferrell, J., Hayward, K., Morrison, W. and Presdee, M. (eds) (2004) 'Fragments of a Manifesto: Introducing Cultural Criminology Unleashed', in *Cultural Criminology Unleashed*. London: GlassHouse Press.

Fitzgerald, M. and Sim, J. (1982) *British Prisons*, 2nd edn. Oxford: Blackwell.

Fletcher, D., Woodhill, D. and Herrington, A. (1998) *Building Bridges into Employment and Training for Ex-offenders*. York: Joseph Rowntree Foundation.

Flint, J. (2006) 'Housing and the New Governance of Conduct', in J. Flint (ed.), *Housing, Urban Governance and Anti-social Behaviour: Perspectives, Policy and Practice*. Bristol: Policy Press.

Folwell, K. (1999) *Getting the Measure of Social Exclusion*. London: London Research Centre.

Forrest, R. (2000) 'Does Neighbourhood Still Matter in a Globalised World?', Occasional Paper Series No. 5. Centre for Comparative Public Management and Social Policy, City University of Hong Kong.

Forrest, R. and Kearns, A. (2001) 'Social Cohesion, Social Capital and the Neighbourhood', *Urban Studies*, 38 (12): 2125–43.

Foster, J. (1990) *Villains: Crime and Community in the Inner City*. London: Routledge.

Foster, J. (1997) 'Challenging Perceptions: Community and Neighbourliness on a Difficult to Let Estate', in J. Jewson and S. Macgregor (eds),

Transforming Cities: Contested Governance and New Spatial Divisions. London: Routledge.

Foucault, M. (1977) *Discipline and Punish: The Birth of the Prison*. London: Penguin.

Foucault, M. (1982) 'The Subject of Power', in H. Dreyfus and P. Rabinow (eds), *Michael Foucault: Beyond Structuralism and Hermeneutics*. Brighton: Harvester.

Friedlander, K. (1947) *The Psycho-analytical Approach to Juvenile Delinquency*. London: Kegan Paul.

Friedman, T.L. (2005) *The World Is Flat: A Brief History of the Twentieth Century*. New York: Farrar, Straus and Giroux.

Fuller, D and Gough, J. (2001) 'Geographies of Poverty', in R. Pain (ed.), *Introducing Social Geographies*. London: Arnold.

Furlong, A. and Cartmel, F. (1997) *Young People and Social Change: Individualization and Risk in Late Modernity*. London: Open University Press.

Gadd, D. and Farrall, S. (2004) 'Criminal Careers, Desistance and Subjectivity: Interpreting Men's Narratives of Change', *Theoretical Criminology*, 8 (2): 123–56.

Gadd, D. and Jefferson, T. (2007) *Psychosocial Criminology: An Introduction*. London: Sage.

Gallo, E. and Ruggiero, V. (1991) 'The Immaterial Prison: Custody as a Factory for the Manufacture of Handicaps', *International Journal for the Sociology of Law*, 19: 273–91.

Galster, G. (2001) 'On the Nature of Neighbourhood', *Urban Studies*, 38 (12) 2111–24.

GangsinLondon (2006) [online] Available at http://www.piczo.com/gangsinlondon (accessed October 2007).

Gans, H. (1968) 'Urbanism and Suburbanism as Ways of Life', in R. Pahl (ed.), *Readings in Urban Sociology*. Oxford: Pergamon.

Garland, D. (2001) *The Culture of Control: Crime and Social Order in Contemporary Society*. Buckingham: Open University Press.

Garland, D. (2002) 'Of Crimes and Criminals: The Development of Criminology in Britain', in M. Maguire, R. Morgan and R. Reiner (eds), *The Oxford Handbook of Criminology*, 3rd edn. Oxford: Oxford University Press.

Garrett, P.M. (2009) 'Pierre Bourdieu', in M. Gray and S.A. Webb (eds), *Social Work: Theories and Methods*. London: Sage.

Giddens, A. (1976) *New Rules of Sociological Method*. London: Hutchinson.

Giddens, A. (1984) *The Constitution of Society*. Cambridge: Polity Press.

Giddens, A. (1987) *Social Theory and Modern Sociology*. Cambridge: Polity Press.

Giddens, A. (1990) *The Consequences of Modernity*. Cambridge: Polity Press.

Giddens, A. (1991) *Modernity and Self-Identity*. Cambridge: Polity Press.

Gilling, D. (2007) *Crime Reduction and Community Safety: Labour and the Politics of Local Crime Control*. Cullompton: Willan Publishing.

Giordano, P.C., Cernkovich, S.A. and Rudolph, J.L. (2002) 'Gender, Crime and Desistance: Toward a Theory of Cognitive Transformation', *American Journal of Sociology*, 107: 990–1064.

Glueck, S. and Glueck, E. (1940) *Juvenile Delinquents Grown Up*. New York: Commonwealth Fund.

Glueck, S. and Glueck, E. (1950) *Unravelling Juvenile Delinquency*. New York: Commonwealth Fund.

Goering, J. and Richardson, T. (eds) (2003) *Choosing a Better Life: Evaluating the Moving to Opportunity Social Experiment*. Washington, DC: Urban Institute Press.

Goffman, E. (1961) *Asylums*. London: Penguin.

Goffman, E. (1967) *Interaction Ritual: Essays on Face to Face Interaction*. New York: Free Press.

Goffman, E. (1968) *Stigma: Notes on the Management of Spoiled Identity*. Harmonsworth: Penguin.

Goffman, E. (1969) *The Presentation of Self in Everyday Life*. London: Allen Lane.

Goffman, E. (1997) 'Self-Presentation: The Presentation of Self in Everyday Life', in C. Lemert and A. Branaman (eds), *The Goffman Reader*. Oxford: Blackwell.

Golledge, R.G., Brown, L.A. and Williamson, F. (1972) 'Behavioural Approaches in Geography: An Overview', *Australian Geographer*, 12: 59–79.

Golledge, R.G. and Stimson, R.J. (1997) *Spatial Behaviour: A Geographic Perspective*. New York: Guilford Press.

Gordon, D.A. (2002) 'Intervening with Families of Troubled Youth: Functional Family Therapy and Parenting Wisely', in J. McGuire (ed.), *Offender Rehabilitation and Treatment: Effective Programmes and Policies to Reduce Re-offending*. Chichester: John Wiley and Sons.

Gore, S.M., Bird, A.G., Burns, S.M., Goldberg, D.J., Ross, A.J. and MacGregor, J. (1995) 'Drug Injection and HIV Prevalence in Inmates of Glenochil Prison' *British Medical Journal*, 310 (6975): 285–89.

Gottfredson, M. and Hirschi, T. (1990) *A General Theory of Crime*. Stanford, CA: Stanford University Press.

Gottman, J.M. (1993) 'Studying Emotion in Social Interaction', in M. Lewis and J.M. Haviland (eds), *Handbook of Emotions*. New York: Guilford Press.

Gove, W. (1985) 'The Effect of Age and Gender on Deviant Behavior: A Biopsychosocial Perspective', in A.S. Rossi (ed.), *Gender and the Life Course*. New York: Aldine.

Graham, J. and Bennett, T. (1995) *Crime Prevention Strategies in Europe and North America*. Helsinki: HEUNI.

Graham, J. and Bowling, B. (1995) *Young People and Crime*. London: Home Office.

Gray, P. (2005) 'The Politics of Risk and Young Offenders' Experiences of Social Exclusion and Restorative Justice', *British Journal of Criminology*, 45 (6): 938–57.

Greater London Authority (GLA) (2002) *London Divided: Income Inequality and Poverty in the Capital*. London: Greater London Authority.

Guerry, A.-M. (1833) *Essai sur la statistique morale de la France*. Paris: Chez Crochard.

Hagan, J. (1993) 'The Social Embeddedness of Crime and Unemployment', *Criminology*, 31: 455–91.

Hagan, J. (1997) 'Crime and Capitalization: Toward a Developmental Theory of Street Crime in America', in T. Thornberry (ed.), *Developmental Theories of Crime and Delinquency*. New Brunswick: Transaction Press.

Hagell, A. Newburn, T. and Rowlingson, K. (1995) *Financial Difficulties on Release from Prison*. London: Policy Studies Institute.

Hägerstrand, T. (1982) 'Diorama, Path and Project', *Tijdschrift voor Economische en Sociale Geographie*, 73: 323–39.

Hakim, C. (2000) *Research Design: Successful Designs for Social and Economic Research*. London: Allen and Unwin.

Hales, G., Lewis, C. and Silverstone, D. (2006) *Gun Crime: The Market in and Use of Illegal Firearms*. London: Home Office.

Hall, P. (1988) *Cities of Tomorrow*. Oxford: Basil Blackwell.

Hall, S. (1991) 'Old and New Identities, Old and New Ethnicities', in A.D. King (ed.), *Culture, Globalization and the World-System*. Basingstoke: Macmillan.

Hall, S. and Winlow, S. (2004) 'Barbarians at the Gate: Crime and Violence in the Breakdown of the Pseudo-Pacification Process', in J. Ferrell, K. Hayward, W. Morrison and M. Presdee (eds), *Cultural Criminology Unleashed*. London: GlassHouse Press.

Hall, S., Winlow, S. and Ancrum, C. (2008) *Criminal Identities and Consumer Culture: Crime, Exclusion and the New Culture of Narcissism*. Cullompton: Willan Publishing.

Halliday, J. (2001) *Making Punishments Work: Report of a Review of the Sentencing Framework for England and Wales*. London: Home Office.

Hallsworth, S. and Silverstone, D. (2009) '"That's Life Innit". A British Perspective on Guns, Crime and Social Order', *Criminology and Criminal Justice: an International Journal*, 9 (3): 359–77.

Hammersley, M. (1992) *What's Wrong with Ethnography?* London: Routledge.

Hamnett, C. (1999) *Winners and Losers: Home Ownership in Modern Britain*. London: UCL Press.

Hancock, L. (2007) 'Is Urban Regeneration Criminogenic?', in R. Atkinson and G. Helms (eds), *Securing an Urban Renaissance: Crime, Community and British Urban Policy*. Bristol: Policy Press.

Haney, C. (2005) 'The Contextual Revolution in Psychology and the Question of Prison Effects', in A. Liebling and S. Maruna (eds), *The Effects of Imprisonment*. Cullompton: Willan Publishing.

Harper, G. and Chitty, C. (eds) (2005) *The Impact of Corrections on Re-offending: A Review of 'What Works'*, 3rd edn. Home Office Research Study 291. London: Home Office Research, Development and Statistics Directorate.

Harris, C.D. and Ullman, E.L. (1945) 'The Nature of Cities', *Annals of the American Academy of Political Science*, 242: 7–17.

Harrison, P. (1983) *Inside the Inner City*. Harmondsworth: Penguin.

Harvey, D. (1972) *Society, the City and the Space Economy of Urbanism*, Resources Paper 18, Commission on College Geography, Washington, DC: Association of American Geographers.

Harvey, D. (1973) *Social Justice and the City*. London: Edward Arnold.

Harvey, D. (1981) 'The Urban Process Under Capitalism', in M. Dear and A. Scott (eds), *Urbanisation and Urban Planning in Capitalist Society*. London: Methuen.

Harvey, D. (1990) *The Condition of Postmodernity*. Oxford: Blackwell.

Harvey, D. (1996) *Justice, Nature and the Geography of Difference*. Cambridge, MA: Blackwell.

Harvey, D. (1997) 'Contested Cities, Social Processes and Spatial Form', in N. Jewson and S. MacGregor (eds), *Transforming Cities, Contested Governance and New Social Divisions*. London: Routledge.

Harvey, J. (2005) 'Crossing the Boundary: The Transition of Young Adults into Prison' in A. Liebling and S. Maruna (eds), *The Effects of Imprisonment*. Cullompton: Willan Publishing.

Hayward, K.J. (2002) 'The Vilification and Pleasures of Youthful Transgression', in J. Muncie, G. Hughes and E. McLaughlin (eds), *Youth Justice: Critical Readings*. London: Sage.

Hayward, K.J. (2004) *City Limits: Crime, Consumer Culture and the Urban Experience*. London: GlassHouse Press.

Hebdige, D. (1988) *Hiding in the Light: On Images and Things*. London: Routledge.

Heidegger, M. (1971) *Poetry, Language, Thought*. New York: Harper and Row.

Henry, S. (1978) *The Hidden Economy: The Context and Control of Borderline Crime*. Oxford: Martin Robertson.

Herbert, D.T. (1982) *The Geography of Urban Crime*. Harlow: Longman.

Herbert, D.T. (1993) 'Neighbourhood Incivilities and the Study of Crime in Place', *Area*, 25: 45–54.

Herrnstein, R.J. and Murray, C. (1994) *The Bell Curve*. New York: Free Press.

Highmore, B. (2002) *Everyday Life and Cultural Theory: An Introduction*. London: Routledge.

Hills, J. (2007) *Ends and Means: The Future Roles of Social Housing in England*. London: Centre for Analysis of Social Exclusion.

Hirschfield, A. and Bowers, K. (1997) 'The Effect of Social Cohesion on Levels of Recorded Crime in Disadvantaged Areas', *Urban Studies*, 8: 1275–95.

Hirschi, T. (1969) *Causes of Delinquency*. Berkeley, CA: University of California Press.

HM Chief Inspector of Prisons (2005) *Report on a Full Announced Inspection of HM YOI Feltham, 15–20 May 2005*. London: Home Office.

HM Prison Service and Commission for Racial Equality (2003) *Implementing Race Equality in Prisons: A Shared Agenda for Change*. London: HM Prison Service.

Hobbs, D. (1985) *Doing the Business: Entrepreneurship, the Working Class, and Detectives in the East End of London*. Oxford: Oxford University Press.

Hobbs, D. (1995) *Bad Business: Professional Crime in Modern Britain*. Oxford: Oxford University Press.

Hollin, C. (1992) *Criminal Behaviour: A Psychological Approach to Explanation and Prevention*. London: Falmer Press.

Holloway, L. and Hubbard, P. (2001) *People and Place: The Extraordinary Geographies of Everyday Life*. Harlow: Prentice-Hall, Pearson Education Ltd.

Holmes, C. (2006) *Mixed Communities: Success and Sustainability*. York: Joseph Rowntree Foundation.

Home Office (1984) *Probation Service in England and Wales: Statement of National Objectives and Priorities*. London: Home Office.

Home Office (2001a) *Prison Statistics England and Wales 2000*. Cm. 5250. London: Home Office.

Home Office (2001b) *Through the Prison Gate: A Joint Thematic Review by HM Inspectorates of Prisons and Probation*. London: Home Office.

Home Office (2002a) *Justice for All*. Cm 5563, 'The Auld Review'. London: Home Office.

Home Office (2002b) 'The Police National Computer and the Offenders Index: Can They Be Combined for Research Purposes?', *Findings*, 170.

Home Office (2003) *Prison Statistics England and Wales 2002*. Cm 5996. London: Home Office.

Home Office (2004a) *Joint Inspection Report into Persistent and Prolific Offenders*. London: Home Office.

Home Office (2004b) *Reducing Re-offending: National Action Plan*. London: Home Office.

Home Office (2006a) *A Five Year Strategy for Protecting the Public and Reducing Re-offending*. Cmnd. 6717. London: Home Office.

Home Office (2006b) *Respect Action Plan*. London: Home Office.

Hood, R. and Sparks, R. (1970) *Key Issues in Criminology*. London: Weidenfeld and Nicolson.

hooks, b. (1990) *Yearning: Race, Gender and Cultural Politics*. Toronto: Between the Lines Press.

Hope, T. (1995) 'Community Crime Prevention', in M. Tonry and D.P. Farrington (eds), *Crime and Justice: A Review of Research*, vol. 19. Chicago: University of Chicago Press.

Hope, T. (2001) 'Crime Victimisation and Inequality in Risk Society' in R. Matthews and J. Pitts (eds), *Crime, Disorder and Community Safety*. London: Routledge.

Horney, J., Osgood, D.W. and Marshall, I.H. (1995) 'Criminal Careers in the Short-Term: Intra-individual Variability in Crime and its Relation to Local Life Circumstances', *American Sociological Review*, 60: 655–73.

Houchin, R. (2005) *Social Exclusion and Imprisonment in Scotland*. Glasgow: Glasgow Caledonian University.

Howard, L. (1994) 'Where Do Prisoners Come From? Some Information About the Home Areas of Prisoners in England and Wales', *Research Bulletin* 36. London: Home Office.

Howard, P., Clark, D. and Garnham, N. (2006) *An Evaluation of the Offender Assessment System (OASys) in Three Pilots 1999–2001*. London: Ministry of Justice.

Hoyt, H. (1939) *The Structure and Growth of Residential Neighbourhoods*. Washington, DC: US Federal Housing Administration.

Hubbard, P., Kitchin, R. and Valentine, G. (eds) (2004) 'Editors' Introduction', in *Key Thinkers on Space and Place*. London: Sage.

Hughes, G. (1996) 'Communitarianism and Law and Order', *Critical Social Policy*, 16 (4): 17–41.

Hughes, G. (2007) *The Politics of Crime and Community*. Basingstoke: Palgrave Macmillan.

Hughes, G. and Rowe, M. (2007) 'Neighbourhood Policing and Community Safety: Researching the Instabilities of the Local Governance of Crime, Disorder and Security in Contemporary UK', *Criminology and Criminal Justice*, 7 (4): 317–46.

Ignatieff, M. (1978) *A Just Measure of Pain: The Penitentiary in the Industrial Revolution 1750–1850*. London: Macmillan.

Irwin, J. (1970) *The Felon*. Englewood Cliffs, NJ: Prentice-Hall.

Irwin, J. and Cressey, D. (1962) 'Thieves, Convicts and the Inmate Culture', *Social Problems*, 10: 142–55.

Irwin, J. and Owen, B. (2005) 'Harm and the Contemporary Prison', in A. Liebling and S. Maruna (eds), *The Effects of Imprisonment*. Cullompton: Willan Publishing.

Jacobs, B.A. and Wright, R. (1999) 'Stick-Up, Street Culture, and Offender Motivation', *Criminology*, 37: 149–73.

Jacobs, J. (1961) *The Death and Life of Great American Cities*. New York: Random House.

Jacobs, J. (1979) 'Race Relations and the Prisoner Subculture', in N. Morris and M. Tonry (eds), *Crime and Justice: A Review of Research*, vol. 1. Chicago: University of Chicago Press.

James, A. (1993) *Childhood Identities: Self and Social Relationships in the Experience of the Child*. Edinburgh: Edinburgh University Press.

Jameson, F. (1984) 'Postmodernism or the Cultural Logic of Late Capitalism', *New Left Review*, 146: 53–92.

Jamieson, R. and Grounds, A. (2005) 'Release and Adjustment: Perspectives from Studies of Wrongly Convicted and Politically Motivated Prisoners', in

A. Liebling and S. Maruna (eds), *The Effects of Imprisonment*. Cullompton: Willan Publishing.

Jencks, C. and Mayer, S. (1990) 'The Social Consequences of Growing up in a Poor Neighbourhood', in L. Lynn and M.G.H. McGeary (eds), *Inner-city Poverty in the United States*. Washington, DC: National Academy Press.

Jenkins, R. (2002) *Pierre Bourdieu*, revised edn. London: Routledge.

Jenkins, R. (2004) *Social Identity*, 2nd edn. London: Routledge.

Jewkes, Y. (2002) *Captive Audience: Media, Masculinity and Power in Prisons*. Cullompton: Willan Publishing.

Jewkes, Y. (2005) 'Loss, Liminality and the Life Sentence: Managing Idenity Through a Disrupted Lifecourse', in A. Liebling and S. Maruna (eds), *The Effects of Imprisonment*. Cullompton: Willan Publishing.

Johnson, R. (2005) 'Brave New Prisons: The Growing Social Isolation of Modern Penal Institutions', in A. Liebling and S. Maruna (eds), *The Effects of Imprisonment*. Cullompton: Willan Publishing.

Johnston, C. and Mooney, G. (2007) '"Problem" people, "problem" places? New Labour and council estates', in R. Atkinson and G. Helms (eds), *Securing an Urban Renaissance: Crime, Community and British Urban Policy*. Bristol: Policy Press.

Johnston, L. MacDonald, R., Mason, P., Ridley, L. and Webster, C. (2004) *Snakes and Ladders: Young People, Transitions and Social Exclusion*. Bristol: Policy Press.

Johnston, R., Forrest, R. and Poulsen, M. (2002) 'Are There Ethnic Enclaves/ Ghettos in English Cities?', *Urban Studies*, 39 (4): 591–618.

Johnston, R.J., Gregory, D., Pratt, G. and Watts, M. (eds) (2000) *The Dictionary of Human Geography*. Oxford: Blackwell.

Jones, G.S. (1971) *Outcast London*. Oxford: Oxford University Press.

Jones, R.S. and Schmid, T.J. (2000) *Doing Time: Prison Experience and Identity Among First-Time Inmates*. Stamford, CT: Jai Press.

Jordan, B. (1996) *A Theory of Poverty and Social Exclusion*. Cambridge: Polity Press.

Jordan, B. (2008) 'Social Capital and Welfare Policy', in D. Castiglione, J.W. van Deth and G. Wolleb (eds), *The Handbook of Social Capital*. Oxford: Oxford University Press.

Jordan, B. and Jordan, C. (2000) *Social Work and the Third Way: Tough Love as Social Policy*. London: Sage.

Joseph Rowntree Foundation (1996) *The Housing Needs of Ex-Prisoners*. Findings: Housing Research No. 178. York: Joseph Rowntree Foundation.

Karp, D.R. and Clear, T.R. (2000) 'Community Justice: A Conceptual Framework', in C.M. Friel (ed.), *Boundary Changes in Criminal Justice Organizations: Criminal Justice 2000*, vol. 2. Washington, DC: National Institute of Justice.

Karsten, L. (2005) 'It All Used to Be Better? Different Generations on Continuity and Change in Urban Children's Daily Use of Space', *Children's Geographies*, 3 (3): 275–90.

Katz, J. (1988) *The Seductions of Crime: Moral and Sensual Attractions in Doing Evil*. New York: Basic Books.

Katz, M.B. (1989) *The Undeserving Poor: From the War on Poverty to the War on Welfare*. New York: Pantheon Books.

Kearns, A. and Parkinson, M. (2001) 'The Significance of Neighbourhood', *Urban Studies*, 38, (12): 2103–10.

Kellner, D. (1992) 'Popular Culture and the Construction of Postmodern Identities', in S. Lash and J. Friedman (eds), *Modernity and Identity*. Oxford: Blackwell.

Kemshall, H. (2007) 'Dangerous Offenders: Release and Resettlement', in A. Hucklesby and L. Hagley-Dickinson (eds), *Prisoner Resettlement: Policy and Practice*. Cullompton: Willan Publishing.

Kershaw, C., Nicholas, S. and Walker, A. (eds) (2008) *Crime in England and Wales 2007/08: Findings from the British Crime Survey and Police Recorded Crime*. Home Office Statistical Bulletin 07/08. London: Home Office.

King, R. and McDermott, K. (1995) *The State of Our Prisons*. Oxford: Clarendon Press.

Kintrea, K., Bannister, J., Pickering, J., Reid, M. and Suzuki, N. (2008) *Young People and Territoriality in British Cities*. York: Joseph Rowntree Foundation.

Kling, J.R., Ludwig, J. and Katz, L.F. (2005) 'Neighbourhood Effects on Crime for Female and Male Youth: Evidence from a Randomised Housing Voucher Experiment', *Quarterly Journal of Economics*, 120 (1): 87–130.

Knight, B.J. and West, D.J. (1975) 'Temporary and Continuing Delinquency', *British Journal of Criminology*, 15: 43–50.

Kobrin, S. (1959) 'The Chicago Area Project: A 25-Year Assessment', *Annals of the American Academy of Political and Social Science*, 322 (1): 19–29.

Kodras, J. (1997) 'The Changing Map of American Poverty in an Era of Economic Restructuring and Political Realignment', *Economic Geography*, 72: 67–93.

Kolvin, I., Miller, F.J.W., Fleeting, M., and Kolvin, P.A. (1988) 'Social and Parenting Factors Affecting Criminal-Offence Rates: Findings from the Newcastle Thousand Family Study (1947–1980)', *British Journal of Psychiatry*, 152: 80–90.

Lander, B. (1954) *Towards an Understanding of Juvenile Delinquency*. New York: Columbia University Press.

Langan, P. and Levin D. (2002) *Recidivism of Prisoners Released in 1994*. Washington, DC: Bureau of Justice Statistics.

Lasch, C. (1980) *The Culture of Narcissism*. London: Sphere.

Lash, S. and Urry, J. (1987) *The End of Organized Capitalism*. Cambridge: Polity Press.

Lash, S. and Urry, J. (1994) *Economies of Signs and Space*. London: Sage.

Laub, J.H. and Sampson, R.J. (2001) 'Understanding Desistance from Crime', in M. Tonry (ed.), *Crime and Justice: A Review of Research*, vol. 28. Chicago: University of Chicago Press.

Laub, J.H. and Sampson, R.J. (2003) *Shared Beginnings, Divergent Lives: Delinquent Boys to Age 70*. Cambridge, MA: Harvard University Press.

Laurini, R. and Thompson, D. (1992) *Fundamentals of Spatial Information Systems*. London: Academic Press.

La Vigne, N. and Kachnowski, V. (2003) *A Portrait of Prisoner Reentry in Maryland*. Washington, DC: Urban Institute.

La Vigne, N., Mamalian, C., Travis, J. and Visher, C. (2003) *A Portrait of Prisoner Reentry in Illinois*. Washington, DC: Urban Institute.

La Vigne, N. and Thomson, G.L. (2003) *A Portrait of Prisoner Reentry in Ohio*. Washington DC: Urban Institute.

Layder, D. (1981) *Structure, Interaction and Social Theory*. London: Routledge and Kegan Paul.

Layder, D. (2004) *Social and Personal Identity: Understanding Yourself*. London: Sage.

Laws, G. (1997) 'Spatiality and Age Relations', in A. Jamieson, S. Harper and C. Victor (eds), *Critical Approaches to Ageing and Later Life*. Buckingham: Open University Press.

LeBel, T.P., Burnett, R., Maruna, S. and Bushway, S. (2008) 'The "Chicken and Egg" of Subjective and Social Factors in Desistance from Crime', *European Journal of Criminology*, 5: 131–59.

Lee, M.R. and Bankston, W.B. (1999) 'Political Structure, Economic Inequality, and Homicide: A Cross-Sectional Analysis', *Deviant Behavior: An Interdisciplinary Journal*, 19: 27–55.

Leech, M. (1992) *A Product of the System: My Life in and out of Prison*. London: Victor Gollancz.

Lefebvre, H. (1976) [1973] *The Survival of Capitalism: Reproduction of the Relations of Production*, trans. F. Bryant. London: Allison and Bushy.

Lefebvre, H. (1984) [1968] *Everyday Life in the Modern World*. New Brunswick, NJ: Transaction.

Lefebvre, H. (1988) 'Towards a Leftist Cultural Politics', in C. Nelson and L. Grossberg (eds) *Marxism and the Interpretation of Culture*. Chicago: University of Illinois Press.

Lefebvre, H. (1991) [1974] *The Production of Space*. Oxford: Blackwell.

Lefebvre, H. (1996) *Writings on Cities*, trans. and ed. E. Kofman and E. Lebas. Oxford: Blackwell.

Lefebvre, H. (2003) [1970] *The Urban Revolution*, trans. R. Bononno. Minneapolis, MN: University of Minnesota Press.

Lefebvre, H. (2008) [1947] *Critique of Everyday Life, Volume I*, trans. J. Moore. London: Verso.

Lefebvre, H. (2008) [1961] *Critique of Everyday Life, Volume II*, trans. J. Moore. London: Verso.

Leibrich, J. (1993) *Straight to the Point: Angles on Giving up Crime*. Otago, New Zealand: University of Otago Press.

Lemert, E.M. (1951) *Social Pathology: A Systematic Approach to the Theory of Sociopathic Behavior*. New York: McGraw-Hill.

Levitas, R. (2005) *The Inclusive Society: Social Exclusion and New Labour*, 2nd edn. Basingstoke: Palgrave Macmillan.

Lewis, O. (1967) *La Vida: A Puerto Rican Family in the Culture of Poverty – San Juan and New York*. London: Secker and Warburg.

Lewis, S., Maguire, M., Raynor, P., Vanstone, M. and Vernard, J. (2003) *The Resettlement of Short-term Prisoners: An Evaluation of Seven Pathfinders*. RDS Occasional Paper No. 83. London: Home Office.

Ley, D. (1985) 'Cultural/Humanistic Geography', *Progress in Human Geography*, 9: 415–23.

Ley, D. (2002) [1978] 'Social Geography and Social Action', in M.J Dear and S. Flusty (eds), *The Spaces of Postmodernity: Readings in Human Geography*. Oxford: Blackwell.

Liebling, A. (1999) 'Prison Suicide and Prisoner Coping' in M. Tonry and J. Petersilia (eds), *Prison, Crime and Justice: An Annual Review of Research*, 26: 283–360.

Liebling, A. (2004) *Prisons and Their Moral Performance: A Study of Values, Quality and Prison Life*. Oxford: Clarendon Press.

Liebling, A. and Maruna, S. (2005) 'Introduction: The Effects of Imprisonment Revisited', in A. Liebling and S. Maruna (eds), *The Effects of Imprisonment*. Cullompton: Willan Publishing.

Liebling, A. and Price, D. (2001) *The Prison Officer*. Winchester: Waterside Press.

Lipsey, M. (1995) 'What Do We Learn from 400 Research Studies on the Effectiveness of Treatment with Juvenile Delinquents?', in J. McGuire (ed.), *What Works: Reducing Reoffending*. Chichester: Wiley.

Lister, R. (2004) *Poverty*. Cambridge: Polity.

Little, M. (1990) *Young Men in Prison*. Aldershot: Dartmouth.

Local Government Association (LGA) (2005) *Going Straight: Reducing Re-offending in Local Communities*. London: LGA.

Loeber, R. and Farrington, D.P. (eds) (1998) *Serious and Violent Juvenile Offenders: Risk Factors and Successful Interventions*. Thousand Oaks, CA: Sage.

Loeber, R. and Wikström, P.-O. (1993) 'Individual Pathways to Crime in Different Types of Neighbourhood', in D.P. Farrington, R.J. Sampson and P.-O. Wikström (eds), *Integrating Individual and Ecological Aspects of Crime*. Stockholm: Liber Forlag.

Longley, P.A. (2004) 'Geographical Information Systems: On Modelling and Representation', *Progress in Human Geography*, 28, (1): 108–16.

Longley, P.A., Goodchild, M.F., Maguire, D.J. and Rhind, D.W. (2001) *Geographic Information Systems and Science*. Chichester: John Wiley and Sons.

Low, M. (1999) 'Communitarianism, Civic Disorder and Political Representation', *Environment and Planning* A, 31: 87–111.

Lowndes, V. and Pratchett, L. (2008) 'Public Policy and Social Capital', in D. Castiglione, J.W. van Deth and G. Wolleb (eds), *The Handbook of Social Capital*. Oxford: Oxford University Press.

Lucas, T. (1998) 'Youth Gangs and Moral Panics in Santa Cruz, California', in T. Skelton and G. Valentine (eds), *Cool Places: Geographies of Youth Cultures*. London: Routledge.

Lupton, R. (2003) *'Neighbourhood Effects': Can We Measure Them and Does it Matter?* CASEpaper 73. London: London School of Economics.

Lynch, J.P. and Sabol, W.J. (2001) *Prisoner Reentry in Perspective*. Washington, DC: Urban Institute.

Lynch, K. (1960) *The Image of the City*. Cambridge, MA: MIT Press.

MacDonald, R. and Marsh, J. (2005) *Disconnected Youth? Growing up in Britain's Poor Neighbourhoods*. Basingstoke: Palgrave Macmillan.

MacIntyre, A. (1985) *After Virtue: A Study in Moral Theory*, 2nd edn. London: Duckworth.

Mack, J. (1964) 'Full-time Miscreants, Delinquent Neighbourhoods and Criminal Networks', *British Journal of Sociology*, 15: 38–53.

Mackie, P. (2008) *This Time Round: Exploring the Effectiveness of Current Interventions in the Housing of Homeless Prisoners Released to Wales*. Swansea: Shelter Cymru.

MacLeod, J. (1995) *Ain't No Makin' It: Aspirations and Attainment in a Low-Income Neighbourhood*. Boulder, CO: Westview Press.

Macnicol, J. (1994) 'Is There an Underclass? The Lessons from America', in M. White (ed.), *Unemployment and Public Policy in a Changing Labour Market*. London: Policy Studies Institute.

Maguire, M. and Nolan, J. (2007) 'Accommodation and Related Services for Ex-prisoners', in A. Hucklesby and L. Hagley-Dickinson (eds), *Prisoner Resettlement: Policy and Practice*. Cullompton: Willan Publishing.

Maguire, M. and Raynor, P. (2006) 'How the Resettlement of Prisoners Promotes Desistance from Crime: Or Does It?', *Criminology and Criminal Justice*, 6 (19): 19–38.

Malinosky-Rummell, R. and Hansen, D.J. (1993) 'Long-Term Consequences of Childhood Physical Abuse', *Psychological Bulletin*, 114: 68–79.

Maltz, M.D. (1984) *Recidivism*. New York: Academic Press.

Marris, P. and Rein, M. (1972) *Dilemmas of Social Reform: Poverty and Community Action in the United States*, 2nd edn. London: Routledge and Kegan Paul.

Martin, D. (1996) *Geographic Information Systems: Socioeconomic Applications*, 2nd edn. London: Routledge.

Martinson, R. (1974) 'What Works? Questions and Answers About Prison Reform', *The Public Interest*, 35: 22–56.

Maruna, S. (1999) 'Desistance and Development: The Psychological Process of Going Straight', *Papers from the British Criminology Conference, Selected Proceedings*, vol. 2. Queens University, Belfast, 15–19 July 1997.

Maruna, S. (2001) *Making Good: How Ex-convicts Reform and Rebuild Their Lives*. Washington DC: American Psychological Association.

Maruna, S. and Farrall, S. (2004) 'Desistance from Crime: A Theoretical Reformulation', *Kölner Zeitschrift für Soziologie und Sozialpsychologie*, 43: 171–94.

Maruna, S., Immarigeon, R. and LeBel, T.P (2004) 'Ex-offender Reintegration: Theory and Practice', in S. Maruna and R. Immarigeon (eds), *After Crime and Punishment: Pathways to Offender Reintegration*. Cullompton: Willan Publishing.

Maruna, S. and LeBel, T. (2003) 'Welcome Home? Examining the "Reentry Court" Concept from a Strengths-Based Perspective', *Western Criminological Review*, 4 (2): 91–107.

Maruna, S. and Toch, H. (2005) 'The Impact of Imprisonment on the Desistance Process', in J. Travis and C. Visher (eds), *Prisoner Reentry and Crime in America*. Cambridge: Cambridge University Press.

Massey, D. (1984) *Spatial Divisions of Labour: Social Structure and the Geography of Production*. London: Methuen.

Massey, D. (1993) 'Power-Geometry and a Progressive Sense of Place', in J. Bird, T. Curtis, T. Putnam, G. Robertson and L. Tickner (eds), *Mapping the Futures*. London: Routledge.

Massey, D. (1997) 'A Global Sense of Place', in T. Barnes and D. Gregory (eds), *Reading Human Geography*. London: Arnold.

Massey, D. (1998) 'The Spatial Construction of Youth Cultures', in T. Skelton and G. Valentine (eds). *Cool Places: Geographies of Youth Cultures*. London: Routledge.

Massey, D. (1999) 'Imagining Globalisation: Power Geometries of Time-Space', in A. Brah, M.J Hickman and M. Mac an Ghaill (eds), *Global Futures: Migration, Environment and Globalization*. Basingstoke: Macmillan.

Massey, D. (2005) *For Space*. London: Sage.

Massey, D. (2007) *World City*. Cambridge: Polity Press.

Massey, D.S. and Denton, N.A. (1993) *American Apartheid: Segregation and the Making of the Underclass*. Cambridge, MA: Harvard University Press.

Mathiesen, T. (1965) *The Defences of the Weak*. London: Tavistock.

Mathiesen, T. (1974) *The Politics of Abolition: Essays in Political Action Theory*. Oxford: Martin Robertson.

Matthews, R. (2002) *Armed Robbery*. Cullompton: Willan Publishing.

Matthews, R. (2009) *Doing Time: An Introduction to the Sociology of Imprisonment*, 2nd edn. Basingstoke: Palgrave Macmillan.

Matza, D. (1964) *Delinquency and Drift*. New York: Wiley.

Mawby, R.I. (1977) 'Defensible Space: A Theoretical and Empirical Appraisal', *Urban Studies*, 14: 169–79.

Mawby, R.I. (1979) *Policing the City*. Farnborough: Saxon House.

Maxwell, J.A. (1996) *Qualitative Research Design: An Interactive Approach*. London: Sage.

May, C. (1999) 'Explaining Reconviction Following a Community Sentence: The Role of Social Factors', *Home Office Research Study*, 192. London: Home Office.

May, J. (1979) *Committee of Inquiry into the United Kingdom Prison Services: Report*. Cmnd. 7673. London: HMSO.

259

Mays, J.B. (1964) *Growing up in the City: A Study of Juvenile Delinquency in an Urban Neighbourhood.* Liverpool: Liverpool University Press.

McDermott, K. and King, R.D. (1988) 'Mind Games: Where the Action is in Prisons', *British Journal of Criminology*, 28 (3): 357–75.

McMurran, M. (2002) 'Alcohol, Aggression and Violence', in J. McGuire (ed.), *Offender Rehabilitation and Treatment: Effective Programmes and Policies to Reduce Re-offending.* Chichester: John Wiley and Sons.

McNeill, F. (2002) *Beyond 'What Works': How and Why Do People Stop Offending?* Briefing Paper, Edinburgh: Criminal Justice Development Centre.

McNeill, F. (2006) 'A Desistance Paradigm for Offender Management', *Criminology and Criminal Justice*, 6 (39): 39–62.

McVie, S. and Norris, P. (2006a) 'The Effect of Neighbourhoods on Adolescent Property Offending', *The Edinburgh Study of Youth Transactions and Crime* 11. Edinburgh: University of Edinburgh.

McVie, S. and Norris, P. (2006b) 'Neighbourhood Effects on Youth Delinquency and Drug Use', *The Edinburgh Study of Youth Transactions and Crime*, 10. Edinburgh: University of Edinburgh.

Mead, G.H. (1934) *Mind, Self and Society.* Chicago: University of Chicago Press.

Mead, L. (1997) *From Welfare to Work: Lessons from America.* London: Institute for Economic Affairs.

Meisenhelder, T. (1977) 'An Exploratory Study of Exiting from Criminal Careers', *Criminology*, 15: 319–34.

Meisenhelder, T. (1982) 'Becoming Normal: Certification as a Stage in Exiting from Crime', *Deviant Behaviour*, 3: 137–53.

Melossi, D. and Pavarini, M. (1981) *The Prison and the Factory: The Origins of the Penitentiary System.* London: Macmillan.

Merton, T. (1938) 'Social Structure and Anomie', *American Sociological Review*, 3: 672–82.

Meyrowitz, J. (1985) *No Sense of Place: The Impact of Electronic Media on Social Behavior.* New York: Oxford University Press.

Miles, M.B. and Huberman, A. (1994) *Qualitative Data Analysis.* Thousand Oaks, CA: Sage.

Miller, W. (1962) *Lower Class Culture as a Generating Milieu of Gang Delinquency.* Indianapolis, IN: Bobbs-Merrill.

Miller, W.R. and Rollnick, S. (1991) *Motivational Interviewing: Preparing People to Change.* New York: Guilford.

Millie, A. and Erol, R. (2006) 'Rehabilitation and Resettlement: A Study of Prolific Offender Case Management in Birmingham, United Kingdom', *International Journal of Offender Therapy and Comparative Criminology*, 50: 691–710.

Mills, C.W. (1959) *The Sociological Imagination.* Oxford: Oxford University Press.

Ministry of Justice (2009a) *Re-offending of Adults: Results from the 2007 Cohort.* London: The Stationery Office.

Ministry of Justice (2009b) *Statistics on Race and the Criminal Justice System 2007/08*. London: Ministry of Justice.

Ministry of Justice (2009c) *Cutting Crime: The Case for Justice Reinvestment*. London: Ministry of Justice.

Modell, J. (1994) 'Book review of 'Crime in the Making: Pathways and Turning Points Through Life', *American Journal of Sociology*, 99: 1389–91.

Moffitt, T.E. (1993) 'Adolescent-Limited and Life-Course Persistent Antisocial Behavior: A Developmental Taxonomy', *Psychological Review*, 100: 674–701.

Mooney, G. (1999) 'Urban "disorders"', in S. Pile, C. Brook and G. Mooney (eds), *Unruly Cities?* London: Routledge.

Moore, J.W. (1996) 'Bearing the Burden: How Incarceration Weakens Inner-City Communities', in K. Fulbright (ed.), *The Unintended Consequences of Incarceration*. New York: Vera Institute of Justice.

Moran, D. (2000) *Introduction to Phenomenology*. Oxford: Routledge.

Morgan, J. (1991) *Safer Communities: the Local Delivery of Crime Prevention Through the Partnership Approach*. London: Home Office.

Morgan, R. (2002) 'Imprisonment: A Brief History, the Contemporary Scene, and Likely Prospects', in M. Maguire, R. Morgan and R. Reiner (eds), *The Oxford Handbook of Criminology*, 3rd edn. Oxford: Oxford University Press.

Morris, L. (1993) 'Is There a British Underclass?', *International Journal of Urban and Regional Research*, 17 (3): 404–13.

Morris, N. (1974) *The Future of Imprisonment*. Chicago: University of Chicago Press.

Morris, T. (1957) *The Criminal Area: A Study in Social Ecology*. London: Routledge and Kegan Paul.

Mouzelis, N. (1995) *Sociological Theory: What Went Wrong? Diagnosis and Remedies*. London: Routledge.

Mowl, G. (2001) 'The Place of Leisure', in R. Pain (ed.), *Introducing Social Geographies*. London: Arnold.

Mumford, L. (1938) *The Culture of the City*. Harmondsworth: Penguin.

Murie, A. (1998) 'Linking Housing Changes to Crime', in C. Jones-Finer and M. Nellis (eds), *Crime and Social Exclusion*. Oxford: Blackwell.

Murray, C. (1984) *Losing Ground*. New York: Basic Books.

Murray, C. (1990) *The Emerging British Underclass*. London: Institute of Economic Affairs.

Murray, C. (1994) *Underclass: The Crisis Deepens*. London: Institute of Economic Affairs.

Musolf, G.R. (2003) *Structure and Agency in Everyday Life: An Introduction to Social Psychology*, 2nd edn. Lanham, MD: Rowman and Littlefield.

Musterd, S. and Ostendorf, W. (1998) 'Segregation, Polarisation and Social Exclusion in Metropolitan Areas', in S. Musterd and W. Ostendorf (eds), *Urban Segregation and the Welfare State: Inequality and Exclusion in Western Cities*. New York: Routledge.

Myrdal, G. (1962) *Challenge to Affluence*. New York: Pantheon.

Nagin, D. and Waldfogel, J. (1995) 'The Effects of Criminality and Conviction on the Labour Market Status of Young British Offenders', *International Review of Law and Economics*, 15: 109–26.

Nelken, D. (1994) 'Community Involvement in Crime Control', in N. Lacey (ed.), *A Reader in Criminal Justice*. Oxford: Oxford University Press.

Nellis, M. (2006) 'NOMS, Contestability and the Process of Technocorrectional Innovation', in M. Hough, R. Allen and U. Padel (eds), *Reshaping Probation and Prisons: The New Offender Management Framework*. Bristol: Policy Press.

Nelson, G. and Prilleltensky, I. (2004) *Community Psychology: In Pursuit of Liberation and Well-Being*. London: Palgrave Macmillan.

Newman, J. (2001) *Modernising Governance: New Labour, Policy and Society*. London: Sage.

Newman, K. (2002) 'No Shame: The View from the Left Bank', *American Journal of Sociology*, 107 (6): 1577–99.

Newman, O. (1972) *Defensible Space: People and Design in the Violent City*. London: Architectural Press.

Newman, S.J. and Harkness, J. (2002) 'The Long-Term Effects of Public Housing on Self-Sufficiency', *Journal of Policy Analysis and Management*, 21 (1): 21–43.

Niven, S. and Olagundaye, J. (2002) *Jobs and Homes: A Survey of Prisoners Nearing Release*. Home Office Research Findings 173. London: Home Office.

Niven, S. and Stewart, D. (2005) *Resettlement Outcomes on Release from Prison in 2003*. London: Home Office.

Oberwittler, D. (2004) 'A Multilevel Analysis of Neighbourhood Contextual Effects on Serious Juvenile Offending: The Role of Sub-cultural Values and Social Disorganization', *European Journal of Criminology*, 1 (2): 201–35.

Office of the Deputy Prime Minister (2005) *Sustainable Communities: People, Places and Prosperity*. Cm 6425. London: HMSO.

Oktay, D. (2002) 'The Quest for Urban Identity in the Changing Context of the City', *Cities*, 19 (4): 261–71.

Ormerod, P. (2005) *Why Most Things Fail: Evolution, Extinction and Economics*. London: Faber and Faber.

Osborn, S.G. (1980) 'Moving Home, Leaving London, and Delinquent Trends', *British Journal of Criminology*, 20: 54–61.

Pacione, M. (2009) *Urban Geography: A Global Perspective*, 3rd edn. Abingdon: Routledge.

Pahl, R.E. (1969) 'Urban Social Theory and Research', *Environment and Planning*, 1 (2): 143–53.

Parker, H. (1974) *View from the Boys*. London: David and Charles.

Parker, H., Aldridge, J. and Egginton, R. (2001) *Drugs Unlimited*. London: Palgrave.

Parker, H., Aldridge, J. and Measham, F. (1998) *Illegal Leisure: The Normalization of Adolescent Recreational Drug Use*. London: Routledge.

Parker, T. (1966) *The Unknown Citizen*. Harmondsworth: Penguin.

Paulus, P.B., McCain, G. and Cox, V. (1981) 'Prison Standards: Some Pertinent Data on Crowding', *Federal Probation*, 15: 48–54.

Peck, J. (2003) 'Geography and Public Policy: Mapping the Penal Scene', *Progress in Human Geography*, 27 (2): 222–32.

Pennant, R. (2005) *Diversity, Trust and Community Participation in England*, Home Office Research Development and Statistics Directorate Paper 253. London: Home Office.

Perlman, J. (1976) *The Myth of Marginality*. Berkeley, CA: University of California Press.

Petersilia, J. (2000) 'Challenges of Prisoner Reentry and Parole in California', *Brief* 12 (3). California Policy Research Center.

Petersilia, J. (2003) *When Prisoners Come Home: Parole and Prisoner Reentry*. Oxford: Oxford University Press.

Phillips, C. (2007) 'Ethnicity, Identity, and Community Cohesion in Prison', in M. Wetherell, M. Lafleche and R. Berkeley (eds), *Identity, Ethnic Diversity and Community Cohesion*. London: Sage.

Phillips, C. and Earle, R. (n.d.) *Ethnicity, Identity, and Social Relations in Prison*. Swindon: Economic and Social Research Council Identities and Social Action Programme.

Philo, C. and Parr, H. (2000) Institutional Geographies: Introductory Remarks. *Geoforum*, 31: 513–21.

Pickles, J. (2002) 'Toward an Economy of Electronic Representation and the Virtual Sign', in M.J. Dear and S. Flusty (eds), *The Spaces of Postmodernity: Readings in Human Geography*. Oxford: Blackwell.

Pile, S. (1996) *The Body and the City: Psychoanalysis, Space and Subjectivity*. London: Routledge.

Pile, S., Brook, C. and Mooney, G. (1999) *Unruly Cities?* London: Routledge.

Pitts, J. (2003) *The New Politics of Youth Crime: Discipline or Solidarity?* Lyme Regis: Russell House Publishing.

Pitts, J. (2008) *Reluctant Gangsters: The Changing Face of Youth Crime*. Cullompton: Willan Publishing.

Pontell, H.N. and Welsh, W.N. (1994) 'Incarceration as a Deviant Form of Social Control: Jail Overcrowding in California', *Crime and Delinquency*, 40: 18–36.

Posner, R. (1985) 'An Economic Theory of Criminal Law', *Columbia Law Review*, 85: 1193–1231.

Power, A. and Tunstall, T. (1997) *Dangerous Disorder: Riots and Violent Disturbances in Thirteen Areas of Britain 1991–92*. York: Joseph Rowntree Foundation.

Presdee, M. (2000) *Cultural Criminology and the Carnival of Crime*. London: Routledge.

Prison Reform Trust (2005) *Recycling Offenders Through Prison*. London: Prison Reform Trust.

Proshansky, H.M., Fabian, A.K. and Kaminoff, R. (1983) 'Place-Identity: Physical World Socialization of Self', *Journal of Environmental Psychology*, 3: 57–83.

Pryor, S. (2001) *The Responsible Prisoner*. London: Her Majesty's Inspectorate of Prisons.

Putnam, R.D. (2000) *Bowling Alone: The Collapse and Revival of American Community*. New York: Simon and Schuster.

Quetelet, A. (1996) [1842] 'Of the Development of the Propensity for Crime', in J. Muncie, E. McLaughlin and M. Langan (eds), *Criminological Perspectives*. London: Sage.

Quinney, R. (1977) *Class, State and Crime: On the Theory and Practice of Criminal Justice*. New York: McKay.

Raban, J. (1974) *Soft City*. London: Hamish Hamilton.

Raine, J.W. (2006) 'NOMS and its Relationship to Crime Reduction, Public Confidence and the New Sentencing Context', in M. Hough, R. Allen and U. Padel (eds) *Reshaping Probation and Prisons: The New Offender Management Framework*. Bristol: Policy Press.

Ramsay, M. (ed.) (2003) 'Prisoners' Drug Use and Treatment: Seven Studies', *Home Office Research Findings* 186. London: Home Office.

Raphael, S. and Winter-Ebmer, R. (1999) *Identifying the Effect of Unemployment on Crime*. Discussion paper 2129. London: Centre for Economic Policy Research.

Ratcliffe, P. (1997) 'Race, Housing and the City', in N. Jewson and S. MacGregor (eds), *Transforming Cities: Contested Governance and New Spatial Divisions*. London: Routledge.

Rawson, R.A. (1999) 'Treatment for Stimulant use Disorders', *Treatment Improvement Protocol [TIP] Series* 33, DHHS Publication No. SMA 99-3296. Rockville, MD: US Department of Health and Human Services, Center for Substance Abuse Treatment.

Raynor, P. (2007) 'Theoretical Perspectives on Resettlement: What It Is and How It Might Work', in A. Hucklesby and L. Hagley-Dickinson (eds), *Prisoner Resettlement: Policy and Practice*. Cullompton: Willan Publishing.

Raynor, P. and Maguire, M. (2006) 'End-to-End or End in Tears? Prospects for the Effectiveness of the National Offender Management Model', in M. Hough, R. Allen and U. Padel (eds), *Reshaping Probation and Prisons: The New Offender Management Framework*. Bristol: Policy Press.

Raynor, P. and Vanstone, M. (1994) 'Probation Practice, Effectiveness and the Non-Treatment Paradigm', *British Journal of Social Work*, 24 (4): 387–404.

Reid-Howie Associates (2004) *The Provision of Housing Advice to Prisoners in Scotland*. Edinburgh: Scottish Executive.

Reiman, J.H. (1979) *The Rich Get Richer and the Poor Get Prison*. New York: John Wiley.

Relph, E. (1976) *Place and Placelessness*. London: Pion.

Rex, S. (1999) 'Desistance from Offending: Experiences of Probation', *Howard Journal*, 38: 366–83.

Rex, S. (2001) 'Beyond Cognitive-Behaviouralism? Reflections on the Effectiveness Literature', in A. Bottoms, L. Gelsthorpe and S. Rex (eds), *Community Penalties: Change and Challenges*. Cullompton: Willan.

Richards, S.C. and Jones, R.S. (2004) 'Beating the Perpetual Incarceration Machine: Overcoming Structural Impediments to Re-entry', in S. Maruna and R. Immarigeon (eds), *After Crime and Punishment: Pathways to Offender Reintegration*. Cullompton: Willan Publishing.

Roberts, J. (1994) 'The Relationship between the Community and the Prison', in E. Player and M. Jenkins (eds), *Prisons after Woolf: Reform through Riot*. London: Routledge.

Roberts, J. (1999) 'Philosophizing the Everyday', *Radical Philosophy*, 98: 16–17.

Robertson, D., Smyth, L. and McIntosh, I. (2008) *Neighbourhood Identity: People, Time and Place*. York: Joseph Rowntree Foundation.

Robinson, G. and Crow, I. (2009) *Offender Rehabilitation: Theory, Research and Practice*. London: Sage.

Robson, B., Parkinson, M., Boddy, M. and Maclennan, D. (2000) *The State of English Cities*. London: Department of the Environment, Transport and the Regions.

Rock, P. (2005) 'Victimisation of the Homeless', *Mannheim Newsletter*, 1: 8–9.

Rojek, C. (1995) *Decentring Leisure: Rethinking Leisure Theory*. London: Sage.

Rose, D. and Clear, T.R. (1998) 'Incarceration, Social Capital and Crime: Implications for Social Disorganisation Theory', *Criminology* 36: 441–79.

Rose, D., Clear, T. and Scully, K. (1999) 'Coercive Mobility and Crime: Incarceration and Social Disorganization'. Paper presented at the American Society of Criminology, Toronto, Canada, 12–15 November.

Ross, K. (1996) 'Streetwise: The French Invention of Everyday Life', *Parallax*, 2: 67–75.

Rothman, D. (1980) *Conscience and Convenience: The Asylum and its Alternatives in Progressive America*. Boston: Little, Brown & Co.

Rotman, E. (1990) *Beyond Punishment: A New View of the Rehabilitation of Offenders*. Westport, CT: Greenwood Press.

Ruggiero, V. (1995) 'Flexibility and Intermittent Emergency in the Italian Penal System', in V. Ruggiero, M. Ryan and J. Sim (eds), *Western European Penal Systems: A Critical Anatomy*. London: Sage.

Ruggiero, V. (2001) *Movements in the City: Conflict in the European Metropolis*. Harlow: Prentice-Hall.

Ruggiero, V. and South, N. (1995) *Eurodrugs: Drug Use, Markets and Trafficking in Europe*. London: UCL Press.

Rusche, G. and Kirchheimer, O. (2003) [1939] *Punishment and Social Structure*. New Brunswick, NJ: Transaction Publishers.

Rutter, M. and Giller, H. (1983) *Juvenile Delinquency*. Harmondsworth: Penguin.

Sampson, E.E. (1989) 'The Deconstruction of the Self', in J. Shotter and K.J. Gergen (eds), *Texts of Identity*. London: Sage.

Sampson, R.J. (2006) 'How Does Community Context Matter? Social Mechanisms and the Explanation of Crime Rates', in P.-O.H. Wikström and R.J. Sampson (eds), *The Explanation of Crime: Context, Mechanisms and Development*. Cambridge: Cambridge University Press.

Sampson, R.J. (2008) 'Moving to Inequality: Neighbourhood Effects and Experiments Meet Social Structure', *American Journal of Sociology*, 114 (1): 189–231.

Sampson, R.J. and Laub, J.H. (1993) *Crime in the Making: Pathways and Turning Points Through Life*. Cambridge, MA: Harvard University Press.

Sampson, R.J. and Laub, J. (1994) 'Urban Poverty and the Family Context of Delinquency', *Child Development* 65: 523–40.

Sampson, R.J. and Laub, J.H. (2005) 'A General Age-Graded Theory of Crime: Lessons Learned and the Future of Life-Course Criminology', in D. Farrington (ed.), *Advances in Criminological Theory*, vol. 14. *Integrated Developmental/Life Course Theories of Offending*. New Brunswick, NJ: Transaction Publishers.

Sampson, R.J., Morenoff, J.D. and Gannon-Rowley, T. (2002) 'Assessing "Neighborhood Effects": Social Processes and New Directions in Research', *Annual Review of Sociology*, 28: 443–78.

Sampson, R.J. and Raudenbush, S.W. (1999) 'Systematic Social Observation of Public Spaces: A New Look at Disorder and Crime', *American Journal of Sociology*, 105: 603–51.

Sampson, R.J., Raudenbush, S.W. and Earls, F. (1997) 'Neighbourhoods and Violent Crime: A Multilevel Study of Collective Efficacy', *Science*, 277: 918–24.

Sanchez-Jankowski, M. (2003) 'Gangs and Social Change', *Theoretical Criminology*, 7 (2): 191–216.

Sapsford, R.J. (1983) *Life-Sentence Prisoners: Reaction, Response and Change*. Milton Keynes: Open University Press.

Sarre, P., Phillips, D. and Skellington, R. (1989) *Ethnic Minority Housing: Explanations and Policies*. Aldershot: Avebury.

Sassen, S. (1991) *The Global City: New York, London, Tokyo*. Princeton, NJ: Princeton University Press.

Scheff, T.J. and Retzinger, S.M. (1991) *Emotions and Violence: Shame and Rage in Destructive Conflicts*. Lexington, MA: Lexington Books.

Schlossman, S., Zellman, G. and Shavelson, R. with Sedlak, M. and Cobb, J. (1984) *Delinquency Prevention in South Chicago: A Fifty-Year Assessment of the Chicago Area Project*. Santa Monica, CA: Rand.

Schmid, C. (1960) 'Urban Crime Areas: part II', *American Sociological Review*, 25 (5): 655–78.

Schuerman, L. and Kobrin, S. (1986) 'Community Careers in Crime', in A.J. Reiss and M. Tonry (eds), *Communities and Crime*. Chicago: University of Chicago Press.

Scott, J. (1994) *Poverty and Wealth: Citizenship, Deprivation and Privilege.* London: Longman.

Scraton, P., Sim, J. and Skidmore, P. (1991) *Prisons Under Protest.* Milton Keynes: Open University Press.

Seale, C. (1998) *The Quality of Qualitative Research.* London: Sage.

Seamon, D. (1979) *A Geography of the Lifeworld: Movement, Rest and Encounter.* London: Croom Helm.

Sen, A.K. (1985) *Commodities and Capabilities.* Oxford: Oxford University Press.

Sen, A.K. (1992) *Inequality Re-examined.* Oxford: Oxford University Pres.

Sen, A.K. (1999) *Development as Freedom.* Oxford: Oxford University Press.

Sennett, R. (1990) *The Conscience of the Eye: The Design and Social Life of Cities.* London: Faber and Faber.

Sharpe, J.A. (1990) *Judicial Punishment in England.* London: Faber and Faber.

Shaw, C.R. and McKay, H.D. (1942) *Juvenile Delinquency and Urban Areas.* Chicago: University of Chicago Press.

Shelter (2007) *Good Practice Briefing: Barred from housing.* London: Shelter [online]. Available at http://england.shelter.org.uk/__data/assets/pdf_file/0006/38715/30484.pdf (accessed January 2010).

Sherman, L.W., Gartin, P.R. and Buerger, M.E. (1989) 'Hot Spots of Predatory Crime: Routine Activities and the Criminology of Place', *Criminology*, 27 (1): 27–55.

Shilling, C. (1993) *The Body and Social Theory.* London: Sage.

Shmuely, A. (2008) 'Totality, Hegemony, Difference: Henri Lefebvre and Raymond Williams', in K. Goonewardena, S. Kipfer, R. Milgrom and C. Schmid (eds), *Space, Difference, Everyday Life: Reading Henri Lefebvre.* London: Routledge.

Shover, N. (1996) *Great Pretenders: Pursuits and Careers of Persistent Thieves.* Boulder, CO: Westview Press.

Silverstone, R. and Hirsch, E. (1992) *Consuming Technologies: Media and Information in Domestic Spaces.* London: Routledge.

Sim, J. (1994) 'Tougher Than the Rest?', in T. Newburn and E.A. Stanko (eds), *Men, Masculinities and Crime: Just Boys Doing Business?* London: Routledge.

Simmel, G. (1969) [1903] 'The Metropolis and Mental Life', in R. Sennett (ed.), *Classic Essays on the Culture of Cities.* New York: Appleton Century Crofts.

Simmie, J., Carpenter, J., Chadwick, A., Martin, R. and Wood, P. (2006) *State of the English Cities: The Competitive Economic Performance of English Cities.* London: Department of Communities and Local Government.

Singleton, N., Meltzer, H. and Gatward, R. (1998) *Psychiatric Morbidity Among Prisoners in England and Wales.* London: Stationery Office.

Skogan, W.G. (1990) *Disorder and Decline: Crime and the Spiral of Decay in American Neighbourhoods.* New York: Free Press.

Smith, D. (1995) *Criminology for Social Work.* London: Macmillan.

Smith, D.J. (2002) 'Crime and the Life Course', in M. Maguire, R. Morgan and R. Reiner (eds), *The Oxford Handbook of Criminology*, 3rd edn. Oxford: Oxford University Press.

Smith, E. and Stewart, J. (1997) 'Probation and Social Exclusion', *Social Policy and Administration*, 31 (5): 96–115.

Smith, S. (1987) 'Residential Segregation: A Geography of English Racism?' in P. Jackson (ed.), *Race and Racism: Essays in Social Geography*. London: Allen and Unwin.

Social Exclusion Unit (SEU) (1997) *Tackling Truancy*. London: HMSO.

Social Exclusion Unit (SEU) (1998) *Bringing Britain Together*. London: HMSO.

Social Exclusion Unit (SEU) (2001) *A New Commitment to Neighbourhood Renewal: National Strategy Action Plan*. London: Cabinet Office.

Social Exclusion Unit (SEU) (2002) *Reducing Re-offending by Ex-prisoners: Report by the Social Exclusion Unit*. London: Office of the Deputy Prime Minister.

Soja, E. (1980) 'The Socio-Spatial Dialectic', *Annals of the Association of American Geographers*, 70: 207–25.

Soja, E. (1995) 'Postmodern Urbanization: The Six Restructurings of Los Angeles', in S. Watson and K. Gibson (eds), *Postmodern Cities and Spaces*. Oxford: Blackwell.

Soothill, K. (1974) *The Prisoner's Release*. London: Allen and Unwin.

Sparks, R., Bottoms, A.E. and Hay, W. (1996) *Prisons and the Problem of Order*. Oxford: Clarendon Press.

Straus, M., Gelles, R. and Steinmetz, S. (1980) *Behind Closed Doors*. New York: Doubleday.

Stretton, H. (1976) *Capitalism, Socialism and the Environment*. Cambridge: Cambridge University Press.

Sun, I., Payne, B. and Wu, W. (2008) 'The Impact of Situational Factors, Officer Characteristics, and Neighborhood Context on Police Behavior: A Multilevel Analysis', *Journal of Criminal Justice*, 36 (1): 22–32.

Sykes, G. (1958) *The Society of Captives*. Princeton, NJ: Princeton University Press.

Sykes, G. and Matza, D. (1957) 'Techniques of Neutralization: A Theory of Delinquency', *American Sociological Review*, 22: 664–73.

Tarling, R. (1982) *Unemployment and Crime*. Home Office Research Bulletin, 14: 28–33.

Taylor, I. (1999) *Crime in Context: A Critical Criminology of Market Societies*. Cambridge: Polity Press.

Taylor, M. (2003) *Public Policy in the Community*. Basingstoke: Palgrave Macmillan.

Taylor, R.B. and Gottfredson, S. (1986) 'Environmental Design, Crime and Prevention: An Examination of Community Dynamics', in A.J. Reiss and M. Tonry (eds), *Communities and Crime*. Chicago: University of Chicago Press.

Thomas, C.W. (1977) 'Theoretical Perspectives on Prisonization: A Comparison of the Importation and Deprivation Models', *Journal of Criminal Law and Criminology*, 68: 135–45.

Thomas, W. and Znaniecki, F. (1920) *The Polish Peasant in Europe and America*. Boston: Gorham.

Thornberry, T. and Krohn, M.D. (1977) 'Peers, Drug Use, and Delinquency', in D.M. Stoff (ed.), *Handbook of Antisocial Behavior*. New York: Wiley.

Thrift, N. (2002) [1983] 'On the Determination of Social Action in Space and Time', in M.J. Dear and S. Flusty (eds), *The Spaces of Postmodernity: Readings in Human Geography*. Oxford: Blackwell.

Thrift, N. (1985) 'Flies and Germs: A Geography of Knowledge', in D. Gregory and J. Urry (eds), *Social Relations and Spatial Structures*. Basingstoke: Macmillan.

Tilley, N. (1993) *After Kirkholt: Theory, Methods and Results of Replication Evaluations*. Crime Prevention Unit Paper 47. London: Home Office.

Titmuss, R.M. (1976) *Commitment to Welfare*. London: Allen and Unwin.

Toch, H. (1992) *Living in Prison: The Ecology of Survival*. Washington DC: American Psychological Association.

Travis, J. and Petersilia, J. (2001) 'Reentry Reconsidered: A New Look at an Old Question', *Crime and Delinquency*, 47: 291–313.

Trickett, A., Ellingworth, D., Hope, T. and Pease, K. (1995) 'Crime Victimisation in the Eighties: Changes in Area and Regional Inequality', *British Journal of Criminology*, 35 (3): 343–59.

Trotter, C. (1999) *Working with Involuntary Clients: A Guide to Practice*. London: Sage.

Tuan, Yi-Fu (1974) *Topophilia: A Study of Environmental Perception, Attitudes and Values*. Englewood Cliffs, NJ: Prentice-Hall.

Tuan, Yi-Fu (1977) *Space and Place: The Perspective of Experience*. Minneapolis, MN: University of Minnesota Press.

Tuan, Yi-Fu (1998) *Escapism*. Baltimore, MD: Johns Hopkins University Press.

Tucker, S.B. and Cadora, E. (2003) 'Justice Reinvestment: To Invest in Public Safety by Reallocating Justice Dollars to Refinance Education, Housing, Healthcare, and Jobs', *Ideas for an Open Society*, Occasional Papers, vol. 3, no. 3. New York: Open Society Institute.

Turnbull, P., Stimson, G. and Stillwell, G. (1994) *Drug Use in Prison*. Horsham, West Sussex: AVERT.

Turok, I., Kearns, A., Fitch, D., Flint, J., McKenzie, C. and Abbotts, J. (2006) *State of the English Cities: Social Cohesion*. London: Department for Communities and Local Government.

Uggen, C., Manza, J. and Behrens, A. (2004) 'Less Than the Average Citizen: Stigma, Role Transition and the Civic Reintegration of Convicted Felons', in S. Maruna and R. Immarigeon (eds), *After Crime and Punishment: Pathways to Offender Reintegration*. Cullompton: Willan Publishing.

Ulmer, J.T. and Spencer, J.W. (1999) 'The Contributions of an Interactionist Approach to Research and Theory on Criminal Careers', *Theoretical Criminology*, 3 (1): 95–124.

Valentine, G. and Longstaff, B. (1998) 'Doing Porridge: Food and Social Relations in a Male Prison', *Journal of Material Culture*, 3: 131–52.
Valentine, G. and McKendrick, J. (1997) 'Children's Outdoor Play: Exploring Parental Concerns About Children's Safety and the Changing Nature of Childhood', *Geoforum*, 28 (2): 219–35.
Visher, C.A. and Travis, J. (2003) Transitions from Prison to Community: Understanding Individual Pathways', *Annual Review of Sociology*, 29: 89–113.
von Eckartsberg, R. (1998) 'Introducing Existential-Phenomenological Enquiry', in R. Calle (ed.), *Phenomenological Inquiry in Psychology*. New York: Plenum.

Wacquant, L. (1997) 'Three Pernicious Premises in the Study of the American Ghetto', *International Journal of Urban and Regional Research*, 20: 341–53.
Wacquant, L. (2001) 'Deadly Symbiosis: When Ghetto and Prison Meet and Mesh', *Punishment and Society*, 3 (1): 95–134.
Wacquant, L. (2002) 'The Curious Eclipse of Prison Ethnography in the Age of Mass Incarceration', *Ethnography*, 3 (4): 371–97.
Wacquant, L. (2008) *Urban Outcasts: A Comparative Sociology of Advanced Marginality*. Cambridge: Polity.
Walker, N. (1991) *Why Punish?* Oxford: Oxford University Press.
Walmsley, D.J. and Lewis, G.J. (1984) *Human Geography: Behavioural Approaches*. London: Longman.
Walmsley, R. (2009) *World Prison Population List* (8th edn). King's College London: International Centre for Prison Studies [online]. Available at http://www.kcl.ac.uk/depsta/law/research/icps/downloads/wppl-8th_41.pdf (accessed January 2010).
Walmsley, R., Howard, L. and White, S. (1992) 'The National Prison Survey 1991: Main Findings', *Home Office Research Study*, 128. London: HMSO.
Ward, T. and Brown, M. (2004) 'The Good Lives Model and Conceptual Issues in Offender Rehabilitation', *Psychology, Crime and Law*, 10: 243–57.
Ward, T. and Maruna, S. (2007) *Rehabilitation*. London: Routledge.
Warr, M. (1998) 'Life-Course Transitions and Desistance from Crime', *Criminology*, 36: 183–216.
Warr, M. (2002) *Companions in Crime: The Social Aspects of Criminal Conduct*. Cambridge: Cambridge University Press.
Weatherburn, D., Bronwyn, L. and Simon, K. (1999) 'Hotbeds of Crime? Crime and Public Housing in Urban Sydney', *Crime and Delinquency*, 45 (2): 256–71.
Weatherburn, D. and Lind, B. (2001) *Delinquent-Prone Communities*. Cambridge: Cambridge University Press.

Weber, M. (1978) *Economy and Society*, vol. I. Berkeley, CA: University of California Press.

Webber, R. (2007) 'The Metropolitan Habitus', *Environmental and Planning A*, 39: 182–207.

Webster, C., MacDonald, R. and Simpson, M. (2006) 'Predicting Criminality? Risk Factors, Neighbourhood Influence and Desistance', *Youth Justice*, 6 (1): 7–22.

Weir, R. and Bangs, M. (2007) *The Use of Geographic Information Systems by Crime Analysts in England and Wales*. Home Office Online Report 03. London: Home Office.

Wellman, B. (1979) 'The Community Question: The Intimate Networks of East Yorkers, *American Journal of Sociology*, 84: 1201–31.

Wellman, B. (1987) *The Community Question Re-evaluated*. Toronto: University of Toronto Press.

Wener, R. and Keys, C. (1988) 'The Effects of Changes in Jail Population Densities on Crowding, Sick Call and Spatial Behavior', *Journal of Applied Social Psychology*, 18: 852–66.

West, D.J. (1982) *Delinquency: Its Roots, Careers and Prospects*. Aldershot: Gower.

Whyte, W.H. (1943) *Street Corner Society*. Chicago: University of Chicago Press.

Wikström, P.-O. (1991) *Urban Crime, Criminals and Victims: The Swedish Experience in an Anglo-American Comparative Perspective*. New York: Springer-Verlag.

Wikström, P.-O. and Loeber, R. (2000) 'Do Disadvantaged Neighbourhoods Cause Well Adjusted Children to Become Adolescent Delinquents? A Study of Male Serious Juvenile Offending, Individual Risk and Protective Factors, and Neighbourhood Context, *Criminology*, 38: 1109–42.

Wikström, P.-O. and Sampson, R.J. (2006) 'Introduction: Toward a Unified Approach to Crime and its Explanation', in P.-O. Wikström and R.J. Sampson (eds), *The Explanation of Crime: Context, Mechanisms and Development*. Cambridge: Cambridge University Press.

Wilde, O. (1999) [1898] 'The Ballad of Reading Gaol', in *De Profundis, The Ballad of Reading Gaol and Other Writings*. Ware: Wordsworth.

Wiles, P. and Costello, A. (2000) 'The Road to Nowhere: The Evidence for Travelling Criminals', *Home Office Research Study*, 207. London: Home Office.

Wilkinson, R.G. (2005) *The Impact of Inequality: How to Make Sick Societies Healthier*. Abingdon: Routledge.

Williams, R. (1973) *The Country and the City*. London: Chatto and Windus.

Willis, P. (1977) *Learning to Labour: How Working Class Kids Get Working Class Jobs*. Farnborough: Saxon House.

Wilson, J.Q. (1975) *Thinking About Crime*. New York: Basic Books.

Wilson, J.Q. and Herrnstein, R.J. (1985) *Crime and Human Nature*. New York: Touchstone Books.

Wilson, J.Q. and Kelling G. (1982) 'Broken Windows', *Atlantic Monthly* (March): 29–38.

Wilson, W.J. (1987) *The Truly Disadvantaged: The Inner City, the Underclass and Public Policy*. Chicago: University of Chicago Press.

Wilson, W.J. (1997) *When Work Disappears*. New York: Alfred A. Knopf.

Woolf, H. and Tumim, S. (1991) *Prison Disturbances 1990*. Cm. 1456. London: HMSO.

Worrall, A. and Hoy, C. (2005) *Punishment in the Community: Managing Offenders, Making Choices*, 2nd edn. Cullompton: Willan Publishing.

Wortley, R. (2008) 'Situational Precipitators of Crime', in R. Wortley and L. Mazerolle (eds), *Environmental Criminology and Crime Analysis*. Cullompton: Willan Publishing.

Young, I.M. (1990) 'The Ideal of Community and the Politics of Difference', in L.J. Nicholson (ed.), *Feminism/Postmodernism*. London: Routledge.

Young, J. (1992) 'Ten Points of Realism', in J. Young and R. Matthews (eds), *Rethinking Criminology: The Realist Debate*. London: Sage.

Young, J. (1999) *The Exclusive Society: Social Exclusion, Crime and Difference in Late Modernity*. London: Sage.

Young, J. (2002) 'Crime and Social Exclusion', in M. Maguire, R. Morgan and R. Reiner (eds), *The Oxford Handbook of Criminology*, 3rd edn. Oxford: Oxford University Press.

Young, J. (2003) 'Merton with Energy, Katz with Structure: The Sociology of Vindictiveness and the Criminology of Transgression', *Theoretical Criminology*, 7 (3): 389–414.

Young, J. and Matthews, R. (1992) 'Questioning Left Realism', in R. Matthews and J. Young (eds), *Issues in Realist Criminology*. London: Sage.

Young, M. and Willmott, P. (1962) [1957] *Family and Kinship in East London*. Harmondsworth: Penguin.

Young, T., Fitzgerald, M., Hallsworth, S. and Joseph, I. (2007) *Groups, Gangs and Weapons*. A Report for the Youth Justice Board of England and Wales. London: Youth Justice Board.

Zamble, E. and Porporino, E.J. (1988) *Coping, Behaviour and Adaptation in Prison Inmates*. New York: Springer-Verlag.

Zamble, E. and Quinsey, V. (1997) *The Criminal Recidivism Process*. Cambridge: Cambridge University Press.

Zukin, S. (1991) *Landscapes of Power from Detroit to Disney World*. Berkeley, CA: University of California Press.

Zukin, S. (1992) 'Postmodern Urban Landscapes: Mapping Culture and Power', in S. Lash and J. Friedman (eds), *Modernity and Identity*. Oxford: Blackwell.

Index